AF537996

Between Tehran and Tel Aviv

Gaza's Story of Unending War

BETWEEN TEHRAN AND TEL AVIV

Gaza's Story of Unending War

Col Rajeev Agarwal

First published in 2026 by

PENTAGON PRESS LLP
206, Peacock Lane, Shahpur Jat
New Delhi-110049, India
Contact: 011-26490600

Typeset in AGaramond, 11 Point
Printed at
Quiinkit Infotech Pvt. Ltd., Gurugram

ISBN 978-81-997728-9-2

Disclaimer: The views and opinions expressed in the book is the individual assertion of the Author. The Publisher does not take any responsibility for the same in any manner whatsoever. The same shall solely be the responsibility of the Author.

www.pentagonpress.in

CONTENTS

SECTION III: IRAN ENTERS THE CONFLICT

SECTION IV: THE RAFAH OFFENSIVE AND THE DANGEROUS ESCALATION

SECTION V: THE DEMOLITION OF HEZBOLLAH AND OUSTER OF ASSAD IN SYRIA

SECTION IX: ISRAEL UPS THE ANTE, QATAR STRIKE AND THE '20 POINT TRUMP PEACE PLAN'

SECTION X: INDIA AND THE GAZA WAR

ANNEXURES

FOREWORD

Few events have the power and potential to change history. In a conflict-ridden and contested region like West Asia, such events must be truly catastrophic or transformative to achieve that. The war in Gaza, unleashed from 7th October 2023, was one such event.

Coming almost against the run of play when many things seemed to be going right for the region, including the Saudi-Iran peace deal in March, the re-entry of Syria into the Arab League, and reports relating to possible normalisation of ties between Saudi Arabia and Israel, the Hamas attacks from Gaza caught the world by surprise. In hindsight, it has been suggested by some commentators that these developments may well have been the very reason for the deadly attacks. This is because it appeared that, as each of the developments that promised to usher in peace and reconciliation in the region, the cause for an independent, sovereign and viable Palestine state was being pushed into oblivion.

On 7 October, Hamas struck Israel at multiple locations, catching it by absolute surprise. As Israeli armed forces and the political leadership scrambled to retaliate, the assault revived for Israelis the painful memories of a strikingly similar surprise attack launched by Egypt and Syria on 6 October 1973 on Yom Kippur, the holiest day in the Jewish calendar, exactly 50 years earlier, and, as before, was viewed as an existential threat to the Jewish state.

In response to the Hamas attacks, Israel launched a military campaign in Gaza aimed at dismantling Hamas's military and leadership infrastructure. An intense cocktail of airstrikes, artillery bombardment, and eventual ground operations in the Gaza Strip, one of the most densely populated territories in the world, became one of the most debated conflicts in the twenty-first century. Governments, international organisations, scholars, and civil society groups found themselves sharply divided over questions of strategy, legality, and morality.

The Israeli game-plan was to hunt down the last of the Hamas cadre in Gaza and, in the process, make the enclave unliveable for years to come. Hence, its armed forces targeted homes, educational institutions, hospitals, aid agencies, and, above all, media personnel – so that the story of Gaza would disappear under the rubble and pass away from human memory. However, brave journalists who recorded the events and academics who have carried out real-time assessments, have ensured that the happenings in Gaza have been preserved as a human document that can be retrieved when the time comes to judge the crimes that were committed and identify the war criminals.

Israel seized the opportunity provided by the attacks to attempt to settle its grievances with its neighbours as well through a series of lethal attacks that targeted hostile leaderships, movements, state administrations and military capabilities. Israel's leadership was able to co-opt into its destructive enterprise the US president and the full backing of American military might as well, directed, in June 2025, at Iran's nuclear program.

The two-year war in Gaza is seared in the memories of most of us who follow events in West Asia. The world watched in despair as Israeli soldiers used their superior military capability to destroy this enclave – bringing down almost every edifice and institution. Over 72,000 Palestinians have been killed in Gaza since October 2023, with several thousand missing under the rubble of their homes. Not surprisingly, most of them are women and children. After two years of war, the conflict between Israel and Hamas in the Gaza Strip finally came to an end with a US-sponsored truce, leaving behind a landscape profoundly altered by destruction, loss, and political uncertainty.

Col Rajeev Agarwal, veteran soldier and outstanding scholar, in this book, *Between Tehran and Tel Aviv: Gaza's story of Unending War*, has provided a substantial and urgently needed account of the war from its inception to the ceasefire promoted by US President Donald Trump who announced it in September 2025 followed up by an endorsement through the UN Security Council Resolution on November 17. His book is an incisive examination of the entirety of the Gaza war. He has carefully placed the conflict in the broader regional and geopolitical context, guiding the reader through the security lapses preceding the war, the gradual escalations, and the various ceasefire efforts that only prolonged the war.

Col Agarwal presents a structural perspective that combines the military and political aspects of the conflict. This is an accessible and comprehensive narrative of the war in Gaza, that also includes the role of regional actors in the conflict and appropriately places them in the broader regional and global context.

In the early part of the book, Col Agarwal has looked at Israel's complex domestic politics – a prime minister under siege, his opportunistic coalition with the extreme right-wing parties in Israel, and the commencement of policies of deliberate provocation and intimidation against the Palestinians. After a detailed look at the October 7 attacks by Hamas, the author discusses the carnage mercilessly wreaked upon the civilians in Gaza by Israel, as residence blocks were bombarded into rubble, and people compelled to flee from one sanctuary to another till they finally realised that Gaza offered no safe haven to anyone.

The author has also examined the futile attempts of President Biden to obtain a ceasefire and the ways in which his feeble efforts were firmly brushed aside by Netanyahu. Besides the study of the complex ramifications of the conflict and the related diplomacy, the author's significant contribution is the analysis that traces the root causes of the conflict to Trump's first term, when the president came under the spell of the beguiling Israeli leader, Netanyahu.

Trump backed almost every item on Israel's agenda – shifting the US embassy to Jerusalem, approving the annexation of the Golan Heights and East Jerusalem by Israel, and even approving a major expansion of settlements in the West Bank. The camaraderie between the two leaders also produced Trump's "Deal of the Century", a peace plan for Palestine that was so heavily loaded in favour of Israel that it quickly withered away and is now largely discredited.

That bond with Trump has served Netanyahu well in the president's second term, such as obtaining the ceasefire in Gaza, putting in place the extraordinary Board of Peace, and then the 12-day assault on Iran in June 2025 in which the US also joined. Though outside the purview of this book, it should be noted that the Netanyahu magic has also ensured the Israeli-US partnership in the ongoing war on Iran.

The final ceasefire agreement of October 2025, emerging from Trump's "20 Point Peace Plan" has silenced the guns in Gaza, though sporadic acts of violence continue to test its efficacy. However, the arrangements relating to the peace process are indeed curious, possibly they are without precedent, as they provide for the US president to preside over a Board of Peace, whose members, selected by Trump, are heads of diverse states with a stake in peace in Gaza. Though several Arab, African and Asian leaders have joined the Board, the US' European partners have not, based on concerns relating to the exclusion of the UN from the peace process. Prospects of lasting peace in Gaza look remote: Hamas is not yet ready to surrender its arms, so that Gaza cannot be completely demilitarised, thus ensuring that Israeli forces will not vacate Gaza. The odds in favour of Gaza returning to another period of conflict are therefore live and real.

The book is a well-researched analysis of events that followed October 7, a chronology which the author has carefully untangled, highlighting the nuances of a very complex conflict. To a reader who has followed the widespread debate amongst different sections of society all around the world, such nuance becomes important to understand when determining questions of sovereignty, self-determination and aspects of international war. The book is thought-provoking, and some of the accounts mentioned raise pertinent questions not just for the Israeli and Palestinian societies, but for everyone who would like to see a resolution to this conflict that, as the title of the book says, has remained elusive.

Col Agarwal's study of the Gaza war is a timely and substantial contribution to contemporary research relating to West Asia. It is replete with important details, backed by credible sources, and offers lucid analyses of events during that turbulent period.

At a time when the global discourse around the conflict is often marked by polarization and emotive rhetoric, this work offers a measured and informed perspective. It is therefore a valuable contribution not only for students of military strategy and international relations, but also for the general reader seeking a deeper understanding of one of the most enduring and complex conflicts of our time.

March 2026 **Talmiz Ahmad**

Former Indian Ambassador to Oman, the UAE and Saudi Arabia, and Distinguished Professor for International Studies, Symbiosis International University, Pune

ACKNOWLEDGEMENTS

This is my first attempt at writing a book and it would not have been possible without the constant encouragement and support of many people who stood by me during the long process of research and writing.

I would like to begin by expressing my deepest gratitude to Meenu, my wife and my two children, Shubham and Pankhuri. Their patience, understanding, and constant encouragement gave me the strength to pursue this demanding project. Writing about a conflict as complex and emotionally charged as the Gaza war required long hours of reading, reflection, and writing, and their quiet support made this journey worth the while. A special word for my parents who have been my guiding light as I grew up.

I am also grateful to many of my friends and seniors who consistently motivated me to keep writing and to pursue this work. Their words of encouragement, ideas and thoughtful conversations helped me sustain my resolve during moments of doubt and fatigue. In particular, I would like to mention my colleagues at MP-IDSA who in my formative years, taught me the ropes of research and writing, especially Dr Arvind Gupta, former DG, IDSA and Deputy National Security Adviser of India, Dr Meena Singh Roy, Former Head of West Asia and Eurasia Centre and Col Vivek Chadha, Head of the Military Centre.

I would like to acknowledge the various media platforms, newspapers, and think tanks that published my articles and analyses on the Gaza war over the past three years. Their willingness to provide space for informed discussion on developments in West Asia not only enriched the public discourse but also helped shape many of the ideas that eventually formed the core of this book. Much of the content in the book has been curated from those ideas and writings.

I would also wish to place on record my sincere gratitude to Shri Shishir Priyadarshi, President of Chintan Research Foundation, Delhi for providing me the space, encouragement, and time to complete this project.

Finally, a big thanks to all the readers who are the most important part of the conversation.

Any shortcomings in this book remain entirely my own.

02 April 2026 **Col Rajeev Agarwal (Retired)**

INTRODUCTION

The pre-emptive strikes on 28 February 2026 by Israel and the USA on Iran, citing 'existential' and 'pre-eminent' threat have plunged the entire West Asian region into the most dangerous conflict in the region, ever. An offensive launched by two of the most modern, lethal and technologically advanced militaries was supposed to bring Iran to its knees, begging for ceasefire in a matter of days. The targeted assassination of Iran's Supreme Leader was supposed to act as a catalyst to bring people out in the streets and force a regime change. However, Iran, contrary to most expectations, is hitting back hard. Fighting a lone battle, it has not only absorbed hundreds of air and missile strikes from the USA and Israel but has unleashed a whole range of attacks through missiles and drones on almost every nation in the region which hosts American bases or has permitted USA and Israel to use its soil or airspace to launch strikes into Iran, including Saudi Arabia, UAE, Bahrain, Jordan, Iraq, Qatar, Oman etc.

What has been witnessed has shocked the world and has gone well beyond the wildest calculations of American and Israeli generals. The targeted assassination of its Supreme Leader and over 40 top generals has not deterred Iran but has, on the contrary, strengthened its resolve to fight back. The inadequacy of the American security umbrella in the Gulf region has been totally exposed while the American defensive systems are being overwhelmed and outnumbered. US bases and embassies have been struck badly, key radars and bases have been destroyed, F-15 fighter jets and MQ-9B drones shot down. A number of places in Israel, key among them being Tel Aviv, Galilee, Haifa etc too have borne the brunt of Iranian missiles and drones.

The closure of the Strait of Hormuz is threatening global oil supplies and a sharp rise in prices of oil and natural gas is having cascading effects on all other aspects of global economy.

These strikes are almost a mirror image of what happened earlier in June 2025 when Israel struck pre-emptively on 13th June, initiating the '12 Day War'. Why is it important? Because the nuclear talks between Iran and the US were progressing well and Iran and the US were scheduled for their fifth round of talks on a possible nuclear deal on 15th June. Obviously, there were no talks thereafter once the war broke out.

How is it similar this time? On 27th February, after the end of the last round of talks in Geneva to negotiate a deal and prevent a war, Omani Foreign Minister Badr Albusaidi announced that Iran has agreed to significant breakthrough" concessions in indirect nuclear talks with the United States, aiming to prevent further conflict. Iran had reportedly agreed to the following:

- Zero Enriched Uranium Stockpiling: Iran has agreed to a policy of "zero accumulation" and "zero stockpiling" of enriched uranium.
- Down-blending Existing Material: Iran agreed to degrade its current, higher-enriched stockpiles into fuel, allowing for full verification by the International Atomic Energy Agency (IAEA).
- "Never, ever" a Bomb: The above two steps will ensure that Iran will not possess a nuclear bomb, making this an unprecedented "very important breakthrough".

As per this, Iran and the US were closer than ever at reaching a nuclear deal which would have ensured that Iran never gets the nuclear weapon. However, Iran had made it clear that its right to enrichment of Uranium, being a signatory of the NPT and its ballistic missile program cannot be part of any negotiations. For Israel, however, the threat posed by its ballistic missile was equal if not more important than the nuclear deal, something that Israel's leadership had often openly spoken of. The next round of 'technical talks' on how to take the discussions and broad understandings of Geneva forward, were to be held in Vienna the following week which obviously did not take place.

The latest conflict therefore once again has highlighted the deep faultlines and animosity that exist, particularly between Israel and Iran. It is also an offshoot of the perennial threat that Israel has faced on its borders from non-state actors and proxies of Iran like the Hamas and Hezbollah who have been fermenting trouble for Israel over the decades. In centre of all this lies a small, thin strip of land, 'Gaza', which has borne the brunt of this animosity through a conflict which was imposed on it, almost against the run of play, in October 2023.

The year 2023 was in fact, a roller coaster one for West Asia. There were exciting and positive developments promising an end to long-term rivalries, paving the way for regional peace and economic prosperity in a conflict-prone region. However, a sudden and unexpected event in the second half of the year threatened to destroy all these efforts in a single sweep. It was the war in Gaza, unleashed following the 7 October terror attack.

What happened? Why did the war break out? Unlike previous conflicts in Gaza, why did it last so much? Why did it engulf the entire region? Why did the international community not intervene and stop it? Why was the human cost so high in this conflict? Many more questions and so few answers!

When 2023 started, things looked good for the region. The Saudi-Iran peace deal was the first major and welcome surprise. On 10 March, China stunned the world when it announced that Saudi Arabia and Iran have agreed to resume diplomatic relations after seven years, in a peace deal brokered by it. Following the Saudi-Iran peace deal, there was a wave of reconciliation among the countries in the region. The Egyptian Foreign Minister visited Syria, the first trip by a top Egyptian diplomat to Syria since its civil war began in 2011. He held talks with his Turkish counterpart on the possibility of restoring ties, during the first visit to Cairo by Turkey's top diplomat since relations ruptured after the overthrow of the Muslim Brotherhood government in 2013 in Egypt. Qatar and Bahrain too announced the restoration of diplomatic ties on 13 April, an important step for unity within the Gulf Cooperation Council (GCC). The re-entry of Syria into the Arab League in April too was a major development, ending 12 years of its exile. Its membership was earlier revoked when civil war broke out in Syria following a violent crackdown on protesters in March 2011 during the 'Arab Spring' protests.

The story of reconciliation in the region in 2023 cannot be complete without the mention of developments in the Saudi-Israel normalisation. It was a process which was well on its way to finality in September, brokered by the USA. Inputs indicated that Saudi Arabia would get iron-clad security guarantees from the USA as well as a civilian nuclear program. Israel, in turn, would be asked to offer 'assurances' to the Palestinian groups without any clear outcome on the two-state solution.

In the midst of this, two more significant developments took place. In August, Egypt, Iran, Saudi Arabia and the UAE were admitted into BRICS, an important multilateral platform, taking global centre stage. And in September, at the G20 summit in Delhi, the India-Middle East-Europe Economic Corridor (IMEC) was announced which had the West Asia region at the heart of it.

What happened then? Why did Gaza happen? Perhaps, many of the above developments contributed to it in some manner, because in all of it, the cause for an independent state of Palestine was getting successively diluted and lost. But obviously, there were many more reasons for it.

The Hamas terror attack on 7 October was nothing like any previous attack witnessed in Israel. Launched on a day of prayer and holiday in Israel, it took the entire security and intelligence network by absolute shock and surprise. Within a few hours, over 1,100 persons had been killed, hundreds more injured and 251 hostages taken across to Gaza by Hamas.

Israel regrouped quickly and unleashed its most ferocious military campaign ever. Vowing to eliminate Hamas from the face of the Earth and flatten Gaza to the ground, the campaign soon turned ugly when reports of hospitals, schools, shelters, UN buildings, etc., being bombed took over the news. Israel was however relentless in its vow to punish Hamas.

Despite international pressure and internal protests, Israel continued to bomb Gaza. Along the way, it expanded its campaign to destroy Hezbollah to the North too. When Iran entered the conflict in April 2024, it threatened to escalate dangerously. The downfall of the Assad regime in Syria in December 2024 was another threat neutralised across Israel's borders. When the USA joined Israel in taking out Iran's nuclear sites in June 2025 during the '12 Day War', Israel got much more than it had hoped for at the start of the war.

There were several attempts at a ceasefire but it was only after Donald Trump became the 47th President of the USA in January 2025 that a proper ceasefire took shape, at least for a few weeks. The eventual end to the war following the adoption of the '20 Point Peace Plan' of Trump in October 2025 may have ended the war but the path towards enduring peace is going to be long and arduous.

This book is a story of the Gaza war. It captures important developments as they happened and relives moments of victory, defeat, death, anxiety and hope along the way. In separately segregated sections, it focuses on not only the 'what' of the war but also raises questions on the 'how' and 'why'. It raises questions on various aspects of the war, how Israel regained military control over Gaza, why multiple ceasefire attempts failed, how Israeli intelligence agencies redeemed themselves, how Iran and Israel engaged in a direct military conflict for the first time, how Israel used this war to eliminate all other threats on its borders and, most importantly, how the war finally ended.

A brief section on India highlights how it managed to keep itself on the right side of the war all throughout. Some key military lessons for India from the war and what could be India's role in Gaza as it searches for long-term peace, adds a clear Indian perspective to it.

Finally, this book is a work curated from the writings and analyses of the war for over three years and it is hoped that it will provide readers a deep insight into how this human tragedy unfolded, many years from now.

April 2026 **Col Rajeev Agarwal (Retired)**

Partition Plan as approved by the UN General Assssembly in Nov 1947

Map as per 1967 Borders

Gaza Map as in October 2023, Prior to 7th October Attack - UN OCHA Oct 2023

SECTION 1

A War that was Waiting to Happen: A Story of Missed Signals and Gross Miscalculations

1

In the Midst of the COVID-19 Pandemic, Gaza Erupts into a Conflict

It is May 2021 and Gaza has just witnessed another sharp, short and bitter conflict!

The guns have fallen silent, fighter aircraft are back to their bases and the two sides, while counting their losses, are trying to hold onto their nerves as the latest conflict between Israel and Hamas in the Gaza Strip has come to a halt after the declaration of an unconditional ceasefire on 21 May 2021. It started off with Hamas firing a barrage of rockets on 11 May into Israeli territory, which was promptly retaliated by the Israeli Defence Forces by launching a precise and punitive attack with missiles and airstrikes on Hamas targets in the Gaza Strip. The final tally of losses reads: more than 200 Palestinians killed including 60 children while on the Israeli side, 13 lives were lost. In the midst of the COVID-19 pandemic raging across the globe, the people in the region hope that this fragile ceasefire holds and that this latest conflict spurs the stakeholders into finding a peaceful resolution to the Palestine issue, simmering since the birth of Israel in 1948.

The trigger to the current conflict is attributed to a number of factors. There is the issue of Israeli police barricading the Damascus Gate in the old city of Jerusalem on 13 April, preventing Palestinian Arabs from offering prayers at the Al-Aqsa-Mosque on the first day of the holy month of Ramadan. The barricading drew widespread anger and protests. There were continued and sporadic protests/clashes thereafter throughout the holy month. Again, on 7 May, the last Friday of Ramadan, Israeli police and the Palestinians clashed after the evening prayers at Al-Aqsa Mosque with the Israeli police entering the mosque and hundreds of Palestinians getting hurt. On 10 May, Hamas gave Israel a warning to withdraw its forces from the Al-Aqsa Mosque area as well as Sheikh Jarrah. The firing of rockets by Hamas into Israel on the night of 10/11 May thereafter sparked the war with Israel launching 'Operation Guardian of Walls'.

Another issue which triggered the conflict was a property dispute in the Sheikh Jarrah neighbourhood of East Jerusalem in Israel where a number of Palestinian residents were agitated over possible eviction from their homes. Reason? It was a case over land-ownership between a few Palestinian and Israeli Jewish families who had settled there in 1967. The case was scheduled to be heard in Israel's Supreme Court on 10 May 2021. On 7 May, there were clashes in the Sheikh Jarrah neighbourhood between the Palestinian residents and right-wing Israelis over the land-ownership case. The court hearing was postponed due to the unrest but the damage had already been done.

Let us explore and analyse the 'Why Now'. The issue of land ownership in the neighbourhood of Sheikh Jarrah is not new. It goes back to the time when Jordan, in 1956, after its capture of the old city of Jerusalem earlier, leased the captured property in Sheikh Jarrah to 28 Palestinian families. After the 1967 Arab-Israeli war, Israel passed a law permitting Jewish families who had been forcefully evicted by Jordan or Britain before 1967, to claim property rights by producing proof of original property ownership. So, this issue was not new. Why it was slated for hearing by the Israeli Supreme Court on 10 May could be an interesting coincidence.

The first clashes started when Israeli police prevented Palestinians from offering prayers at their holy place on 13 April, the first day of the holy month of Ramadan. Again, a curious coincidence! The second major clashes and Israeli forces entering the mosque on 7 May, the last Friday of Ramadan, raise another interesting choice/coincidence of dates. For any Muslim, two things are beyond debate. The holy month of Ramadan and the significance of the Al-Aqsa Mosque. Is there an argument that Israel wanted to provoke a violent reaction?

The US-Israel relations too are a significant factor. With Joe Biden as the President, Israel was feeling unsure of the unflinching support it had enjoyed earlier under President Trump. The readiness of the Biden administration to commence nuclear talks with Iran and delink monetary aid to Palestine from the Israeli equation hurt Israel. BBC News reported on 7 April that *"US President Joe Biden's administration plans to provide $ 235 m (£ 171 m) of aid to Palestinians, restoring part of the assistance cut by Donald Trump. Two-thirds will go to the UN's agency for Palestinian refugees, Unrwa, which has suffered a financial crisis since it lost $ 360 m of US funding in 2018. Mr. Biden wants to 'restore credible engagement' by the Palestinians in long-stalled peace talks with Israel*". This announcement interestingly was exactly one week before the first trigger to the present conflict.

The Iran factor too is interesting in relation to the conflict. The talks on the possibility of the revival of the Joint Comprehensive Plan of Action (JCPOA) or the Iran Nuclear Deal were held in Vienna between the EU and Iran during this period. While nothing concrete had materialised out of it yet, there were reports of a massive explosion at the Natanz nuclear plant of Iran on 11 April, which Iran blamed on Israel. While Iran did not retaliate militarily, the opportunity presented to Hamas in Israel must have been more than welcome. Obviously, with Iran presidential elections scheduled for 18 June, a conflict in Israel works well with the top leadership and the hardliners in Iran.

There is also the issue of elections to the Palestinian Legislative Assembly which were scheduled for 22 May. Palestinian Authority President Mahmoud Abbas abruptly called it off on 29 April. Hamas thought that it had the upper hand and the cancellation therefore was an act of sabotage against its political interests. Again, the timing of it and Hamas's eagerness to exploit this situation militarily looks quite obvious. Therefore, the clashes on 7 May and storming of the mosque by Israeli forces was a perfect opportunity for Hamas.

There are also the larger issues of the Abraham Accords, which brought Israel closer to the Arab world as well as the resolution of the GCC crisis earlier in the year and the returning of Qatar in the fold of GCC. Both these threatened the dilution of the Palestine cause in the larger Muslim world. Coupled with it, reports of talks between Egypt and Israel in March 2021 on expanding their ties in the region would have served no good purpose to the Palestine cause.

On the Israeli front, there was an important political interplay, i.e., the national elections. In four elections over one year, Prime Minister Netanyahu had failed to secure a majority. On 4 May, he failed to meet the deadline to conjure up numbers to form a government, just three days before the Israeli forces stormed the Al-Aqsa Mosque on 7 May. Should this too be called a coincidence?

Let us discuss the objectives and outcomes. In Netanyahu's own words, he said he was "determined to continue this operation until its objective is achieved: to restore quiet and security to you, citizens of Israel". Have the Israeli military operations before the ceasefire achieved those objectives? Has Hamas been so degraded that it poses no military threat in the near future to Israel? Has the top leadership of Hamas been taken out? Sadly, to most of the questions, the answer may be a 'No'.

Lastly, who has gained and how much? Israel, and particularly Prime Minister

Netanyahu, has clearly demonstrated its will to take punitive military action when threatened and have succeeded in shoring up national support. Wars are always a close rallying point for national leadership and Israel is no different. Hamas too, on the other hand, has gained in its standing among the Palestinian and Arab leadership. In a future election to the Palestine Legislative Assembly, it may emerge victorious. Also, the conflict did not result in a ground invasion or capture of Gaza, as was initially feared, a positive for Hamas. Iran, playing its role quietly in the background, has avenged the Natanz attack (maybe) and its open support to the Hamas cause has won it important stakes in the Muslim world where many of the other important Muslim countries offered feeble support to Palestine.

Hundreds of lives were lost and thousands of families were rendered homeless: can this be a result of so many curious coincidences over such a short period of time? When the dust settles over this conflict, the manner of its escalation and timing will always be a point of debate.

2

Another Conflict in Gaza: Deepening the Divide

There was a sense of relative peace in Gaza since the last confrontation in May 2021. The calm was shattered again when, on 5 August 2022, Israel launched an offensive code-named '*Operation Breaking Dawn*' in Gaza Strip, targeting the Palestinian Islamic Jihad (PIJ). The offensive lasted three days and, as claimed by Israel, was provoked by "imminent threat of attack against Israeli civilians posed by the PIJ." Official figures put casualties in the Gaza Strip at 44 killed, including 16 children and 360 wounded while only three civilians in Israel suffered injuries.

As a pre-emptive measure, Israeli forces arrested Bassam al-Saadi, the head of the PIJ in the West Bank and his close aide, Asharaf al-Jada, on 1 August in Jenin. As per a statement from Israel's Security Agency, Shabak, PIJ was increasing its military presence in the West Bank and Al-Saadi was the mastermind behind it. Israel therefore took the initiative and launched the attacks. Among the prominent targets were PIJ's Northern commander, Taysir Al-Jabari, whose apartment was blown up by a missile strike on 5 August, followed by the killing of Khaled Mansour, commander of the Southern Region, the next day and one of the founders of the Al-Quds Brigades group in the Gaza Strip. The targeting and killing of Al-Jabari was tactically very important as he was one of the most prominent leaders of the movement after the death of Baha Abu Al-Ata, who too had been eliminated in an Israeli strike in November 2019.

After three days of firing, on 7 August 2022, Israel and the PIJ agreed to an Egypt-brokered ceasefire. Hamas, which governs the Gaza Strip, did not join PIJ directly in the fight, but offered 'moral' support. International reactions were mixed and on expected lines. US President Biden reiterated the USA's support for Israel's "right to defend itself against attacks" while the UN Special Coordinator for the Middle East Peace Process, Tor Wennesland, expressed concern about civilian casualties, and later welcomed the ceasefire. UK Foreign Secretary Liz Truss expressed her country's support for Israel and its right to self-defence. Iran expectedly had a combative response with its Commander of the Iranian Revolutionary Guards, Major General Salami, promising that "the Israelis will pay yet another heavy price for their recent crime." Russia laid the blame for the escalation on Israel, saying fighting started after the Israeli Air Force attacked the Gaza Strip, causing Palestinian terror groups to respond.

Though the fighting has stopped, at least for the time being, this isn't the first time a major conflict has occurred between Israel and the Palestinian groups. In fact, a brief look back into time clearly depicts an episodic and a rather deliberately orchestrated nature of these conflicts.

Soon after Hamas took over the reins of the Gaza Strip in 2007, Israel declared Gaza to be 'hostile territory' and put in place a naval blockade across it coupled with a series of other severe restrictions. But the first major conflict came on 4 November 2008, when Israel launched a raid on the Gaza Strip aimed to destroy a tunnel on the Gaza-Israel border dug by militants to infiltrate into Israel; in the process six Hamas operatives were killed. It led to escalation of hostilities leading to 7 December when Israel launched '*Operation Cast Lead*', a 22-day military assault on the Gaza Strip, which included a ground offensive too, launched on 3 January 2009. With heavy casualties in the Gaza Strip and under intense international pressure, both parties announced a ceasefire on 18 January, a day before President Obama was sworn in as US President.

Four years later came the next conflict, '*Operation Pillar of Defence*'. On 14 November 2012, Israel launched an attack in its claimed attempt to prevent rocket attacks from Gaza and protect its citizens in South Israel. It commenced with the targeted assassination of Ahmed Jaabari, the head of Hamas' military wing, and was subsequently followed by the killing of Hamas' Central Command chief, Ahmad Abu Jalal, on 16 November. The operation lasted eight days.

Less than two years later, on 18 July 2014, Israel launched an attack on Gaza named '*Operation Protective Edge*'. It was triggered by the Israeli response to the kidnapping and murder of three Israeli youth by Palestinians from the West Bank on 11 June which was followed by Israeli military raids in Palestinian cities and villages. Israel also carried out bombing attacks in the Gaza Strip. Palestinian factions in Gaza, in return, began firing rockets into Israel, prompting Israel to launch '*Operation Protective Edge*'. A ceasefire was finalized on 26 August, bringing the end of yet another bloody chapter in the region. Incidentally, it was the first time that Israel put into operation its anti-missile defence system 'Iron Dome' which has proved hugely successful in thwarting rocket and missile attacks into Israeli territory.

Post 2014, although minor cross-border skirmishes and rocket/missile attacks continued, the next major conflict came after almost six years in May 2021, '*Operation Guardian of Walls*'. Egypt's mediated ceasefire brought an end to the conflict on 21 May.

The above-mentioned conflicts clearly indicate the episodic nature of conflicts. Also, these conflicts have not moved towards the possibility of a two-state solution but have slowly led to one where the regional countries as well as the world in general are losing interest and hope in the cause.

The Abraham Accords of 2020 that established Israel's formal diplomatic ties with Arab countries – the UAE, Bahrain, Sudan and Morocco – are an indication that the region now thinks beyond Israel as enemy or problem No.1. There have been reports of Israeli and Saudi leadership forging communications, which would have been unthinkable in the past. Turkey is mending its ties with Israel while Egypt continues to be a key peace mediator for Israel and Palestine when required. The ever increasing settlements and therefore the areas that can possibly be offered as a part of a future Palestine state are shrinking by the day. Against these factors, the frequently occurring Israel-Palestine conflicts are not serving the cause for a viable two-state solution.

3

Netanyahu Faces Troubles at Home: Is there Another Conflict Round the Corner?

It is April 2023 and the 7 October Hamas terror attack is still a long way off. Meanwhile, in Israel, there is internal turmoil.

When Prime Minister Benjamin Netanyahu won the parliamentary elections in November 2022 and finally managed to muster a full majority in the Knesset (Israel's Parliament) after a turbulent political period of three years since 2019 over which Israel had to hold five Knesset elections, it was greeted with cautious optimism. 'Bibi', as he is popularly known, was back in power as Prime Minister 17 months after losing the elections in June 2021 to Naftali Bennett. The victory was greeted with optimism because the return of Netanyahu with a full majority (however thin) offered hope for a period of internal political stability. Caution because, knowing Netanyahu and his traditionally aggressive 'security oriented' policies, there is always a fear of blowback for Israel in the region. The ride so far has however been far from smooth with Netanyahu facing serious challenges both within the country as well as in the region.

Internal Troubles

Internally, the Israeli government has been facing stiff resistance over some of the controversial reforms that Netanyahu proposed within months of taking over as the PM, primary among them being the judicial reforms. The judicial reforms are aimed to substantially constrain the authority of the judiciary and give the government near-complete control over the appointment of judges. The reforms triggered widespread protests on the streets of Israeli cities with citizen groups, including workers' unions and even reservists of the Israeli Defence Forces, calling the bill a murder of democracy. It also led to Netanyahu firing his Defence Minister Yoav Gallant on 26 March, when the latter insisted on a pause to the judicial reforms. Although Yoav Gallant was reinstated on 10 April, the event exposed the deep fragility within the coalition government.

Netanyahu's troubles have, however, not subsided with the reinstatement of the Defence Minister. The rather unprovoked attacks on Palestinian worshippers at the holy Al-Aqsa Mosque in East Jerusalem twice in the first week of April, not only provoked various armed groups in the West Bank, Gaza Strip and Syria but also drew sharp criticism from the Arab countries in the region. Israeli police claimed that they were forced to enter the mosque compound after 'masked agitators' locked themselves inside with fireworks, sticks and stones, but there are not many who are ready to buy this argument, especially as the worshippers were offering prayers in the holy month of Ramadan. Provoked by Israeli raids on worshippers at Al-Aqsa Mosque, al-Quds Brigades, the armed wing of the Palestinian Islamic Jihad movement, fired six rockets from Syria on 9 April, drawing immediate retaliation from Israel. Armed clashes were reported across the Gaza Strip and the occupied West Bank escalating the security situation all around Israel.

Earlier, at least 10 Palestinians were killed on 22 February in fighting with Israeli forces in the West Bank town of Nablus, sparking unrest in the area. This was soon followed by a retaliatory action in which two Israeli brothers were shot dead in a terror attack on 26 February in the West Bank town of Huwara. Concerned over the escalating situation and the upcoming period of Ramadan, Khaldoon Al Mubarak, senior adviser to UAE President Mohamed bin Zayed Al Nahyan, was despatched to meet PM Netanyahu on 23 March to convey a message to the Israeli government concerning its treatment of Palestinians. "The direction of this government goes completely against the Abraham Accords," Mubarak was quoted as having told Netanyahu.

Regional Developments

In the midst of this internal turmoil, two major developments were reported from the region having a direct bearing on Israel. On 28 February 2023, the UN reported that Iran had enriched parts of uranium to 84 per cent purity, causing alarm that Iran was on the threshold of developing a nuclear weapon. Just a few days later, on 10 March, China stunned the world when it announced that Saudi Arabia and Iran had agreed to resume diplomatic relations after seven years in a peace deal brokered by it. Both these announcements had a profound impact on Israel's regional policies. Israel has been propagating stiff action (including military) against Iran to counter its nuclear program which, it alleges, has a strong military dimension and poses an existential threat to Israel. A firm critic of the Iran Nuclear

Deal, it was the first to welcome when President Trump pulled out of the Iran Nuclear Deal in May 2018, calling it 'the worst deal ever'. Recent reports of Iran enriching uranium to very high levels, almost weapon grade, can therefore be no good news for Israel.

The other development, that is, Saudi-Iran rapprochement, may raise more concern in the Israeli establishment than even nuclear enrichment by Iran. The Saudi-Iran peace deal, signed in March 2023, threatens to put to waste years of back-door attempts towards reconciliation with the Arab world in general and Saudi Arabia in particular. In the past few years, there were even reports of Saudi going slow on the Palestinian issue as also trying to find a way to fit Israel into the regional framework where the sole aim seemed to unite, 'against Iran'. This seemed logical to some extent because Iran was the common enemy for Israel as well as Saudi Arabia, especially since Iran-backed proxies had upped the ante and targeted Saudi Arabia with drones and long-range weapons since 2019. The Abraham Accords signed in August 2020 were an initiator towards this process, deliberately keeping Saudi Arabia out of it while incorporating its powerful ally, the UAE, to test the waters. The Saudi-Iran peace deal is therefore a huge setback to Israel's regional calculus. If Iran no longer remains 'enemy No.1' for the Arab world, how does Israel find support for its anti-Iran crusade in the region?

This is not all. Along with the Saudi-Iran peace deal, there seems to be a wave of reconciliation among the Arab countries in the region. Egyptian Foreign Minister Sameh Shoukry visited Syria on 27 February, the first trip by a top Egyptian diplomat to Syria since its civil war began in 2011, in a signal towards possible warming ties between Syria and Arab states. Earlier, in March, Egypt's foreign minister held talks with his Turkish counterpart, Mevlut Cavusoglu, on the possibility of restoring ties during the first visit to Cairo by Turkey's top diplomat since relations ruptured after the overthrow of the Muslim Brotherhood government in 2013 in Egypt. Qatar and Bahrain too have announced restoration of diplomatic ties on 13 April, an important step towards unity within the GCC.

There are also serious developments towards getting Syria back within the fold of the Arab League. During President Assad's visit to the UAE on 19 March, UAE President Sheikh Mohamed bin Zayed Al-Nahyan told Assad, "Syria has been absent from its brothers for too long, and the time has come for it to return to them and to its Arab surroundings." On 14 April, GCC foreign ministers and their counterparts from Egypt, Jordan and Iraq met in Jeddah upon the invitation of Saudi Arabia's Foreign Minister Prince Faisal bin Farhan to discuss Arab developments. "The ministers discussed the efforts that aim to reach a political solution…which preserves Syria's unity, security, stability and Arab identity and that brings Syria back to the Arab fold," a statement issued by the Saudi foreign ministry said.

Looking Ahead

The developments in the Arab world mentioned above leading towards larger reconciliation in the Arab world and a peace deal with Iran could permanently alter the decades-old geopolitics of the West Asian region. With the mainstreaming of Iran in the region, Israel will have to rethink its strategy, especially with the Iran nuclear deal going nowhere and Iran steadily enriching uranium to higher grades. The reluctance and, in fact, the inability of the USA to influence geopolitics in the region is another dampener for Israel. Also, China's active and assertive diplomatic involvement in the region and Russia leaning towards China and the countries in the region for support in view of Western sanctions on it owing to the war in Ukraine, may make it tough for Israel, especially if it keeps resorting to frequent armed actions against the Palestinians in the Gaza Strip and/or the West Bank. Its strategy of 'enforcing peace through security' and a fast-fading option of a viable two-state solution for Palestine will require a serious review, going forward. Israel needs to stay ahead of the curve to reap the benefits of its diplomatic overtures in the region in the past few years, lest it finds itself left out in the region once again, turning back the clock to the 1990s, a period of hostility and isolation.

4

Israel's Operations in Jenin Camp, West Bank: A Warning Sign Ignored

It is July 2023 and the slow build-up to 7 October has started taking shape, away from the public eye or Israeli vigil.

The Israeli raid on the Jenin Camp in the West Bank on 3 July 2023 is the fiercest and largest military operation comprising land as well as air forces (including drones and armed helicopters) in the West Bank in over two decades. Accusing Palestinian militant groups of using Jenin Camp for basing fighters within the densely-populated refugee camp, the Israeli military claimed that it had hit a weapons production and explosives storage facility during the assault, reducing threats of future attacks into Israeli territory. Code named '*House and Garden*', Israel's military called it an 'extensive counter-terrorism effort' adding that the raid was intended to "break the safe-haven mindset of the camp, which has become a hornets' nest".

During the two-day operation in Jenin which houses more than 14,000 refugees, 12 Palestinians were killed and more than 150 were injured. The assault destroyed more than 300 homes and damaged over 400, forcing more than 3,000 Palestinians to flee the camp. The joint air and ground operations in Jenin is the first one of such intensity since the 2002 battle of Jenin, when more than 50 Palestinians and 23 Israeli soldiers were killed. The current military operation, the culmination of a large number of smaller but connected armed skirmishes in the West Bank in over a year, has brought the official death toll of Palestinians killed in that year in the West Bank to 133.

Israel's military operations against Palestinian militant groups have generally been targeted inside the Gaza Strip, which is governed by Hamas since 2007, one of the rival factions in the Palestinian authority, the other one being Fatah, which governs the West Bank. Soon after Hamas took over the governance of the Gaza Strip in 2007, Israel declared Gaza to be 'hostile territory' and put in place a naval blockade across it. The first significant conflict came when on 4 November 2008 Israel launched '*Operation Cast Lead*', a raid in the Gaza Strip to destroy a tunnel on the Gaza-Israel border dug by militants to infiltrate Israel. Many episodic conflicts later, in May 2023, Israel launched '*Operation Shield and Arrow*' into the Gaza Strip, as Israel's response to an escalation of rocket and mortar fire by PIJ, which itself was a response to the death of a senior member of the group's West Bank branch while on hunger strike in an Israeli prison.

However, over the past two years, there has been a drastic escalation in the number of attacks from and into the West Bank. Jenin Camp has been in the news for becoming a hotbed of militants and a safe hiding place for them. Over the last one year, the intensity of engagement with Israeli forces has intensified. In August 2022, Israeli forces arrested Bassam al-Saadi, the head of the PIJ in the West Bank, and his close aide Asharaf al-Jada in Jenin. Earlier, on 26 January 2023, Israeli forces killed seven gunmen and two civilians in a raid in Jenin. Just a few days ago, on 25 July, three Palestinians were killed by Israeli troops in Nablus, West Bank. Israel's army, in a statement, said that armed terrorists had opened fire on its soldiers from a vehicle in the Nablus neighbourhood and that its troops had fired back to neutralize the threat.

Plenty for Israel to Ponder

With no let-up in the threat from the Gaza Strip, escalation of violence in the West Bank cannot be good news for Israel in any manner. To add fire in this emerging situation, PM Netanyahu's reported statement to the Knesset (Israeli parliament) committee members in a closed-door meeting stating on 1 July (reported by *The Jerusalem Post*) that Palestinian hopes of establishing a sovereign state "must be eliminated," cannot be termed reconciliatory in any manner.

The continuance of settlements for Israeli citizens in the West Bank too is a sore point. On 26 June 2023, the Israeli Defence Ministry planning committee approved more than 5,000 new housing units in the West Bank. Peace Now, an Israel-based advocacy group opposed to settlements, in a statement condemned the move stating that "the approval of nearly 5,700 housing units today and over 13,000 in the first half of this year alone should make it clear that the government is rushing headlong towards an annexation coup". The USA, principal ally of Israel, too has been critical of continued expansion of Israeli settlements in the occupied West Bank. US State Department spokesperson Matthew Miller expressing concern said, "We are deeply troubled by the Israeli government's reported decision to advance planning for over 4,000 settlements in the West Bank." Wasel Abu Yousef, a Palestinian official in the occupied West Bank, called the move an "open war against the Palestinian people."

The Abraham Accords with the aim of mainstreaming Israel in the region too is likely to suffer setbacks with the ongoing developments. The UAE, one of the signatories of the Abraham Accords and which has restored full diplomatic ties with Israel, has been very critical of Israel's military actions. Immediately after the Jenin raid, the UAE Ministry of Foreign Affairs (MoFA) called for the immediate halt of repeated and escalating campaigns against the Palestinian people. There have been a lot of back channel talks on brokering diplomatic ties between Saudi Arabia and Israel. However, incidents like this are a dampener on such efforts. Israel has to remember that Muslim solidarity is the glue that binds the nations in the region. Saudi Arabia, being the leader of Muslim nations, will therefore weigh its prospects very carefully before taking any decision on relations with Israel. Also, despite the fact that there is a creeping wariness on the Palestine issue among the Arab countries due to its never-ending cycle of conflict and very little hope of any solution in the near future, it is very unlikely that these nations will abandon the Palestinian cause in the near future.

Internally too, PM Netanyahu has found the going tough, especially over the judicial reforms. After months of protests and opposition, the bill was finally passed on 24 July 2023 by the Knesset promulgating a law that prevents the courts from reviewing the 'reasonableness' of government and ministerial decisions.

Looking Ahead

The recent armed conflicts in the West Bank have extended the Palestinian conflict to both sides of Israel. The use of excessive fire power in the Jenin raid was perhaps avoidable and invited widespread condemnation from the region and the global community.

Also, provocative steps like building of additional settlements in the occupied West Bank draw widespread criticism and shrink the geographical area finally available for a 'two-state solution'. Lastly, the raids like the one on Jenin Camp only result in alienating the two sides further and diminishing prospects of any early solution to the conflict.

5

The 7 October Terror Strike: A War that was Waiting to Happen

In the early hours of 7 October 2023, while the world was still asleep and Israel was on a holiday celebrating Simchat Torah, the day when Jews complete the annual cycle of reading the Torah scroll, Hamas struck Israel at multiple locations through multiple modes, catching it by absolute surprise. As Israeli armed forces and the political leadership scrambled to retaliate, the surprise assault revived the painful memories of a strikingly similar surprise attack launched by Egypt and Syria on 6 October 1973 on Yom Kippur, the holiest day of the Jewish calendar, exactly 50 years earlier.

The assault from Hamas began with thousands of rockets fired into Israel in the wee hours of the morning of 7 October. Various reports estimate the count of rockets to be between 5,000 and 7,000. Surprisingly, unlike in the past when the famous Israeli anti-missile and rocket system, the 'Iron Dome', fended off more than 90 percent of the rockets, this time, hundreds of these rockets from Gaza found their mark in Israeli territory. This was followed simultaneously by raids launched across land, air and sea. Defying years of blockade over sea, Hamas militants launched small boats and landed on Israeli beaches, firing indiscriminately. In a rather unique and audacious attempt, a number of Hamas operatives launched themselves in the air, piloting powered hang gliders, crossing over the fence and landing in Israeli territory. Simultaneously, Hamas broke through the border crossings in pickup trucks and motorcycles across more than 20 locations, blowing up parts of Israel's highly fortified fence at a number of places, storming into Israeli towns along the Gaza border, targeting and shooting at residents and Israeli soldiers. In no time, over 200 people in Israel were killed with over 300 injured. A police station was captured and a number of Israeli soldiers and civilians taken hostage and driven into Gaza. The 'shock and awe' tactics applied by Hamas took Israel and the entire world by storm as the timing,

Hamas Attack on 7th October 2023 - Lemonde International 11 Oct 2023

ferocity of the attack and the large number of casualties, including hostages, were perhaps the largest in the last five decades.

Israeli forces soon recovered and launched a ferocious air and artillery offensive on Gaza, targeting key military and command positions of Hamas. The ground troops regained control of the breached crossings and were able to neutralize most of the Hamas operatives who had infiltrated into Israeli territory. The war wages on and Israel with its military superiority will eventually prevail, but the damage would already have been done by then, both in terms of prospects of a long-term peace in the region as well as Israel's reputation as impenetrable and formidable territory. Questions will be asked and analysed as to how Hamas was successful in launching its largest ever military incursion into Israel and how the most technologically advanced and effective intelligence system failed to give any lead input on the attack.

The Missed Signals

The first indicator has to be the rapid increase in violence and conflict in the West Bank for the past two years. Right from the time Hamas took political control of Gaza and started governing it from 2007 onwards, the most frequent conflicts with Israel have occurred across Gaza. The West Bank had relatively been an 'island of peace' while the Gaza Strip was the focus of conflict. It is only in the last two years that Palestinian Islamic Jihad (PIJ) has taken the fight against Israel from across the West Bank. The skirmishes in the West Bank had three major effects; it kept Hamas and Gaza out of the limelight, escalated the scope of conflict to both ends of Israel's border with Palestinian territory and added to the animosity against Israel as the official death toll of Palestinians killed that year in the West Bank touched 150.

Targeting Palestinians going for worship at the Al-Aqsa Mosque in East Jerusalem has to be another important red flag. The Al-Aqsa in East Jerusalem, which Israel captured in the 1967 Six-Day War, hosts Islam's third-holiest site, Al-Aqsa Mosque and the Dome of the Rock, a seventh-century structure believed to be where the Prophet Muhammad ascended to heaven. The rather unprovoked attacks on Palestinian worshippers at the Al-Aqsa Mosque twice in the first week of April 2023, provoked various armed groups in the West Bank, Gaza Strip and Syria and drew sharp criticism from the Arab countries in the region. More recently, on 17 September, Israeli settlers forced themselves into the Mosque complex while the forces attacked Palestinian worshippers at Bab as-Silsila, one of the main entrances to the Al-Aqsa Mosque compound. Saudi Arabia, the UAE and Egypt immediately condemned the storming of Al-Aqsa Mosque. Saudi Arabia's Foreign Ministry called the Israeli actions "a blatant violation of all international norms and conventions, and a provocation to the feelings of Muslims across the world." Despite this, on 4 October, Israeli Jews again entered the Al-Aqsa Mosque complex while the Palestinian worshippers were held off by the Israeli forces. All this led to build-up of rage within the Palestinian community. In fact, Hamas military commander Muhammad Deif coined the ongoing Hamas operation as "*Operation Al-Aqsa Deluge*", in retaliation for Israel's 'desecration' of the Al-Aqsa Mosque on the Temple Mount in Jerusalem.

Talks on Saudi-Israel normalization have to be mentioned here. Inputs indicated that Saudi Arabia could get iron-clad security guarantees from the USA as well as a nuclear program. Israel would be asked to offer 'assurances' to the Palestinian groups but there would be no clear outcome on the two-state solution. In the last week of September 2023, Israeli Tourism Minister Haim Katz became the first Israeli minister to head an official delegation to Saudi Arabia to take part in a conference of the United Nations Tourism Organization. He was followed soon by Communications Minister Shlomo Karhi on 3 October, leading an Israeli delegation to the Universal Postal Union's 2023 Extraordinary Congress. Saudi Crown Prince MbS as well as Israel's PM Netanyahu too spoke publicly of the possibility of a deal. If Saudi Arabia and Israel were to establish formal diplomatic relations without a permanent solution to the establishment of a viable and independent Palestine, it would deal a death blow to the struggle of over 75 years by the Palestinians.

Iran has to be a big factor whenever there is the question of Israel. The resurgence of Iran was one big factor perhaps ignored by Israel. The Saudi-Iran peace deal in March 2023 has given a fresh lease of life to Iran in the region. Its nuclear program continues unabated and the nuclear deal talks are in a deep freeze. Even reports of Iran enriching uranium up-to 84 percent could not force any action against the program. Iran refusing access to IAEA inspectors into its nuclear sites and shutting down cameras only drew muted protests. Another boost to Iran was the prisoner exchange with the USA on 18 September, mediated by Qatar, wherein five American prisoners were released by Iran in exchange for six billion US dollars. The US Department of Defence's 2023 Strategy for Countering Weapons of Mass Destruction Report 2023, released in the first week of October 2023 stated that Iran is not pursuing a nuclear weapons program at that time, but has the capacity to produce enough fissile material for a nuclear device in less than two weeks. All this should have raised hackles in Israel. If Iran no longer remains 'enemy No.1' for the Arab world and the rest, how then will Israel find support for its anti-Iran crusade in the region?

PM Netanyahu too has to take a major share of the blame for this war. His continued provocations, despite calls for restraint from the USA as well as Arab countries, did not prevent Israel from provoking Palestinians in the West Bank, especially at the Al-Aqsa Mosque.

Surrounded by hostile neighbours, Israel could not have afforded to have missed all the red flags. How could Hamas in Gaza be let off while attention was diverted to PIJ in the West Bank? Hamas used the opportunity to collect weapons and resources to plan an attack of the most audacious nature in fifty years. Palestinian worshipers in Al Aqsa should not have been so blatantly attacked, that too during the period of Ramadan. Israel could not have relied on unconditional support from the UAE and other nations in the region just because the Abraham Accords had been signed and there is a wave of rapprochement in the region.

Looking Ahead

Israel, with its military superiority, will eventually prevail. The question is, at what cost. Some analysts are calling this attack Israel's 9/11. Whatever it might be, it has changed the landscape of Israel's security forever. The notion of Israel's invincibility and its impenetrable border fence has been shattered. Hamas would have calculated the cost of the attack. For them it was not about winning the war, but getting their voice heard. If only Israel had been vigilant, it would have known that the war was coming home and that too at such an unprecedented scale.

6

How the 7 October Nightmare Unfolded?

As Israel regains military control over the Gaza crossings, the visuals of burnt vehicles and buildings, abducted soldiers and people, blood-soaked belongings of the dead and the overall scene of death and destruction is overwhelming and tragic. Stories of horror will be spoken and analysis of the intelligence shortcomings and complacency analysed over and over again, but to comprehend the real perspective of the terror attack, it is extremely important to understand how the terror unfolded on 7 October. Most of the inputs have been stitched together from information published in media outlets and successive information shared by the Israeli Defence Forces (IDF).

The Hamas terror strike on 7 October included multiple military and civilian targets, including border villages and towns along the Gaza border, music festivals (Super-Nova and Psyduck), and adjacent areas. The complexity and modus operandi of the attacks appear to demonstrate a significant level of planning, coordination and detailed prior knowledge of the targets selected.

As per a report compiled by a team from the United Nations Special Representative of the Secretary-General on Sexual Violence in Conflict (SRSG-SVC), the attackers came equipped with high-calibre and military-grade weapons and equipment ranging from rocket propelled grenades, automatic rifles, often reported by witnesses as M16s or Kalashnikovs, ample ammunition, grenades, explosives, flammable substances, and restraints including zip ties. As per eyewitness accounts and stakeholder interviews and material evidence examined by the UN Team, people were shot, often at close range; burnt alive in their homes as they tried to hide in their safe rooms; gunned down or killed by grenades in bomb shelters where they sought refuge; and hunted down at the Nova music festival site as well as in the fields and roads adjacent to it. Other violations included sexual violence, abduction of hostages and corpses, public display of captives, both dead and alive, mutilation of corpses, including decapitation, and the looting and destruction of civilian property.

How the Hamas Terror Attack Unfolded

Huge Rocket Barrage – 03.30 GMT: At about 6:30 a.m. local time in Israel, a loud and massive barrage of rocket fire was reported over Southern Israel, with sirens heard as far away as Ashkelon, Ashdod, Sderot, Tel Aviv and Beersheba. Hamas claimed that it launched 5,000 rockets in the initial barrage. However, Israel estimated it at around 2,500. Mohammed Deif, head of the Qassam Brigades, the military wing of Hamas, simultaneously announced it to the world in his message, "We announce the start of Operation Al-Aqsa Flood." Israel's famous Iron Dome missile defence system kicked but it was quickly overwhelmed by the volume of incoming rocket fire.

Infiltration and Attack – 04:40 GMT: At around 7.40 a.m. local time, under the cover of the massive rocket barrage, Hamas fighters in small groups breached the Gaza border at multiple points. There were reports of Hamas fighters flying over the Gaza fence in powered parachutes from at least 5-6 places. A number of Hamas fighters in pickup trucks and motorcycles then broke through the border barrier between Gaza and Israel. One video showed at least six motorcycles with fighters crossing through a hole in a metal barrier. They entered southern Israel and occupied Israeli villages and towns close to the border, killing soldiers and civilians.

The largest massacres took place at the Supernova music festival being held outside Kibbutz Re'im in southern Israel and in the kibbutzim of Be'eri and Kfar Aza. About 250-260 young Israelis were killed and many others abducted by Hamas. Recounting the horror, Ortel, one of the lucky survivors, said that the first sign that something was wrong was when a siren went off at around dawn, warning of incoming rockets. "They turned off the electricity and suddenly out of nowhere they [militants] came inside with gunfire, opening fire in every direction," she told Israel's Channel 12. She added, "Fifty terrorists arrived in vans, dressed in military uniforms. They fired bursts, and we reached a point where everyone stopped their vehicles and started running. I went into a clump of trees, a bush like this, and they just started spraying people. I saw masses of wounded people thrown around."

Hamas also broke through the naval blockade and crossed into Israel from the sea in motorboats. A video of a motorboat carrying Hamas fighters heading towards Zikim, an Israeli coastal town with a military base, was soon circulating on social media. A photograph later released by Hamas also showed a bulldozer tearing down a section of the fence across Gaza.

Border Towns Raided – 07:00 GMT: By 10 a.m. local time, reports started coming in of Hamas raids across a number of border towns too. By that time, Hamas fighters had stormed six military bases: Erez at the northern end of the Gaza Strip, Nahal Oz opposite Gaza City, two others near the Beeri kibbutz, the Gaza division headquarters at Reim and two in the south close to the Egyptian border. Hamas also raided the Israeli border town of Sderot, a border community, Be'eri, and the town of Ofakim 30km (20 miles) east of Gaza, burning down buildings and taking captives.

By the end of the day, Hamas had killed almost 1,200 people in Israel and taken 251 hostages.

Israel Strikes Back

Although shocked, the IDF was quick to regroup. The initial focus was on regaining control inside Israel, defending towns, responding to infiltrations, and mobilizing forces. While reinforcements were rushed to locations where Hamas was inflicting casualties and damage, the Israeli Air Force was quickly airborne and by 9.30 a.m. local time, key known Hamas locations were being bombarded. In places like Sderot and Ofakim where Hamas had successfully infiltrated, Israeli forces were engaged in fighting Hamas fighters trying to secure areas.

At 11.30 a.m., in a broadcast to the nation, Prime Minister Benjamin Netanyahu declared, "We are at war." By the afternoon, a nationwide emergency had been sounded and around 360,000 reservists were called up to bolster the fighting strength. Israel announced *'Operation Iron Swords'*, a full-scale military operation to counter-attack and eliminate the threat. By the end of the day, all incursion points had been sealed and a search-and-clearance operation was underway.

SECTION 11

Israel's Counter Attack

7

As Israel Vows to Punish Hamas: What are its Options?

It is 9 October 2023. The horrifying sounds and visuals of the surprise and audacious attack in the early hours of 7 October 2023 are still echoing as Israeli forces regain control of the situation across the Gaza strip. The attack by Hamas, launched across land, air and sea, was planned and executed with precision. The 'shock-and-awe' tactics took Israel and the entire world by storm as the timing and ferocity of the attack leading to a large number of casualties, including hostages, were perhaps the largest in the last five decades. Israeli forces soon recovered and launched a ferocious air and artillery assault on Gaza targeting key military and command positions of Hamas. The ground troops too have regained control over the breached crossings and were able to neutralize most of the Hamas operatives who had infiltrated into Israeli territory.

Israel has vowed to punish Hamas as never before. PM Netanyahu pledged revenge stating, "*We will take mighty vengeance for this wicked day. Hamas launched a cruel and wicked war. We will win this war but the price is too heavy to bear*". Defence Minister Yoav Gallant, while briefing the NATO defence ministers in Brussels on 12 October said, "*Hamas is the 'ISIS' of Gaza. The 'ISIS' of Gaza will not exist on our borders. The IDF will destroy Hamas. And we will hunt down every last man, with the blood of our children, on his hands.*" Israel mobilized over 400,000 of its reserves and is moving in tanks, artillery and troops while its aircraft, missiles and artillery continue to bombard and destroy known Hamas locations in Gaza.

Military Capabilities: A Study in Contrast

A broad comparison between the military might of Israel and Hamas quickly reveals that it is a war of two unequal forces. Israel has a well-organized, structured and equipped modern military, while the Hamas has fighters who have been mustered, indoctrinated, equipped and trained as any other terrorist organization in basic combat, guerrilla warfare, suicide attacks, etc.

As per 'Military Balance 2023' Report, Israel has an active military of 169,500 with the Army at 126,000 comprising the bulk. It has a system of conscription wherein all able-bodied Jews and Druze are required to train and serve for periods varying from 24 months (for women) to 48 (for officers). It is an undeclared nuclear weapons power with a capability to deliver nuclear weapons by sea and air. Its Army comprises 3 Corps, 2 Armoured Divisions, 1 Multidimensional Division, 1 Special Operations Brigade, 1 Para Brigade, 3 Artillery Brigades and many other military formations. As per Global Power rankings, Israel is the fourth-largest military in the region with only Turkey, Egypt and Iran ahead of it. Globally, it is ranked at number 18.

It has more than 1,000 Merkava main battle tanks (MBT), 1,200 armoured personnel carriers (APC), 530 artillery guns, including 30 multiple rocket launchers (MRL) and a host of other weapon and surveillance systems. Its Navy is potent with 5 submarines, 3 landing craft, 1 naval commandos unit and almost 50 other patrol and combat boats. Its Air Force comprises the most modern fighter aircraft in the form of F-15s, F-16s and F-35s, with a total of almost 350 aircraft split into 14 squadrons of fighters, 2 of AH-64 Apache attack helicopters and many other aircraft in different support roles. It has a whole range of armed and unarmed UAVs, including the famous Heron armed UAVs as well as a range of missiles and anti-missile systems including the long-range M901 Patriot PAC-2 with a range of 160 km and the short range Iron Dome (anti rocket system). To top it all, Israel has a military budget of around $23.4 billion.

On the other hand, Hamas is a loosely structured group with a militant ideology. It was founded in 1987 by Sheikh Ahmed Yassin, a Palestinian cleric, after the first intifada, the uprising against Israeli occupation of Palestine. Its military wing was formed later in 1990. The military does not have any conventional forces or weapons. It does not have any MBT, artillery, combat ships, etc. The fighters are estimated to be around 25,000 to 30,000 who are primarily trained in guerrilla warfare and terrorist tactics. Apart from basic hand-held weapons, Hamas is known to have in its arsenal an array of short-range rockets. It is known to possess the Russian-made Kornet platform and the Iranian Fajr family of anti-tank weapons. It is also known to have Iranian-origin Fateh-110 ballistic missiles, which have a range of up to 185 miles. All in all, the group is thought to have around 10,000 rockets at any given time which it is able to replenish regularly. As for mobility, it is known to use fast-moving light vehicles like jeeps, pickup trucks and motorbikes. The use of tunnels deep under the Gaza fence, placement of IEDs and carrying out of spectacular attacks in Israel has been its general modus operandi. The matchup is, therefore, between a strong, conventional, modern and technologically superior military and a loosely formed, ill equipped but highly motivated small and unconventional force.

Options for Israel

Israel is still coming to terms with the scale and brutality of the Hamas 7 October attack. Having vowed total annihilation of Hamas, it is likely that the Israeli ground offensive will be punitive and long. There are fears that they could follow a 'scorched earth policy' in areas known to be Hamas strongholds. Israel has already issued a warning to Gaza to vacate its northern part and evacuate its 1.1 million citizens to safer areas.

Israel therefore has two options. It could launch a full-scale ground or air offensive like never before in Gaza and totally overrun and occupy it. However, 'what next' would be a difficult question to answer. Israel has already indicated that it has no intention of occupying and governing Gaza forever. Also, in case of a full-fledged offensive, there will be widespread destruction and death. The likelihood of the war spreading beyond the Gaza Strip is very likely. Already, there are signs of the Palestine Islamic Jihad (PIJ) in the West Bank assembling its men to launch an attack while Hezbollah is already engaged in an artillery battle from Syria. Israel too has launched strikes into Lebanon and Syria with the airports in Damascus and Alleppo being hit on 12 October. If the war prolongs and spreads, it will no longer remain a case of a war against the terror attack of Hamas but can become a war for Palestine and of Muslim solidarity. On 12 October, Crown Prince Mohammed bin Salman while speaking to Palestinian President Mahmud Abbas said that Saudi Arabia continued "to stand by the Palestinian people to achieve their legitimate rights to a decent life, achieve their hopes and aspirations, and achieve just and lasting peace". There are chances that Egypt could be forced to join the war if too much pressure is exerted on its Sinai border.

There is also the question of what would be the end game in such a scenario. A massive and destructive ground offensive would practically put to rest any flicker of hope for a viable Palestine state. That would mean continued hostility around Israel and its occupied territory for decades to come. Episodic conflicts as have been witnessed since 2007 would continue giving neither side a chance to move towards peace or prosperity.

On the other hand, were Israel to launch a sharp and swift offensive specifically targeted against the Hamas and thereafter agree to a ceasefire as before, there could be initial heartburn and dissatisfaction among the Israeli people that their country has not avenged the Hamas brutality fully. However, it might give peace a chance in the future and keep alive the flame of hope for a possible 'Two-State Solution'.

Looking Ahead

Israel is ready to launch the ground offensive into Gaza and it is going to be brutal. Will Israel go for a tactical military victory, overrun Gaza and occupy it, putting to waste years of efforts towards reconciliation in the region or will it show strategic restraint and restrict the offensive in time and space to its immediate military goals, keeping in sight the long-term geo-political and economic interests in mind?

Israel and Palestine are bound together by geography and destiny and therefore any decision is likely to impact both equally. In moments of inflamed passions and despair, it is the leadership which has to rise above the din to take hard but just decisions. For Israel, it is a choice between 'tactical victory' and 'strategic restraint'.

8

Challenges before Israel as the Initial Outrage of Hamas Terror Wears off

It is 17 October. Over the past ten days, the Israeli Air Force has conducted retaliatory and punitive airstrikes against known and suspected Hamas locations in Gaza. Israel has released images and videos of their aircraft targeting buildings in Gaza, reducing them to rubble. Israel has cut off the supply of electricity, water, food and medicines to Gaza as punishment for the entire Gaza population. The images on the TV screen and newspaper reports are now filled with the Israeli military targeting Gaza and the death and destruction being caused there. While the world continues to support Israel and its right to defend itself, concerns are mounting and questions are being asked over the legitimacy, scope and depth of the punitive Israeli strikes into Gaza.

The Changing Narrative

In today's age of the Internet and social media, perceptions are built and destroyed sooner than can be managed. Many voices of support that condemned Hamas initially are rethinking their strategy as the war spreads. Saudi Arabia, which had condemned the Hamas terror strike, in a cabinet meeting on 17 October chaired by King Salman in Riyadh, renewed the Kingdom's categorical rejection of calls for the forced displacement of the Palestinian people, demanded an immediate ceasefire and the lifting of the siege of Gaza. In a statement on 17 October, following a strike on a Gaza hospital which reportedly killed around 500 people, the UAE along with foreign ministries of Egypt, Jordan, Saudi Arabia and Qatar condemned Israel. The UAE along with Russia also called for an emergency UN Security Council meeting over the attack. Jordan too cancelled the proposed Summit of the US President and Arab leaders in Amman on 19 October. Egypt has traditionally been the peace broker in most Israel-Gaza conflicts and has facilitated the movement of Gaza residents and food and aid delivery through its crucial border crossing with Gaza, the Rafah Crossing. It too initially called for exercising the utmost restraint and avoiding exposing civilians to further risks immediately after the Hamas attack, but it has refused to open its crucial Rafah border crossing and has condemned Israel for forcing almost 1.1 million people to leave their homes in North Gaza and move southwards. In a joint statement with Turkey, during the visit of Turkish Foreign Minister Hakan Fidan to Cairo on 14 October, they stated, "*We reject the policy of Palestinians' being removed from their homes in Gaza and exiled into Egypt. We are fully against it and stand with Egypt.*"

India has tried to maintain a fine balance. Indian PM Modi was among the first world leaders to condemn the terror attack and extend support to its strategic ally, Israel. However, on 12 October, it reiterated its principled support for the establishment of a 'sovereign, independent and viable' state of Palestine. There have been widespread support marches and demonstrations in support of Palestine all over the world including the USA, Europe, Australia, etc.

The Humanitarian Crisis

Following the Hamas attack, Israel declared a 'complete siege' of the territory, saying electricity, food, fuel and water would be cut off. Israel's Defence Minister Yoav Gallant said, "We are fighting animals and are acting accordingly." The Israeli infrastructure minister added, "What was in the past will no longer be in the future." Later, Israel ordered people in North Gaza to move to South Gaza as it prepared to target Gaza city. It gave 24 hours to 1.1 million people to leave. Such a vast displacement over such a narrow geographical area, that too with the Rafah Crossing still closed, was an impossible and inhuman task and was widely condemned. To add to it, there were reports of Israeli aircraft bombing places in South Gaza on 17 October, causing casualties and destruction, including among people who were moving southwards from North Gaza. As per reports, more than 100 people were killed in the city of Khan Younis in South Gaza as well as a building at the Rafah Crossing. With the mass exodus of people and essential supplies cut off, the UN warned on 17 October that Palestinian civilians in the Gaza Strip are being "packed into an ever-smaller area" and life-saving essentials have essentially run out, appealing for a humanitarian truce to allow access to aid. "We can't move humanitarian trucks and convoys while active bombardment is ongoing," UN spokesman Stephane Dujarric said. The World Food Programme (WFP) too warned on 17 October that shops were unable to replenish supplies and would run out of food stocks in "less than a week." The WHO and the UN have said that thousands of Palestinians trapped in Gaza are likely to die in the coming days if they are denied access to urgently needed relief supplies, especially medicines. Media reports indicate that a number of hospitals, ambulances and even UN facilities have borne the brunt of Israeli airstrikes. At least 11 UN staff and personnel, as well as 30 students at UN schools, have already been killed in the Gaza Strip. The Palestine Red Crescent Society (PRCS) on 18 October condemned "the intentional targeting of medical teams" adding that targeting medical personnel is a grave breach to international humanitarian law and humanity. The UN has said around 4,200 people have been killed since Hamas invaded Israel on 7 October. More than 2,800 of such deaths and nearly 11,000 wounded were reported in Gaza with another 1,400 deaths and more than 4,100 injured in Israel.

As per the Committee to Protect Journalists (CPJ) report, as of 18 October, at least 17 journalists have been killed in this war which includes 13 Palestinian, 3 Israeli, and 1 Lebanese, mostly while reporting in the Gaza Strip. The latest setback however is the unfortunate strike on Al-Ahli al Arabi hospital in Gaza on 17 October which killed over 500 people. Although Israel tried to present proof that it was a misguided rocket from PIJ that had struck the hospital, there are very few takers, especially in the region. With an accident of such mammoth proportions, emotions are likely to get inflamed, slowly turning the tide against Israel.

The Hamas Challenge

The military fight between Israel and Hamas is of two unequal forces. Israel has a well-organized, structured and equipped modern military, while the Hamas has fighters who have been mustered, indoctrinated, equipped and trained as any other terrorist organization in ground combat, guerrilla warfare, suicide attacks, etc. Hamas has laid an intricate structure of tunnels inside Gaza often called the 'Gaza Metro' which is up to 30 metres deep at some places and which often open inside schools and hospitals. Hamas has claimed that the total network is almost 500 km long, all within Gaza. It is used not only for movement but also to store weapons and rockets as well as to cross into Israel below the fence. This was a challenge for the Israeli army in the past and is likely to pose a huge problem this time also. The densely populated area in the very thin Gaza Strip is a nightmare for any conventional army fighting a guerrilla force and Hamas will pose a great challenge for the Israeli army. The use of Israeli tanks and armoured vehicles will be limited as there is inadequate space for manoeuvring in Gaza due to densely located buildings with narrow roads and alleys. In such a scenario, the advantage is always with a force like Hamas which is able to launch 'sneak attacks' and bog down an enemy's armoured columns. Another problem posed by Hamas is the support it is getting from groups like Hezbollah which has opened a war front into Israel across Lebanon and Syria, the PIJ which is mustering its cadres to take on Israeli forces in the West Bank and the massive moral and financial support it gets from Iran. Hamas aims to draw Israeli forces into a long-drawn battle of attrition which will eventually force a ceasefire after Hamas and Gaza have suffered huge losses. But then, that is a price that they are willing to pay in their fight against Israel.

Looking Ahead

For Israel, hard decisions loom ahead. First and foremost is the question, what would constitute a victory? Israel has stated that it aims to finish Hamas forever. Is it possible? In the previous two ground invasions during '*Operation Cast Lead*' in 2008-09 and '*Operation Protective Edge*' in 2014, Israel had aimed to degrade Hamas to a point that it ceased to be a threat. It didn't happen and Hamas regrouped every time. If Israel tries to decimate Gaza and flatten it with a 'scorched earth' policy, it will be a humanitarian disaster of unparalleled proportions, something that even the USA will not be able to support Israel on. Plus, it will draw in many more players into active war, which Israel, the USA or the region can ill afford. Iran, principal benefactor of Hamas, has already warned Israel of pre-emptive strikes if it tries to escalate the conflict. The USA, Israel's strongest and closest ally too has taken stock of the ferocity of Israeli attacks and in a statement on 16 October stated it would be a mistake for Israel to occupy Gaza again

Israel also has to carry out introspection of its own actions over the past decades. It is the victim this time of a terror attack which cannot be condoned in any manner. But what about its own actions? There is no denying the fact that Israel has been in occupation and control of most of Palestinian land all these years. Even when it withdrew from Gaza in 2005, it had not eased blockades and restrictions, especially after Hamas came to power in 2007. The West Bank continues to be completely under Israeli occupation. The number of settlements in West Bank is growing at an alarming rate leaving practically no space for a viable Palestine State to ever take shape. Its offensive actions against Palestinian worshippers at Al-Aqsa Mosque cannot be justified in any manner.

'*Once you take away hope, there is no more fear and therefore you have nothing to lose*'. In a manner, therefore, Hamas or the Palestinians fighting for a sovereign Palestine state could argue that they have been driven to the brink in the past few years with very little hope. For Israel, however, coping with unimaginable brutality and tragedy, it is about revenge and rage. The challenge is to find a path which satisfies both, giving a flicker of hope to one while satisfying the rage within the other.

News trickling in on 18 October indicates that the USA has vetoed a UN Security Council resolution that would have called for 'humanitarian pauses' to deliver lifesaving aid to millions in Gaza. The visit of President Biden to Israel on the same day and this development indicate a very dark phase of death and destruction in the region as Israel readies for a massive ground offensive. Tough decisions await Israel that are likely to have long-lasting if not a permanent imprint on the future of Israel and Palestine.

9

Israel Presses on with its Ground Offensive Amidst Mounting International Pressure

It is 28 October and the Gaza war is intensifying.

The Israeli Air Force is pounding Northern Gaza as it 'shapes the battlefield' before its battle tanks and ground forces launch the much-anticipated ground offensive. Targeted ground raids with tanks and armoured personnel carriers (APC) have been undertaken to strike and knock out key Hamas leaders as well as command-and-communication installations in Gaza, especially in Northern Gaza. Media reports indicate that over 100 fighter aircraft struck around 150 'underground targets' in Northern Gaza on the night of 27/28 October 2023. Armoured tanks and battle formations have meanwhile lined up waiting for the green signal to cross into Gaza. In the early hours of 28 October, an Israeli strike knocked out a key communication tower plunging Gaza into an Internet and communication blackout. Inputs from the battlefield and statements by key Israeli commanders indicate that a full-scale offensive is imminent. However, with each passing day, pressure as well as opposition to the extremely punitive strikes undertaken by Israel resulting in the deaths of thousands of civilians in Gaza, is building. Amidst this, questions are being asked whether Israel can undermine the appeals and warnings from around the region and globe and still launch a full-scale offensive.

Increasing International Pressure

The visuals and memories of the barbaric Hamas attack of 7 October still haunt Israel and the international community. However, the resultant air and artillery strikes by Israel in the past three weeks, killing thousands of innocent civilians including women and children, has forced the international community to stand up and recognise that Israel too is blameworthy of 'war crimes'. The UN General Assembly, in its special session on 27 October, adopted a resolution sponsored by Jordan calling for an 'immediate, durable and sustained humanitarian truce' between Israeli forces and Hamas militants. It also demanded 'continuous, sufficient and unhindered' provision of lifesaving supplies and services for civilians trapped in the enclave. The resolution was passed with 120 votes in favour, 14 against and 45 abstentions. Gilad Erdan, Ambassador of Israel to the UN, immediately denounced the resolution stating that "today is a day that will go down in infamy and that the UN holds not even one ounce of legitimacy."

Earlier, Brazil's President denounced the Israeli strikes stating that this is not war but genocide, which has already killed about 2,000 children who had nothing to do with it. UN agencies too have been sounding alarms over the humanitarian crisis caused by the complete blockade of Gaza enforced by Israel and the death and destruction being caused on civilians by Israeli strikes which have already resulted in deaths of over 7,000 civilians and displacement of over one million of the population. On 17 October, the UN warned that Palestinian civilians in the Gaza Strip are being "packed into an ever-smaller area" and life-saving essentials have run out, appealing for a humanitarian truce to allow aid access. The WHO and the UN have said that that thousands of Palestinians trapped in Gaza are likely to die in the coming days if they are denied access to urgently needed relief supplies, especially medicines.

Within the region too, voices against Israel's aggression are becoming louder and fiercer. The OIC issued a statement on 27 October expressing deep pain and distress over events in Palestine as a result of wanton Israeli aggression and appealed for collective help and aid to the Palestinians. Nine Arab countries on 26 October issued a joint statement condemning the targeting of civilians and violations of international law in Gaza adding that Israel's right to self-defence after the devastating 7 October attack did not justify neglecting Palestinians' rights. The nine Arab countries include Bahrain, Egypt, Jordan, Kuwait, Morocco, Oman, Qatar, Saudi Arabia and the UAE. At the 9th meeting of GCC Ministers for Islamic Affairs on 25 October, Saudi Minister of Islamic Affairs Sheikh Dr. Abdullatif Al-Sheikh reiterated the steadfast commitment of the Gulf Cooperation Council (GCC) to stand with the Palestinian people stating that it is a cause that unifies Islamic and Arab nations, transcends boundaries and impacts humanity as a whole. Saudi Foreign Minister Prince Faisal bin Farhan bin Abdullah, speaking during the UN Security Council debate on 25 October accused the international community of neglecting to work to immediately stop the collective punishment carried out by the Israeli war machine against the people of Gaza and attempts at forced displacement that "will not bring us any closer to the security and stability that we all seek." Turkey has taken a more confrontationist stand with its President stating that Hamas is not a terrorist organization but a patriotic liberation movement fighting to protect Palestinian lands and people. Egypt too is raising the ante slowly especially after a few missiles have landed in its territory. The Rafah Crossing was hit on 10 October and again on 27 October; an unidentified projectile hit two Egyptian Red Sea towns, wounding at least six people in Taba and an electricity plant in the town of Nuweiba prompting Egyptian President Al Sisi to issue a warning on 28 October of possible expansion of conflict, adding that the region risked becoming a 'ticking time bomb'. Qatar, which hosts the Hamas HQ, too has been belligerent stating that Israel is "solely responsible for the ongoing escalation due to its continuous violations of the rights of the Palestinian people, including the recent repeated incursions into the Al-Aqsa Mosque under the protection of the Israeli police." On 25 October, Qatari PM Sheikh Mohammed bin Abdulrahman al-Thani added in a press conference with the Turkish foreign minister in Doha that "Qatar condemns the collective punishment policy" on Gaza.

The Military Challenge

The ground offensive into Gaza is not going to be a cakewalk and Israel knows it well. Its experience of the previous two ground offensives during '*Operation Cast Lead*' in 2008-09 and '*Operation Protective Edge*' in 2014 have made it very clear that it is going to be a battle of attrition, in a territory which the Hamas has prepared well and where it has mastered the skills of fighting. The intricate network of 500 km of underground tunnels poses a formidable challenge. The heavily concretised and deep tunnels are mostly undamaged as Israeli bombs and missiles do not have the capability to penetrate below 30 metres, that is, 150 feet of earth. Added to this is the fact that the tunnels run under densely-built buildings which camouflage their visibility and cushion the shock of missile/bomb attacks. These tunnels are reportedly also the place where Hamas has kept over 220 hostages from Israel, adding to the challenge in targeting the tunnels. Plus, these tunnels have numerous escape routes as well as cut-offs, meaning that only small portions are damaged during direct Israeli attacks on the tunnels. They also store weapons and rockets as well as house critical command elements of Hamas operations.

Despite warnings from PM Netanyahu, it is unlikely that Hezbollah will pull out from the war, opening a second front against Israel. The Palestinian Islamic Jihad (PIJ), against which Israel has been engaged in numerous skirmishes over the past two years, is already upping the ante in the West Bank. Israeli raids into Jenin Camp in the West Bank in July this year as well as frequent targeting of Palestinian worshippers in Al-Aqsa Mosque has kept the temperature high in the West Bank and despite being occupied by Israel, indications are that the West Bank and the PIJ will keep Israeli forces occupied too.

The question of Iran in any Israeli conflict cannot be ignored. It is monitoring the developments closely and has already warned that it can launch a pre-emptive strike if provoked. The USA has warned Iran to keep out of the conflict. On 27-28 October, US forces targeted some key IRGC posts of Iran in Syria as a warning. But with Iran considering Israel as 'enemy No.1' and being a key benefactor of the Hamas as well as Hezbollah, its entry into the conflict, albeit by proxy, is a very likely possibility. Although the USA has moved aircraft carrier-based forces into the region, Iran is unlikely to be deterred.

Israel Remains Resolute

Despite all the challenges and pressures, Israel stands defiant and resolute. It is banking on its military superiority and support from its staunchest ally, the USA, to lend critical support, especially against any other power like Iran getting directly engaged in the war. Israel has tried to build a narrative that this war is about the right of existence of the Jewish people. On the question of occupying or governing Gaza, Israel has left it unanswered for the time being, saying that it will be a call taken once the dust settles. Israel has called the UN a useless body and has called for the resignation of its Secretary-General.

As the ground offensive slowly rolls into Gaza, it is bound to be a bloody and messy war, lasting over weeks and months. Hamas will definitely suffer heavy losses, but will it be obliterated is a question for serious debate. However, there is little doubt over the mass casualties that innocent civilians will suffer in Gaza and the destruction that Gaza will have to bear, something that might take decades to rebuild.

This conflict has definitely changed the regional landscape forever and perhaps is an important and irreversible inflection point in global geopolitics, the consequences of which will reverberate for decades and among generations to come.

10

Israel Needs to Fight a Smart War: Have a Smarter Exit Strategy

The war is well and truly on. Israel is pounding Gaza with bombs and rockets like never before. In over 26 days of the war, Israel has already carried out more than 6,000 strikes, flattening buildings and infrastructure in Gaza. Target-based ground raids with tanks and armoured personnel carriers (APC) have been on for the past week to strike and knock out key Hamas leaders as well as command and communication installations in Gaza, especially in Northern Gaza. Israel has announced that its military operations are now in Phase-2 and are poised for further escalation. Some troops and formations are already in Gaza while others wait on the border with Gaza, lined up for a full scale offensive.

In the midst of all this, two major incidents have drawn worldwide condemnation of Israel's military tactics. The first was a reported Israeli bombardment on 17 October that struck al-Ahli Arab Hospital in central Gaza, killing an estimated 500 people, including patients and a large number of civilians, who had sought refuge and safety in the complex. Again, on 31 October, an Israeli airstrike on the Jabalia refugee camp in Gaza completely destroyed the camp, killing at least 50. This time, however, Israel owned up to the strike stating that "elimination of Hamas commander Ibrahim Biari] was carried out as part of a wide-scale strike on terrorists and terror infrastructure belonging to the Central Jabalia Battalion". The continuing Israeli strikes on Gaza, killing over 8,000 civilians has forced the international community to stand up and recognise that Israel too is blameworthy of 'war crimes'.

Within the region too, each Israeli strike causing civilian deaths is resulting in voices against Israel's aggression becoming louder and fiercer. After the Israeli strike on Jabalia camp, Saudi Arabia condemned in 'the strongest terms' the inhumane targeting by Israeli occupation forces of the Jabalia camp, while the UAE warned Israel that "the continuation of the senseless bombing will lead the region to repercussions that are difficult to remedy". Qatar, Turkey and even Egypt have already taken a more belligerent view of the Israeli strikes.

Israel has to thus realize that it can't fight a war against everyone at the same time. With every strike resulting in damage to a hospital or a refugee camp, the list of friends will grow slimmer and the 'opposition' will become stronger. It has to thus act intelligently and work on a war plan which is smart but not necessarily brutal.

Smart War Plan

Israel has vowed to flatten Gaza to the ground and eliminate Hamas from the face of the Earth. Israel has to however factor in many vital questions in its war plans. Can it obliterate Hamas from the face of the Earth? The answer is obviously 'no'. It may take out many of its key leaders, destroy part of its famous underground tunnel network, degrade its military potential and war waging capability but Hamas, which enjoys ideological and financial support across many groups and countries in the region, can always regroup and recoup its military capabilities over time, owing majorly to external support.

The second question: can operations in Gaza be short and swift? The answer is again, 'no'. The densely populated and very thin Gaza Strip is a nightmare for any modern, conventional army fighting an unconventional enemy like Hamas. The fact that Hamas merges with the population and blatantly makes use of facilities like hospitals, schools and camps as shields, makes it difficult for any army to strike without causing huge collateral damage. Hamas, with its knowledge of the area and skilful guerrilla tactics, always has a 'defender's advantage' and can launch 'sneak attacks' to bog down the pace of Israeli attacking columns. The buildings and narrow lanes severely restrict the use of Israeli tanks and armoured vehicles as there is very little space for manoeuvring.

The next question is: can Israel rescue over 220 hostages through a massive ground offensive? The answer is again, 'no'. Hamas has kept the hostages dispersed and deep inside tunnels. It has no qualms of using them as human shields. What Israel requires therefore is not a massive ground offensive but intelligent, small team-based precise operations, based on specific intelligence to rescue hostages. It has already rescued five hostages through such operations in the past two days.

US President Biden, in a rather unusual acceptance of errors by the USA, cautioned Israel against repeating the mistakes of the US war strategy in the wake of the 9/11 attacks on US soil. Israel would do well to learn from it. It has to be prepared for a long drawn battle before it achieves its military and political objectives. It has to prevent strikes like the one on the hospital on 17 October and the refugee camp on 31 October to keep key friends on its side. It should use its superior military technology and long cultivated human intelligence to slowly but steadily eliminate the Hamas leadership and rescue as many hostages as possible. Its key partners like the USA, Australia, UK, etc., have to be tapped to coordinate intelligence before executing precise operations.

Its war strategy has to also ensure that the scope of the war remains limited to Gaza as much as possible, despite provocations from groups like Hezbollah and PIJ. At the same time, it needs to review measures not to alienate people, regional countries and global aid agencies by permitting critical aid into Gaza including fuel. Yes, some amount of aid might land up in the hands of Hamas, but that has to be factored in. A difficult option of fighting through aid leakages should be preferable when compared to an easy punitive option of starving and killing the entire population in Gaza. Also, calling the UN as a useless organisation and demanding the resignation of its Secretary-General serves no good purpose for Israel.

It also has to take measures to shape the political narrative intelligently. Amidst a rapidly changing narrative against it, it should try and rally support within key Arab capitals especially Riyadh and Abu Dhabi to cool down tempers before it completely loses the battle of perception. An assurance that it will moderate its strikes to save precious civilian lives despite carrying on with its military objectives could go a long way towards it. The possibility of a viable and independent Palestine state too has to be kept alive by Israel in every possible discussion. Else, this could become a 'fight to the finish', something which even Israel would not be able to control in the end.

Smart Exit Strategy

It is always easy to launch a war but very difficult to decide when to exit and how to exit. Ceasefires most often are forced due to stalemated situations, international pressure or humanitarian crises and often less due to achievement of military and political objectives. The US war in Afghanistan is a classic example which was launched as a result of national outrage to 'finish the al-Qaeda'. Commencing in October 2001, it dragged on till USA exited finally in a messy pullout in August 2021. The US war in Iraq in 2003 is yet another example of operations being launched without a clear exit strategy. The ongoing Russia-Ukraine war is due to complete two years but there is yet no sight of a ceasefire soon.

Israel needs to be vigilant to these possibilities. It will do well to learn from these examples and plan a clear and smart exit strategy rather than getting bogged down in an irretrievable situation. If that be the case, it needs to identify its military and political objectives clearly, which also need to be realistic and achievable without attracting retribution from the entire Arab world.

Way Forward

The next few weeks are crucial for Israel as well as the region. Israel would do well to realize even now that the brutality of Hamas cannot be answered by even more brutal attacks on innocent children and civilians in Gaza. The goals have to be realistic and achievable rather than those born out of rage and revenge. The war will end one day and Israel should be ready to see the reality 'eye to eye', then. This is not a war to the end of time or the end of humanity. The sooner Israel realizes and moderates its war plans accordingly, the better it will find its place in the region and globe, for the 'day after'.

11

One Month On: Is Israel Losing the Plot, Friends and Support?

It is 30 days since the dastardly terror attack by Hamas on 7 October, the bloodiest day in Israel's history. Israel has since then carried out intense punitive strikes into Gaza at regular intervals. Such has been their intensity that the Hamas terror attack today seems a distant memory as the news and TV are daily full of destruction and deaths of thousands in Gaza. In its 30 days of its *'Operation Iron Swords'*, Israel has already carried out more than 6,500 strikes, flattening buildings and infrastructure in Gaza. There have been calls from all over including the USA, Israel's staunchest ally and the UN among many others, for Israel to exercise restraint and minimize civilian casualties. However, Israel in its vow to flatten Gaza and eliminate Hamas, is not listening.

Israeli Strikes and Increasing Loss of Civilian Lives

Meanwhile, reports of daily Israeli strikes on hospitals, refugee camps, schools and UN and international aid establishments resulting in mass civilian casualties are increasing. In the early hours of 5 November, a strike at the Maghazi refugee camp in Central Gaza resulted in the deaths of at-least 33 people and complete destruction of the camp. A strike on an UN-run school near Jabalia refugee camp resulted in the killing of over 15 people on 4 November. A day earlier, an Israeli bomb struck an ambulance evacuating the injured close to Al-Shifa hospital in Gaza, killing 15 people instantly. Another strike targeted Al-Fakhoura School in Northern Gaza causing more than 150 deaths.

International Condemnation

The International Red Cross and other international agencies have reported that over 9,700 civilians have already been killed in Gaza, including over 4,800 children. The WHO, UN Relief and Works Agency, UN Population Fund and UNICEF put out a joint statement on 4 November stating that almost 420 children are being killed or injured in Gaza every day.

On 4 November, US Secretary of State Blinken visited Israel twice in one month and advised PM Netanyahu against punitive strikes causing death and destruction of civilians. He reiterated President Biden's appeal to permit a humanitarian pause so that essential aid could be delivered to the suffering population. There have been calls on Israel to permit essential aid like food, water, medicines and fuel into Gaza but Israel has not yet relented except to permit 10-20 trucks of only food and water to enter Gaza. Fuel is not being permitted at all in the fear that it may be pilfered by Hamas to power its diesel generators to supply oxygen in its deep network of tunnels.

Within the region, each reported assault by Israel resulting in civilian deaths is leading to voices against Israel's aggression becoming louder and fiercer. Immediately after the strike on Jabalia camp on 31 October and the strikes on an ambulance and school on 3 November, Saudi Arabia, with which Israel was in an advanced stage of establishing formal ties, condemned in the strongest terms the inhumane targeting by the Israeli occupation forces, while the UAE, also warned that the continuation of the senseless bombing will lead the region to face repercussions that are difficult to remedy. Bahrain, another signatory of the Abraham Accords with Israel, recalled its ambassador from there and cut off economic ties. Back home, PM Netanyahu is facing intense pressure with people demanding his immediate resignation and asking for concrete actions for the immediate release of hostages while some former government and military officials are questioning the logic of punitive strikes on civilians.

Losing the Plot

Meanwhile, Israel is continuing with its targeted raids in Gaza. Its ground forces have encircled Gaza city and are in the process of carrying out 'neutralization operations'. Israel has announced that its military operations are now in Phase-2 and a full-scale ground offensive could be round the corner. Ground raids with tanks and armoured personnel carriers (APC) are being undertaken to strike and knock out key Hamas leaders as well as command and communication installations. Israel has clearly stated that there will be no let-up in its operations until the entire Hamas leadership, cadres and war waging capability is eliminated. It has also made it clear that there will be no humanitarian pause unless all hostages are released.

Thirty days into the conflict, Israel's ongoing actions still seem to be born out of rage and revenge.

The media is facing the brunt of Israel's revenge. As of 4 November, at least 36 journalists have already been killed in Gaza by Israeli strikes. Israel also has to take note that the war has already become a war for Palestine and that the Hamas terror attack has been subsumed in the evolving narrative. The speech of the Hezbollah chief on 3 November is significant, during which he swore allegiance to Hamas and Palestine but refrained from signalling an all-out war against Israel for the time being. If the war escalates any further and Israeli strikes continue to pound Gaza killing innocent civilians, Hezbollah could well unleash its complete war machinery, something which could enlarge the scope of war farther within the region and which will then be very difficult to contain. The USA is clearly cognizant of it. US Secretary Blinken, in a surprise visit to the West Bank on 5 November, met Palestinian President Mahmud Abbas and assured him of the USA's commitment towards delivery of life-saving humanitarian aid and that Palestinians should not be forcibly displaced, a direct message to Israel to exercise restraint.

Losing Support?

Pressure is mounting on Israel. Calls for a ceasefire are growing louder by the day. Protests are being held across the globe in support of the Palestinians and condemning Israeli strikes on civilians. On 4-5 November, thousands took to the streets in Washington, London and Berlin in support of the Palestinians. A number of countries like Jordan, Bahrain, Bolivia, Colombia, Chile, Turkey, Brazil, Honduras, etc., have recalled their ambassadors from Israel. With Bahrain cutting off economic ties and the UAE upping the ante against Israeli strikes on civilians, the future of the Abraham Accords and support for Israel in the region is slowly melting away.

PM Modi, one of the most influential global leaders and one who enjoys a great personal rapport with PM Netanyahu, has held discussions with the UAE, Egypt, Jordan, Saudi Arabia, the USA, UK and many others on the deteriorating situation in Gaza. India, itself a victim of terror for decades, well appreciates the sentiments within Israel's leadership; however, how long will it keep ignoring gross 'war crimes' in the name of revenge, is an important question to watch out for in the coming weeks. Dr. Jaishankar, External Affairs Minister, in a media interaction on 4 November stated that the situation is extremely complex with a lot of possibilities, which may not lead to a good outcome. In the context of Israel's strikes on Gaza killing innocent civilians, he added that humanitarian laws need to be respected and that India stood firm in its support to a 'Two-State' solution.

Another important factor for the nations, especially in Europe, slowly expressing lack of support to Israeli strikes, goes much beyond the humanitarian issue. It is about safety and economics. Europe is still reeling from the economic backlash of the Russia-Ukraine war. The economic sanctions imposed on Russia as well as it cutting off energy supplies has made a huge dent in the GDP of European nations. With another winter setting in and alternative supplies of natural gas and oil not yet reconciled, Europe cannot afford another prolonged war. In case the war prolongs and spreads beyond Gaza into the region, there is the likelihood of a significant spike in global oil prices which will have a ripple effect on all sections of trade and economy, something that the world cannot afford right now. Also, with a large Muslim population in these countries, including thousands of migrants taken into Europe as a result of wars in West Asia, there are fears of anti-Israel protests as well as targeting of the 'white population'. Many such incidents have already begun in various cities of Europe.

For the USA too, it is again a tricky situation. It has expressed unequivocal support to Israel in its 'right to self-defence'. However, with each ill-directed strike killing civilians in Gaza, it is difficult to manage the narrative at home. For the past decade, it has resolved not to get directly involved in any military conflict in West Asia. It has also made it clear that it will not place boots on the ground. The US President, Defence Secretary Lloyd Austin and Secretary of State Antony Blinken have made it clear in private conversations with Israel, emphasizing that eroding support will have dire strategic consequences for Israel Defence Forces operations against Hamas and that there is limited time for Israel to try to accomplish its stated objective before uproar over the humanitarian suffering and civilian casualties and calls for a ceasefire reaches a tipping point. The USA also moves into its election cycle of presidential elections next year and limits of its support would need to be tempered accordingly. In such a situation, the USA would want the war to remain confined to Gaza and end soon.

Time to Pause and Review Strategy

Israel would do well therefore to pause and review its overall strategy. It has to realize that with every strike resulting in damage to a hospital, school or a refugee camp, the list of friends is growing thinner. Its allies and friends too cannot support Israel blindly while all that Israel focuses on is extracting revenge for 7 October. War is a dirty business and brutalities, though unfortunate, do take place in battle. War has to be therefore fought with a cool and calculated mind and not based solely on revenge. Any response has to be calibrated and force applied proportionate to the effect desired. Operations have to be launched with clearly spelt out and realistic goals while keeping friends and allies on Israel's side. Israel cannot afford to lose the plot, lest it is forced into a prolonged conflict which it could ill afford and a war which will still not get it what it wants – complete destruction of Hamas. Thus, Israel would do well to listen to its friends while there is still time and opportunity.

12

Two Months into the War in Gaza: Red Lines Blur

There was a slight glimmer of hope during the seven-day temporary humanitarian truce from 24 to 30 November in Gaza that it could culminate in a lasting ceasefire. However, with Israel resuming its operations on 1 December in Southern Gaza with renewed force, the future presents a rather bleak picture.

In the 49 days before the truce came into effect on 24 November, Israel conducted over 7,500 strikes by air and artillery and moved ground troops and tanks into Gaza, cutting off Northern Gaza completely. In this intense targeting, more than 12,500 Palestinian civilians, mostly women, children and elderly, lost their lives.

Vowing revenge against Hamas, Israel was expected to unleash its full military potential to seek out and eliminate its operatives, commanders, command centres, etc. In the process, however, Israel's strikes on hospitals in Gaza, UN-run facilities, schools and refugee camps causing mass casualties of innocent civilians led to global outrage. Coupled with it was the complete blockade of Gaza restricting any critical humanitarian and medical aid from entering Gaza. ICRC President Mirjana Spoljaric, during her visit to Gaza on 4 December, expressed grief at the humanitarian suffering, stating "I have arrived in Gaza, where people's suffering is intolerable. It is unacceptable that civilians have no safe place to go, and with a military siege in place there is also no adequate humanitarian response currently possible".

In the current phase of the war, Southern Gaza is bearing the brunt of Israeli attacks. In the six days since the truce failed on 1 December, Israel has already struck more than 700 targets there. It has issued repeated warnings to people to move more south, especially away from the city of Khan Younis where it suspects a major Hamas command centre. It may be recalled that Israel had similarly warned people in Northern Gaza in October, forcing around 1.1 million people to abandon their homes and move south. It also conducted specific and sustained operations on Al Shifa Hospital in Gaza city claiming it was a major command and control centre of Hamas. Although Israeli forces did capture some weapons from the hospital and discovered an underground tunnel network in the hospital compound, it could not conclusively prove its claims. It is now pinning its hopes on the city of Khan Younis in southern Gaza to conclusively unravel and destroy Hamas's command network. Ground forces too have moved in on 4 December to complement the air strikes as Khan Younis and other parts of Southern Gaza are being targeted and isolated.

However, what is more important than the ongoing Israeli offensive in Southern Gaza is what the expected end state of Gaza is. Is Israel planning to push out people from Southern Gaza too as it has done in Northern Gaza. If 'yes', where will these three million people go if they escape alive? In the beginning of the war, most of the neighbouring Arab countries had stated that any kind of forced vacation of the population from Gaza would be a red line and would not be accepted. When Israel asked people to move south from Gaza city, King Abdullah II of Jordan had said specifically on 18 October, "This is a red line ... no refugees to Jordan and also no refugees to Egypt. This is a situation that has to be handled within Gaza and the West Bank". Egyptian President Abdel Fattah al-Sisi echoed the same adding that "if mass displacements take place, the Palestinian state that we are talking about and that the world is talking about will become impossible to implement." Observers are calling this mass displacement a 'Second Nakba' on the lines of the first Nakba which led to the displacement of over 7.5 lakh Palestinians after the 1948 Israel-Palestine War.

To an objective observer, the red lines were violated the day the people in northern Gaza were asked to shift en masse. With the same now happening in southern Gaza, the problem has become more acute. None of the neighbouring countries or any other Arab/Muslim nation is willing to take in Palestinian refugees. There were some reports that Israel has prepared a contingency plan to vacate Gaza and keep the displaced in a small tented area in northern Sinai and the Negev desert.

What is even more disturbing is the rather ambivalent stance taken by the regional countries on the war. Apart from statements to condemn Israeli strikes on hospitals, etc., no concrete and collective stand has been taken. Despite extraordinary summits of the OIC, Arab League, GCC, etc., no clear word has come from the region. There were reports of a recent suggestion from Qatar that the Arab nations should halt oil and gas supplies to the world if the bombing of Gaza does not stop. No Arab country has offered any support to this as yet. The 44th session of the GCC Supreme Council held in Doha on 5-6 December hasn't come up with any concrete reaction to Israeli bombing in Gaza. All this only amplifies the sentiment that prevailed within the region before the war that the countries in the region were losing interest in the Palestine issue.

If Gaza is completely overrun, Israel may be able to claim military victory over Hamas. It may also remove the threat of any terror attack from Gaza into Israel forever and render the underground tunnel network unusable. With Gaza gone, there would be only limited stretches of West Bank left for Palestinians to claim as their homeland. Will this be sufficient for a viable two-state solution? Will eliminating the terror threat from Gaza eliminate threats altogether for Israel? The answer to both is clearly 'No'. Reflecting on the same, on 3 December, the French President stated that "there is no lasting security for Israel in the region if its security is achieved at the cost of Palestinian lives". Anti-Semitic attacks across the world are increasing by the day. Mass protests have been held in support of Palestine across global capitals. Building upon the frustration of having lost the chance of an independent Palestine state, rogue attacks against Israeli citizens and Jews across the world could increase. Hamas may be defeated and maybe even eliminated but history suggests that ideologies like this do not die, especially if they enjoy external support. If not Hamas, another group could rise and take the fight to Israel.

The continuing offensive in southern Gaza indicates the worst fears coming true; total obliteration and de-population of the Strip. If Gaza is lost forever, so will the hopes of millions of Palestinians praying for their own independent nation. Two months into the war, there are no signs of a ceasefire or a negotiated settlement. Meanwhile, Israel continues to pound Gaza vowing to eliminate Hamas, with thousands of innocent people being caught in the crossfire and nowhere to go.

13

'Right to Self-Defence' vs. R2P

It is 26 December and the war rages on. The world was outraged when Hamas attacked Israel on 7 October and killed over 1,200 Israeli citizens including infants, children, women and elderly in a single day; the world was outraged. When Israel vowed to eliminate Hamas and flatten Gaza, the world seemed to nod and support it.

However, as the war progressed and strikes into Gaza have become more destructive and indiscriminate Israel has often been accused of failing to adhere to the principle of proportionality, especially with regard to the destruction of civilian infrastructure and mass deaths of innocent civilians. The war has been on for more than 75 days and has killed over 20,000 persons, including over 8,000 children. Israel's insistence to continue its blockade of Gaza is severely restricting the entry of critical medical supplies and humanitarian aid, despite UN agencies pleading that lack of aid will result in additional mass deaths. In such a situation, can Israel claim that its strikes even now fall within the purview of 'self-defence' or could the globally accepted principle of R2P (Responsibility to Protect) be extended to this war to restrain Israel, negotiate a ceasefire, rush in humanitarian aid and stop the 'genocide' in Gaza?

What is R2P? The Responsibility to Protect, known as R2P, is an international norm that seeks to ensure that the international community never again fails to halt the mass crimes of genocide, war crimes, ethnic cleansing and crimes against humanity. The concept emerged in response to the failure of the international community to adequately respond to mass atrocities committed in Rwanda and the former Yugoslavia during the 1990s. It was unanimously adopted in 2005 at the UN World Summit and is articulated in paragraphs 138 and 139 of the World Summit Outcome Document. It states that each individual State has the responsibility to protect its populations from genocide, war crimes, ethnic cleansing and crimes against humanity. This responsibility entails the prevention of such crimes, including their incitement, through appropriate and necessary methods.

The international community, through the United Nations, also has the responsibility to use appropriate diplomatic, humanitarian and other peaceful means, in accordance with Chapters VI and VIII of the Charter, to help to protect populations from genocide, war crimes, ethnic cleansing and crimes against humanity.

R2P stipulates three pillars of responsibility. Pillar 1 stipulates that every state has the responsibility to protect its populations from four mass atrocity crimes: genocide, war crimes, crimes against humanity and ethnic cleansing. Pillar 2 states that the international community has the responsibility to encourage and assist individual states in meeting that responsibility. Pillar 3 stipulates that if a state is manifestly failing to protect its populations, the international community must be prepared to take appropriate collective action in a timely and decisive manner and in accordance with the UN Charter.

R2P has been invoked in more than 80 UN Security Council resolutions concerning crises in the Central African Republic, Côte d'Ivoire, Democratic Republic of the Congo, Liberia, Libya, Mali, Somalia, South Sudan, Syria, and Yemen, as well as thematic resolutions concerning the prevention of genocide, prevention of armed conflict and restricting the trade of small arms and light weapons. The Responsibility to Protect has also been invoked in more than 50 Human Rights Council resolutions and 13 General Assembly resolutions.

The last time this principle was applied was when the UN invoked it in Libya in 2011 after the outbreak of 'Arab Spring' protests against Libya's long-time dictator, Muammar al-Qaddafi. NATO forces intervened in Libya in order to protect civilians from Qaddafi's forces. The Qaddafi regime was toppled; however, the mission quickly morphed into a destabilizing regime-change operation. As a result, civil war rages in Libya and the country continues to be unstable and violent for more than a decade after the military intervention. Subsequently, Russia and China effectively blocked any such resolution on Syria, Myanmar, etc.

Although R2P in its written form technically applies to situations where regimes are carrying out genocide against its own population, the question remains whether it can be applied to situations akin to the current humanitarian crisis wherein Israel is bombing the Gaza Strip, forcibly evacuating people out of their homes and effectively de-populating the area. As Israel has controlled entry and exit into Gaza Strip for decades, does it not owe the responsibility to protect innocent people and permit critical humanitarian aid? Does its reasoning that the Hamas commanders and operatives are hiding among the civilian population and in tunnels beneath hospitals and schools give it a licence to target hospitals, schools, UN facilities, etc., without any concern for collateral damage?

As per some calculations, in just over two months, the Israeli offensive has wreaked more destruction than the razing of Syria's Aleppo between 2012 and 2016, Ukraine's Mariupol in 2022 or, proportionally, the Allied bombing of Germany in World War II. It has killed more civilians than the US-led coalition did in its three-year campaign against the Islamic State group and more than double of what has happened in almost two years of the Russia-Ukraine war. The USA is majorly complicit as it continues to supply military aid and arms to Israel. Last week, however, President Joe Biden publicly acknowledged that Israel was losing international legitimacy for what he called its 'indiscriminate bombing.'

Calls for a ceasefire are growing louder by the day. Protests are being held across the globe in support of the Palestinians and to condemn Israeli strikes on innocent civilians trapped in a very thin geographical area with nowhere to go. Thousands across the world have taken to the streets. Atleast 97 journalists have already been killed in this war, while 136 UN personnel too have lost their lives.

Israel has tried to build a narrative that this war is based on its right to self-defence, about the right of existence of the Jewish people and the state of Israel. However, with increasing civilian casualties by the day in Gaza, the plea of self-defence is on very thin ice. Also, there are no signs of Hamas being eliminated. On the other hand, continuing reports of Israeli troops in Gaza being ambushed is leading to increasing Israeli military casualties. With no signs of over 140 hostages still with Hamas being released, anger at home is growing. The killing of three Israeli hostages in Gaza by the Israeli army on 15 December, despite being unarmed and waving white flags has caused outrage in Israel, with people demanding Netanyahu's resignation or dismissal. Former PM of Israel Ehud Olmert in a news column on 22 December has said that Israel now faces the choice between a ceasefire as part of a deal that may bring home the hostages in the hope that most of them are alive, and a ceasefire with no deal, no hostages, no apparent achievement, with a total loss of the remnants of international public support for the State of Israel's right to exist without terror threats from murder organizations. French President Macron on 20 December was quoted stating that fighting terrorism did not mean 'flattening Gaza' and called for the protection of civilians and "a truce leading to a humanitarian ceasefire." The entry of Ansarullah of

Yemen in targeting and blocking Israeli-flagged ships from crossing the crucial choke route across the Gulf of Aden threatens to enlarge the conflict and also strangle Israel economically.

It is thus quite clear that Israel needs to review its strategy. It has to realize that the war in Gaza has moved well beyond its 'right to self-defence' and its continuing strikes can no longer be condoned. The global community too cannot hide behind the veil of 'what can we do' as continuing inaction and failure to protect innocent civilians can have far-reaching implications for the prospects of peace in the region and the collective global responsibility to protect in the future. The failure of the UN Security Council to include 'ceasefire' in its resolution passed on 22 December only reflects the complete breakdown of international order. An early ceasefire is an urgent need coupled with massive and internationally collaborated humanitarian assistance before the lights are knocked out of the remaining population in Gaza. The ongoing negotiations in Egypt for a ceasefire and return of hostages offers a glimmer of hope that this humanitarian disaster could end soon, hopefully as early as the rise of the sun in the New Year of 2024.

14

Three Months into the War, Key Iranian Assets Targeted: Will Iran take the Bait?

Three months after one of the deadliest conflicts in the region broke out in the early hours of 7 October 2023, there are no signs of the fighting coming to a close. Estimates suggest that already more than 22,000 civilians have been killed in Gaza including 9,000 children.

Two issues have been of primary concern ever since the war broke out. Firstly, how soon will the war end. The second concern was whether the conflict would spread across the region and more countries joined in it.

On the first, Israel has dismissed all calls for an early end to the war stating that it is ready to fight a prolonged war to achieve its military objective of eliminating the Hamas threat forever. Although Israel had expected that with its military superiority and technical prowess, it would be able to hunt down and eliminate Hamas soon, it is, however, nowhere close to it. On 29 December 2023, the Israeli Chief of Staff of the Army was quoted stating that Israel does not have a magic solution to eliminate Hamas. Thus, despite enjoying limited military success and incurring significant losses, Israel is expected to continue its military operations for some time more at least.

The second concern is even trickier and dangerous. Till now, the conflict has been largely confined to the Gaza Strip. There have been exchanges of rocket attacks and even drone strikes in Syria and Lebanon where Hezbollah is active. There has also been an increase in violence in the West Bank too, mostly instigated by attacks perpetrated by Israeli settlers on Palestinians. The latest entrant into the conflict was the Houthis who have blocked the passage of Israel-flagged ships or ships carrying cargo bound from/to Israeli ports. Despite the best efforts of the USA, including deploying an aircraft carrier-led fleet, the Houthis are determined to attack Israel with attacks on its ships. In fact, on 26 December, while briefing Knesset lawmakers, the Israeli Defence Minister Yoav Gallant said, "We are in a multi-front war. We are being attacked from seven fronts; Gaza, Lebanon, Syria, Judea and Samaria (the West Bank), Iraq, Yemen and Iran. We have already responded and acted on six of those fronts."

As the war continues, it is Israel that is enduring increasing casualties and economic costs. The rest of the Muslim countries around it wait and watch, without getting directly involved in the military conflict while the three 'H's of Iran, that is, Hamas, Hezbollah and Houthis, are taking the fight to the Israeli defence forces.

Provocations and Attacks on Iran

As a result, in the past week or so, there has been a spate of attacks on Iran and its assets in the region. A terror attack on 3 January involving twin explosions at an event near the tomb of Islamic Revolutionary Guard Corps (IRGC) General Qassem Soleimani in the Iranian city of Kerman, killed almost 100 people, marking it as the worst terror attack since Iran's Revolution in 1979. It may be recalled that Qaseem Suleimani was killed on 3 January 2020 in a US drone strike in Baghdad, Iraq. On 2 January, Hamas's deputy leader abroad, Saleh al-Arouri, considered the de facto leader of Hamas's military wing in the West Bank, was killed in an Israeli strike in the Beirut suburb of Dahiyeh. The assassination of Arouri came barely a week after the killing of Seyed Radhi Mousavi, Iran's most influential military commander in the Levant, in a suspected Israeli airstrike in Syria's capital, Damascus, on 25 December. Mousavi, a Quds Force general, was the most senior IRGC commander killed since Soleimani. On 4 January, another blow was dealt when a suspected US drone attack killed Mushtaq Talib Al-Saidi, deputy commander of operations, in the Iraqi capital for Harakat, Al-Nujaba, a pro-Iran militia group. Earlier, on 18 December 2023, around 70 per cent of Iran's petrol stations had their services disrupted after a massive cyberattack by the hacker group Gonjeshke Darande, which translates to 'Predatory Sparrow', linked to Israel's Mossad.

The terror strike on 3 January and the assassinations of prominent leaders is a clear attempt to provoke Iran to join the war directly. Iran has already despatched its warship, the *Alborz*, on 1 January to the Red Sea, one day after the US Navy destroyed and sank three Houthi small boats. Iran's President, in a public statement, has pledged to avenge the death of IRGC commander Mousavi.

However, this is not the first time that Iran is under attack. There is a consistent history of attacks on Iran's assets in the recent past. Shortly after the assassination of Qaseem Suleimani in January 2020, a cyberattack on 19 May 2020 hit Iran's computers that regulate maritime traffic at Shahid Rajaee port on Iran's southern coast in the Persian Gulf, causing mass disruption and a huge traffic jam of ships that waited for days to dock. On 27 November 2020, Mohsen Fakhrizadeh, a prominent nuclear scientist and often called the 'father of Iran's covert nuclear weapons program,' was assassinated in a roadside attack about 40 miles east of Tehran. In a series of attacks in 2021, an explosion at the Natanz nuclear plant on 11 April hit the power supply for centrifuges and caused major damage. Shortly thereafter, on 23 June 2021, a suspected Israeli drone struck a facility in Karaj for manufacturing centrifuges for the nuclear program. All this happened while the nuclear deal talks had just resumed, after President Biden assumed office in January 2021.

Later, on 26 October 2021, a cyberattack disabled the system at over 4,300 petrol pumps that allows Iranians to use government-issued cards to purchase fuel at a subsidized rate. Last year, on 28 January 2023, drones equipped with explosives struck a weapons factory in central Isfahan just before midnight.

Will Iran take the Bait?

The attacks against Iran and its assets in the past week are a clear provocation that Iran is expected to react to. The Islamic State (IS), which has often operated against Iranian groups in Syria, has owned responsibility for the terror attack of 3 January. It has been suspected to collaborate discreetly with the USA in the past few years to specifically target Iranian interests and therefore this angle of being responsible for the terror attack can't be ruled out. Iran has, however, not been known to join battle directly, as has been seen through past instances, despite the serious provocations quoted above. Even at the height of the Persian Gulf crisis in June 2019 which brought the USA and Iran closest ever to a direct conflict, Iran did not force initiation of any conflict.

To further assess this, there are four important factors to consider. Firstly, Iran has proxies and militias all over the Levant which are ideologically and financially supported by it. These militia groups conduct operations to further Iran's political and military agenda and, so far, they have been highly effective. Secondly, Iran has been under continuous Western sanctions for many decades. Severe restrictions have been placed on the sale of its crude oil and gas too. It would be ill-advised on Iran's part to incur a huge military expenditure on a war during this sanction regime when the low-cost option of fighting through proxies is working effectively. Thirdly, Iran has often been pitched against the entire Sunni Muslim world in the region. Any initiation of conflict on the part of Iran, if it does not include other countries of the region as well, may undo all the efforts at reconciliation in the past few years with the Arab world, especially the Saudi-Iran peace deal brokered by China in March 2023. Lastly, Israel, the USA and some countries in the Western world have been looking for opportunities for a military conflict with Iran so that its nuclear apparatus can be specifically targeted. Iran's nuclear program is considered very close to the regime and has been a major rallying point for the country in the past decade or so. Iran would not want this to be jeopardized in any manner.

Iran has traditionally been known to be resilient and patient. It has always chosen its own methods to extract revenge, which do not necessarily involve direct military conflict. The last direct military conflict that Iran fought was the Iran-Iraq war in 1980-88. It is thus very unlikely that Iran would take the bait this time and launch a full-scale military conflict. It is likely to continue targeting the USA and Israel through its proxies in the region. However, will others stop provoking Iran any further? What are the redlines beyond which Iran will not restrain itself? As this conflict prolongs, how is Iran going to posture itself? As the Israel-Hamas conflict progresses into the year, some of the questions will get progressively answered, hopefully with answers which do not escalate the ongoing conflict any further.

15

Four Months into the Conflict, No Signs of Truce

It is February 2024 and the war in Gaza has been on for four months, but it shows no signs of slowing down or ending. Gaza has been punished and pulverized with non-stop bombardment, aerial strikes and a massive ground offensive, which has led to an unprecedented humanitarian crisis. Over 28,000 people have been killed and over 67,000 severely injured. Almost the entire population of around 2.3 million in Gaza has been displaced and the 41-km long Gaza Strip has been reduced to rubble, making it virtually un-inhabitable, perhaps for a long time. International aid agencies and the UN have repeatedly called for a ceasefire and permission to move in food and critical medical aid but Israel has been unrelenting in its pledge to flatten Gaza and eliminate Hamas from the face of the Earth.

The Ceasefire Proposal

In the midst of the raging war, a number of attempts have been made for a ceasefire or a humanitarian pause, through the UN General Assembly, UN Security Council and regional countries. The latest attempt was a negotiated ceasefire deal which was drafted between officials from the USA (through Director CIA), Egypt, Qatar, and Israel in Paris on 28 January. The deal proposed a call for a ceasefire of six weeks coupled with the first phase of civilian hostage releases with three Palestinian prisoners exchanged for each civilian hostage from Gaza. That ratio could go up for exchange of Israel Defence Forces soldiers and a longer pause beyond the six weeks for the later phases could be negotiated later. Israel however, immediately voiced concerns over 'some conditions that were not acceptable'. The proposal was then presented to Hamas which in turn came up with an even more expanded ceasefire proposal on 7 February suggesting a ceasefire of 135 days during which all hostages would be freed, Israel would withdraw its troops from Gaza and an agreement would eventually be reached on an end to the war. Israel was quick to dismiss the offer with PM Netanyahu calling it 'delusional'.

The rejection of this proposal puts an end to any hopes of an early ceasefire although US Secretary of State Blinken, after his tour of the region last week where he engaged with Saudi Crown Prince Mohammed bin Salman (MbS) in Riyadh as well as PM Netanyahu in Tel Aviv, was hopeful when he said that although, "there are some clear non-starters in Hamas's response, we do think it creates space for agreement to be reached".

Israel Continues to Flatten Gaza

Meanwhile, Israel has upped the ante in its offensive. In the latest inputs coming from the war zone, its military is flattening all buildings and constructions along the border of Israel and Gaza to create a clear and well-defined 'buffer zone' for the future. There are reports of intensification of operations in Khan Younis city in Southern Gaza where even refugee camps and hospitals are not being spared. A number of videos have surfaced online in which Israeli troops have been caught on camera killing unarmed people in cold blood, raiding hospitals disguised as civilian medics, etc. The Rafah Crossing near the Egypt border, which has come under immense pressure due to the influx of Palestinian refugees from Northern Gaza, is also being struck by Israel. Despite warnings by Egypt that Rafah is a 'red line' and should not be violated, the attacks from Israel are unrelenting in their timing and scope. On 9 February, PM Netanyahu issued a directive to his military to prepare a plan to evacuate civilians from Rafah ahead of an expected invasion there.

Is Saudi Arabia Having a Rethink?

Immediately after the 7 October attack, Saudi Arabia condemned the Hamas terror strike, but later on 12 October, Crown Prince MbS assured Palestinian President Mahmud Abbas that Saudi Arabia continues "to stand by the Palestinian people to achieve their legitimate rights". However, Saudi Arabia has stayed on the sidelines as the conflict escalated and casualties mounted, letting Qatar and Egypt take the lead. There were even reports that Saudi Arabia and possibly the UAE were permitting Israeli cargo to be carried on land routes across the desert to avoid Houthis which was targeting their ships in the Red Sea.

More recently, however, there seems to be a shift in the Saudi position. In a statement on 7 February, the Saudi Foreign Ministry stated that it has communicated its firm position to the US administration that there will be no diplomatic relations with Israel unless an independent Palestinian state is recognized on the 1967 borders with East Jerusalem as its capital and that the Israeli aggression on Gaza Strip stops and all Israeli occupation forces withdraw from there. It was soon followed by reports of a consultative ministerial meeting on the Gaza war hosted by Saudi Arabia on 8 February which included the UAE, Egypt, Jordan and Palestine where they reaffirmed their support for Palestine. Soon thereafter, reacting to Israel's plans to launch massive operations in Rafah, the Saudi Foreign Ministry issued a statement on 10 February warning of very serious repercussions of storming Rafah. These bold announcements are a definite sign of Saudi's changing positions. Although it may be too early to say, Saudi Arabia may finally be ready to take the lead to end this war.

Pressure on the USA to Pull the Plug

On the American side, its confused and muddled strategy of engagement continues. On one hand, it has continuously been propagating the end of the conflict while on the other it has been reluctant to end financial and military support to Israel. With domestic support lessening and presidential elections nearing, it may have to take hard decisions soon. On 6 February, the US House, by a vote of 250 to 180, voted against the legislation that would send $17.6 billion aid to Israel. A number of US Senate leaders, especially Bernie Sanders, have openly voiced their concern on the USA supporting Israeli genocide. A case filed by South Africa against Israel in the International Court of Justice last month has made its effect. Secretary Blinken, despite his tour to the region on 6-7 February, failed to get the ceasefire deal through.

On 8 February, it became evident that the USA may no longer be able to blindly support Israel against massive domestic and global opposition when President Biden was reported to have stated that Israeli response in Gaza was 'over the top'. The USA has also given Israel 45 days to report on allegations of violations of international law by its forces; else it could lose US aid. Continued attacks on US troops in Syria and Iraq and its fledgling naval campaign against Houthis from Yemen in the Red Sea could be major contributing factors too. As per inputs, the USA is also planning to withdraw all its troops from Syria and Iraq in the next three months. It will therefore be interesting to see if and for how long the Biden administration continues supporting Israel's uncontrolled war in Gaza.

Israel is Feeling the Heat

Israel, or PM Netanyahu specifically, is however determined to push for absolute victory in Gaza. Netanyahu earlier had confirmed fears that many had over the years when he said that he has no intention of working towards a two-state solution. However, with the war prolonging and casualties rising, there is growing opposition in Israel against Netanyahu. On one such occasion, relatives of hostages burst into an Israeli parliamentary meeting on 22 January demanding immediate exchange of hostages. Members of his war cabinet have also openly come out in dissent. Minister Gadi Eisenkot, who is a former IDF Chief of Staff, and Benny Gantz, leader of the National Unity party who joined the war cabinet, have openly questioned Netanyahu's insistence on continuing military operations rather than focusing on getting the hostages back. There are reports that of the 130 hostages estimated to be in Hamas custody, 32 have already been killed in crossfire in Gaza and therefore demands for an early ceasefire and hostage exchange are growing by the day.

Iran-supported proxies are intensifying their operations especially in the North through the Hezbollah and Houthis and are inflicting huge economic costs by not permitting Israeli-flagged ships to transit the Red Sea. Russia has come out in open support of the Palestinian cause and its Air Force has reportedly joined air patrols in the so-called Bravo Line that divides the Golan Heights between Syria and Israel to prevent Israeli air strikes into Syria. With the USA now demanding answers, Egypt lining up troops and tanks at the Rafah border and Saudi Arabia adopting a proactive stand, Israel is definitely feeling the heat.

Options to End War in Gaza

Netanyahu Out

PM Netanyahu is the most crucial factor of the puzzle. Either he is brought around to realistically review the desired end state in the war or domestic pressure could force his ouster, leading to a more pragmatic leader taking charge to end the war and get the remaining hostages back.

USA Pulls the Plug

The USA is the second-most important player in the game. There are signs of fatigue, disappointment and domestic pressure on continuing to blindly support Israel. It has already warned Israel against any rash military action against refugees in Rafah. If Netanyahu goes ahead with it, it may be the perfect excuse for the USA to pull the plug.

Regional Actors Unite

Till now it is mainly Qatar and Egypt which have pursued peace options while Iran has exercised its military power through its proxies. Turkey has been mobilizing the political discourse against Israel while Saudi Arabia and the UAE have watched silently from the sidelines. Neither the Arab League nor the GCC have been able to come up with any firm, bold and unified stand on the war. Saudi Arabia and Egypt hold the key in the region for a possible end to the war. If Egypt and Saudi Arabia, along with others like Qatar and Turkey issue clear and unambiguous warnings to Israel, it may have a very strong deterring effect.

India as a Wildcard

India has a unique position in this war. It enjoys close ties with Israel and both countries have close cooperation and understanding on terror. India has maintained its traditional stand on support for Palestine and the 'two-state solution'. It is well known that Netanyahu and Modi have a close personal rapport and understand each other well. India's successful G20 presidency in 2023 has increased its weight as a 'global leader'. A quiet word from Modi, explaining the realities and course of action possible, could well do the trick.

Looking Ahead

The Gaza war is at a very dangerous phase. Any possible action by Israel in Rafah could draw in many more players into the conflict and unleash a war which will then be very difficult to contain or end. Hopefully, better sense will prevail.

16

Gaza on the Brink as the War Enters Attrition Phase

The war has entered its sixth month with no signs of any letup in hostilities.

On 11 March 2024, 67 Palestinians were reported killed in Israeli airstrikes in Gaza, bringing the Palestinian death toll to over 31,100 since the war began. Of these, more than two-thirds are women and children. This was incidentally the first day of the holy month of Ramadan, a month of peace and fasting, a date which was hoped to usher in a ceasefire, but sadly, there is neither any ceasefire nor any respite from Israeli attacks on Gaza.

Ceasefire Proposals

There have been numerous attempts to negotiate a ceasefire, mainly with Egypt and Qatar taking the lead.

Days before the onset of Ramadan, another attempt at a ceasefire was made through the collective efforts of the USA, Qatar and Egypt, proposing an agreement in which Hamas and Israel would release each other's hostages in return for a six-week ceasefire and more aid to Gaza. Hamas however dismissed it, stating that it wants a permanent ceasefire instead of a six-week pause, and a 'complete withdrawal' of Israeli forces from Gaza alongwith the release of Palestinian prisoners. Israel, on the other hand, has no intention of vacating Gaza anytime soon. Any faint flicker of hope was extinguished when Israeli troops fired on Palestinians gathered to collect food aid in the south-west of Gaza City on 29 February, killing at least 112 persons, an act which drew unanimous condemnation from the world, including the USA. With no convergence on essential conditions for a ceasefire and continued attacks by Israel on civilians in Gaza, the prospects of a truce look distant and bleak.

War Enters Attrition Phase

The war is well into its sixth month and any calculations that Israel may have made for an early end owing to its overwhelming military superiority being able to crush Hamas in no time and overrun Gaza in weeks, have been proven wrong. Hamas has withstood the Israeli onslaught and has, in fact, inflicted sizeable casualties and damage on the Israeli forces in return. While the Hamas terror attack was a major embarrassment for the Israeli intelligence, the prolonged and almost un-winnable war is slowly becoming a bigger embarrassment for Israel.

At the start of the conflict, it was estimated that Hamas had around 25,000 to 30,000 fighters primarily trained in guerrilla warfare and terrorist tactics.

However, almost six months later, it is estimated that only 30 percent of Hamas fighters have been eliminated along with a few middle and high ranking commanders. Hamas's fighting potential remains intact. The supply of rockets and ammunition has not dried up nor has Israel been able to destroy Hamas's war-waging capability. The famous underground tunnel network in Gaza, the 'Gaza metro' though targeted and destroyed at many places, remains in large part, intact and undiscovered. Also, the mastermind of Hamas's military operations, Yahya Sinwar, continues to evade Israeli forces. Besides, with every civilian killed in Gaza, the increasing hatred for Israel is resulting in swelling support and joining of new ranks into the Hamas.

On the other hand, Israel withdrew a large number of combat formations from Northern Gaza in January after it effectively cut it off from the rest of the Gaza Strip. It redeployed some of the combat formations in the south, especially in Khan Younis, and disbanded many reservists who were sent back to anchor critical portions of Israel's economy, leaving Israeli formations depleted. In addition, the Israeli army has lost over 600 officers and troops and over 1,500 have sustained severe injuries. On 23 January, Israeli forces suffered their worst loss in a single day when 24 soldiers died in a Hamas attack in Gaza.

Israel Faces the Heat

As the war drags along, Israel is facing the heat from multiple fronts. Militarily, it has suffered heavy casualties, both in terms of personnel and equipment. Its economy is shrinking rapidly, with some estimates showing a decline of almost 20 percent. Exports are being severely affected and the naval blockade by the Houthis in the Red Sea has effectively blocked Israeli cargoes transiting the sea route despite heavy US naval presence, forcing it to take a longer route around the Cape of Good Hope in South Africa, thus largely increasing transit and insurance costs. Its sea ports of Eilat and Haifa have witnessed huge losses with a drastic drop in economic activities.

Domestically, there is growing opposition to PM Netanyahu, especially because of his inability to negotiate the return of hostages.

Internationally too, anger and opposition against Israel is on the rise. Many of its allies have publicly condemned Israeli actions. The UK, France, Spain and many other countries have announced that they may take unilateral decisions to recognize the state of Palestine while Brazil, which holds the G20 Presidency this year, has broken off diplomatic ties with Israel. South Africa's case of genocide by Israel is another pressure point on Israel.

The USA, which is now in the thick of its presidential election cycle, has also repeatedly asked Israel to ensure that civilian casualties are minimized. It has also stated that any offensive in Rafah is a 'red line' which Israel should not cross. Russia too has upped its game in the conflict despite being heavily committed in its war in Ukraine. It hosted leaders of different Palestine factions including Hamas in Moscow on 26 February and has declared that Russia will do what is required for the establishment of a Palestine state. It has already committed its air power in the region through combat air patrols in Syria along the Golan Heights.

Within the region, there are clear indications of growing solidarity in the Muslim world. Egypt has already amassed troops on the border opposite the Rafah Crossing and the Saudi Arabia-led Arab League has hardened its stand on Israel. Iran-backed proxies continue to target Israel. There were reports of Iraq-based militias striking Tel Aviv airport on 12 March through drones while Hezbollah rained more than 100 rockets in Northern Israel in one day on 11 March including the highly potent Burkan IRAM rockets, inflicting damage on military infrastructure.

What Next

With Netanyahu unyielding on his threat of a ground offensive in Rafah and dismissing the 'red line' caution from President Biden, things don't look good for the region. The holy month of Ramadan has started with increased violence. Israel's recent decision to construct 3,500 more settlements in the West Bank and its presentation of a 'post war plan for Gaza' have only added fuel to the fire.

In the midst of this ongoing conflict and failing ceasefire attempts, there was a report of the Indian NSA visiting Israel and meeting PM Netanyahu on 11 March in a rather hurriedly and discreetly arranged meeting, once again raising questions if India can emerge as a peacemaker where all others have failed. Meanwhile, the conflict drags on. With the international community clueless and none of the warring parties ready to relent, the war looks set for a long drawn out battle of attrition.

17

Gaza Needs a Smart and Urgent Exit Strategy

On 25 March 2024 there was finally some good news about the ongoing conflict in Gaza when the UN Security Council adopted a resolution demanding an immediate ceasefire in Gaza during Ramadan, while also calling for the immediate and unconditional release of all hostages. This was the Security Council's first successfully passed resolution calling for a ceasefire since the onset of the war in the Gaza Strip. The previous four resolutions in the UN Security Council had failed due to veto, thrice exercised by the USA. The USA, however, abstained this time and 'let the resolution pass'.

The resolution drew mixed reactions. Israel was the first to react, with PM Netanyahu alleging that the USA had "abandoned its policy in the UN" and was therefore harming both the war effort and the effort to release the Israeli hostages in Hamas custody. Israel also cancelled the scheduled visit of its ministerial delegation to Washington which was scheduled to discuss the offensive in Rafah and other options. In an almost immediate U-turn, under Israeli pressure, the USA came out with a statement that the UN Resolution is 'non-binding' and that Israel can continue what it is doing in Gaza, making a mockery of the whole process in the UN Security Council. Hamas, on the other hand, initially welcomed the ceasefire resolution, but a day later on 26 March, reiterated its position on a permanent ceasefire accompanied with a complete withdrawal of Israeli forces from Gaza. As a result, the initial euphoria and hopes for an early ceasefire has very quickly turned into a 'back to square one' position.

The War Continues Unabated

With no assurance that the ceasefire will actually take shape, it is now back to the joint efforts of Egypt and Qatar, who have been separately negotiating for an early ceasefire. Meanwhile, Israel has upped the ante in the past few days. It launched an attack on Al Shifa Hospital in Gaza for the second time, again resulting in heavy civilian casualties. The airstrikes and bombing in Rafah too have intensified in the past few days. Reports also indicate Israel targeting Southern Lebanon, killing civilians. Meanwhile, Hezbollah too has intensified its missile strikes into Northern Israel, inflicting damage to key military assets and loss of lives. Houthis in the South continue to disrupt and block Israeli, US and UK ships in the Red Sea, inflicting heavy economic losses on Israel and its allies. As per latest estimates, the war in Gaza has already resulted in the loss of over 32,000 lives.

War Objectives and their Status

When Israel launched its counter-offensive into Gaza on 7 October, it had stated three clear aims; to flatten Gaza to the ground, eliminate Hamas from the face of the Earth and to get back all its hostages. With the war well into its sixth month, it is important to review each of these aims. Yes, Israel has flattened Gaza, in fact so badly that many who have been on the ground seem to suggest that Gaza has been reduced to rubble and virtually un-inhabitable, for years. Israel has also, in the past few weeks, flattened a kilometre-wide stretch along the border with Gaza, which it intends to convert into a buffer zone later.

Secondly, the destruction of Hamas. Best estimates suggest that Israel has succeeded in eliminating only 30 percent of the estimated 30,000 Hamas fighters. Hamas's fighting potential however remains intact and the supply of rockets and ammunition has not dried up. Also, the mastermind of Hamas's military operations, Yahya Sinwar, continues to evade Israeli forces.

Thirdly, except for the exchange of a few hostages during a brief humanitarian pause last November, Israel has not been able to obtain any more. Plus, 30-32 hostages have already been reported killed in crossfire, including some by Israeli forces, leading to uproar and protests against Netanyahu in Israel.

For Hamas, it was a question of two clear objectives. First, to remind the world that while talks of normalization and reconciliation between Israel and the Arab world could go on, the cause for a Palestinian state could not be lost sight of. Second, to expose to the world, and especially its support base, the false sense of invincibility of the Israeli military and its intelligence services. On both counts, Hamas has succeeded so far.

Smart Exit Strategy

It is always easy to start a war but very difficult to decide when and how to call it off.

Israel therefore has to be mindful of the possibilities and the consequences of a prolonged conflict which has military, economic as well as political costs. The Israeli army has already lost over 600 officers and troops and over 1,500 injured severely. Its economy is shrinking rapidly, showing a decline of almost 20 percent.

Politically, it is becoming difficult for Netanyahu to hold on to his position, domestically and internationally. The USA has made it clear that Israel has to restrain itself and cannot bank upon blanket support to any Israeli action in Gaza.

Israel had launched the offensive in a state of rage and revenge. However, after the initial onslaught, instead of reviewing its war strategy and politico-military objectives, it continued to unleash punitive strikes into Gaza. Militarily, Gaza has been defeated. Hamas, as an organization, is however, unlikely to be eliminated from the face of the Earth. What is the most viable option then for Israel? An early ceasefire, withdrawal of forces from Gaza Strip and using the recently flattened one-km strip along the Gaza border as a surveillance-cum-buffer zone, under 24x7 surveillance, to prevent the recurrence of 'another 7 October', could be a possibility. As regards hostages, Hamas would most likely agree to exchange hostages once Israel agrees to the above.

SECTION III

Iran Enters the Conflict

18

Iran Enters Conflict: Vows Massive Retaliation

On 1 April, the ongoing war in Gaza took a dangerous turn, bringing the entire region to a precipice of an all-out war, when an Israeli strike in Syria targeted the Iranian Consulate in Damascus resulting in the death of seven members of the Islamic Revolutionary Guard Corps (IRGC) including General Mohammad Reza Zahedi, the senior most commander in Lebanon and Syria. There was immediate outrage and condemnation from all quarters as the attack on an embassy/consulate complex is considered as an attack on the sovereign land of a country and therefore a direct attack on Iran. Iran's Supreme Leader, Ayatollah Ali Khamenei, promptly announced that Israel would be punished for the attack, while President Ebrahim Raisi said it will "not go unanswered." Fearing reprisal against its troops in the region, the USA was quick to state that it had no prior information of the strike and that "we had nothing to do with it".

While the Israeli army and PM Netanyahu may have finally succeeded in provoking Iran to join the war, this time, it may have taken one risk too many and stretched the envelope too far. It may be recalled that on 3 January, twin explosions at an event to commemorate the death anniversary of General Qassem Soleimani, Islamic Revolutionary Guard Corps (IRGC) Commander, near his tomb in the Iranian city of Kerman, killed almost 100 people, marking it as the worst terror attack since Iran's Revolution in 1979. This time however, Israel has struck on the 'sovereign land' of Iran, taking the consequences to a totally different level.

Fearing fierce retaliatory response, Israel put its armed forces on full alert. Air defence and anti-missile systems are monitoring the skies while GPS systems have been disabled to disrupt guidance to incoming missiles. People are being moved to bomb shelters and there are reports of people evacuating in large numbers from border areas in Israel. There was utter chaos in the Israeli Knesset on 3 April when Israeli demonstrators stormed in demanding the resignation of Netanyahu's government. There are reports that Israel is also evacuating its embassies in the region. There is almost a sense of inevitability that Iran will come hard on Israel. The question in everybody's mind is when and how.

How Could Iran Respond?

As a policy, Iran has not been known to engage itself in a direct military conflict. In fact, the last time that it fought a direct military war was the 1980-88 Iran-Iraq war. Even at the peak of the Persian Gulf crisis in June 2019 which brought the USA and Iran closest ever to a direct conflict, Iran did not initiate any conflict. Over the past 30-odd years, Iran has developed a well-spread network of militias and proxies who have been fighting its battles in the region. The famous 'Three H's, that is, the Hamas, Hezbollah and Houthis, are the prominent ones besides several other smaller yet effective militia groups. It has equipped and trained these proxies and militias with potent weapons systems including modern systems like armed drones, short and medium range missiles, etc. Also, these militias are closely embedded within the local population across the Levant, making it easier for them to operate and merge to disappear.

Iran may therefore once again decide to use these proxies and militias, this time however in a more targeted and concentrated form to inflict massive strikes on Israel and assets of its allies like the USA and the UK in the region. In case Iran does decide to retaliate directly, this would be the first in decades, and could set off a conflict which could then spiral totally out of control. Here it may be noted that Iran has a unique system as regards its armed forces. It has its regular armed forces which comprise all elements of the army, air force and navy. Besides, it has the IRGC which too has its own army, navy and air force and is equally potent, if not more. The IRGC also has the Al Quds forces which primarily operate outside the country. And of course, it has one of the most advanced and potent ballistic missiles programs which can easily cover the entire region. Iran thus has multiple options to respond to Israel.

When Could Iran Strike?

Iran has made it clear that it will respond at a time and place of its own choice. The fifth of April is the last Friday of Ramadan and therefore an auspicious day. It is also celebrated as 'Al Quds Day' in Iran. Coming as a response to the killing of a senior Al Quds Commander, 5 April could be a possible day of choice. However, Iran may let this day pass owing to the religious sentiments of the people, knowing that any strike will in return also invite counter strikes. The next choice could be 7 April when the war would complete six months. However, it may not have resonance in Iran with regard to timing its response.

The next possibility is 12 April, if Iran decides to let the holy month of Ramadan and the festival of Eid pass before it pushes the button. Whatever may be the date and time, the potency and might of the Iranian military response cannot be underestimated in any manner. Combined with Hezbollah's arsenal of rockets and missiles, Iran, with its own arsenal of armed drones and hypersonic missiles, can overwhelm any battlefield before the adversary has a chance to respond.

Effect on the Region

In the past six months, all efforts have been made by every stakeholder to see that the Gaza conflict stays localized. However, recent developments have brought in a sense of unavoidability of an escalation. Iran has called upon all Islamic countries to unite against Israel. On 4 April, the UAE suspended all diplomatic coordination with Israel while other countries including Saudi Arabia have strongly condemned the Israeli attack on the Iranian consulate. Major consultations between foreign offices and National Security Advisers are currently on to see how to take this situation forward. Egypt has already amassed its troops, tanks and guns in Sinai Rafah in anticipation of an Israeli offensive in Rafah.

If Iran does strike Israel directly or indirectly, there are going to be direct consequences in Syria, Iraq and Lebanon. There are reports of Iran mustering up a resistance force in Jordan also. Egypt may be forced to join the war in case its 'red lines' are crossed. Russia, which had already positioned its air assets in Syria for combat air patrols in January, has now reportedly started moving in additional forces in Golan Heights. Syria. Saudi Arabia and the UAE which have so far tried to remain insulated from the ongoing conflict may be forced to join, at least in cutting off ties with Israel and stopping its access to overland trade routes through them across the Arabian Desert. In case of an escalation, the Red Sea region is definitely set for heightened battles too. This would also be the first instance where Iran and the Arab world may be fighting a war against Israel as Iran was not part of earlier Arab-Israeli wars, the last one being in 1973.

Effect on India

West Asia has become one of the most closely integrated regions with India in the past decade. Both regions have found strategic convergence on multiple issues with trade, energy and security being most prominent. Any war or instability in the region would have a direct effect on India. Once the war escalates, the first casualty is definitely going to be oil prices which could shoot through the roof, further increasing the economic instability in the region which has already been adversely affected due to closure of trade routes in the Red Sea. Increase in oil prices and disruption in trade could disrupt positive economic growth. With 8.5 million Indian diaspora in the region, the threat of an escalation could trigger demands for the evacuation of Indians from there. Although India has mastered the art and science of evacuation in past years, it would still be a logistic nightmare. India's National Security Adviser (NSA) Doval was at the SCO-NSA meeting in Astana, Kazakhstan, on 3 April and would have definitely discussed ongoing developments with Iran's NSA and the possible options of retaliation.

Looking Ahead

Iran is an ancient civilizational state and has been known to be resilient and patient. It has often chosen its own type of methods of extracting revenge, which do not necessarily involve direct military conflict. This time however, the situation is different. Does Iran think that the 'Red Line' has been crossed? Does Iran think that Israel has been isolated enough, stretched thin and politically weakened enough to deliver the 'death blow'? Will Iran, in an escalated conflict, take the decision to cross the nuclear threshold and become a nuclear weapons power? These are questions that the Iranian leadership must be war-gaming as they prepare for the strike.

As the people gather for prayers on the last Friday of the holy month of Ramadan, the region and the world wait with bated breath and a fear that the spark may have finally been lit in the haystack, the fire from which could engulf the region in no time.

19

Israel Withdraws *from* Gaza and Iran Keeps the Region Guessing: A Lull *before* the Storm?

The Gaza war has taken a dramatic turn in the past few weeks after the Israeli strike on 1 April targeting the Iranian Consulate in Damascus. It is difficult to say what angered Iran more; the death of a prominent IRGC commander or the fact that the attack targeted its consulate building in a foreign land, which, as per international conventions, is treated as sovereign territory and any military attack on it, therefore, is an act of war.

The attack and the Iranian pronouncements in the days following it have led to a mad scramble in Israel. It has recalled military personnel from leave and has put all surveillance systems on full alert. The USA too is on the alert and is busy safeguarding its assets in the region. Despite the USA claiming that it had no knowledge of the attack, Iran has made it clear that it was a party and that it had given the green signal for it.

In a surprise move, on 7 April, Israel suddenly decided to pull out troops from Gaza, especially southern Gaza, where it had been conducting ground operations for the past few months. The IDF confirmed the development and stated that its 98th Division had 'concluded its mission' in Khan Younis and was leaving the Gaza Strip to 'recuperate and prepare for future operations.' One brigade has been left in a small enclave which divides the Gaza Strip into two halves, north and south. IDF Chief of Staff Lt. Gen. Herzi Halevi added that despite the withdrawal of all the army's manoeuvring ground forces from the Gaza Strip, the war against Hamas continues and is far from over.

As the news of withdrawal filtered in, speculative inputs started flooding the media space, some suggesting that Iran has told the USA that if Israel withdraws its forces from Gaza and signs a permanent ceasefire deal, it might escape its retaliation. Other reports suggested that Hamas and Israel had almost concluded a ceasefire deal and the pre-emptive withdrawal was part of it. Still others suggested that Israel was redeploying forces to meet the Iranian offensive in the north. Iran and the USA soon dismissed any reports of a 'deal' while Hamas also denied any deal. PM Netanyahu, in his typical belligerent self, announced that there is no backing down and that the date for a ground offensive in Rafah has been set.

Iran's Retaliation

Iran has vowed retaliation and hinted at 'direct strikes' more than once in recent days. Whether it will choose the option of retaliating with strikes originating from Iranian soil is however another question. The pressure on Iran this time to retaliate directly is however stronger, more due to the fact that the Israeli strike had targeted its consulate which is 'sovereign territory'.

In a build-up to the retaliatory strikes, Iran has already commenced 'battle drills'. Its Foreign Minister was in Oman and Syria in the past few days. Although the Oman visit was reported as talks towards coordination with Yemeni groups, it is well known that Oman has traditionally been the interlocutor between Iran and the USA and even Israel. The visit to Damascus was to inaugurate the new consulate building, as a show of solidarity after the strike on the consulate as also a direct dare to Israel. Reports filtering in over the past two days also indicate that Iran has banned civilian flights in the airspace for the next 48-96 hours, and has declared a large zone within Iran as a 'no fly zone' which generally indicates a missile test. Could it also be a nuclear weapon test?

With Iran's nuclear program progressing unchecked after the last round of talks failed in August 2022, it has surely accumulated enough highly enriched uranium (weapon grade) for a few warheads and definitely has the required technological knowledge or capability. It can't therefore be ruled out although it may be slightly premature at this juncture for Iran to reveal this trump card. However, it all depends on what Iran is planning as its politico-military objectives in this war. Iran's Foreign Minister has also reportedly called his counterparts in Saudi Arabia, the UAE, Iraq and Qatar which is standard diplomatic protocol with allies before it takes a major military or diplomatic step. It may be recalled that Iran's NSA was in Astana, Kazakhstan, last week, days after the Israeli strike on Iran's consulate in Damascus and would have consulted with China, Russia and others on possible options of retaliation.

Iran has also upped the ante in calling for Muslim unity against Israel and has urged all countries in the region to stop all trade with Israel immediately. In response, UAE has announced on 10 April that it is imposing major trade restrictions on Israel till there is a permanent ceasefire in Gaza. Some reports have indicated a plan to block the Strait of Hormuz also which could have a direct and immediate impact on crude oil prices, a common denominator affecting the global economy.

How Will Iran Retaliate?

It is quite clear that Iran is going to strike back. However, the 'how' is the most important question in everybody's mind right now. A massive coordinated strike across all fronts is the more likely option. A massive rocket barrage from Northern Lebanon by Hezbollah, missile strikes (carrying Iranian ballistic missiles) from Syria, drone strikes originating from Yemen or the Persian Gulf, and ground attacks by small guerrilla teams from Gaza, Lebanon, and even Sinai is a possible scenario. A freshly assembled resistance force attacking Israeli assets across Jordan too is a possibility. A sea blockade in the Persian Gulf is likely. Pointed terror strikes on Israeli or US embassies in the region may also be a part of the plan.

In the build-up to the strikes and preparing the battlefield, Iraqi resistance forces have already struck key points in Israel including Haifa and Eliat ports by drones. Strikes from Hezbollah have been successful on Israel's key surveillance and communication posts along the border in the north.

When will the Strikes Come

It is difficult to say whether Israel has been successful in finally baiting Iran to join battle directly this time or whether Iran was waiting for such a 'red line' to be crossed so that it could declare war legitimately on Israel. Either way, the battle lines are clearly drawn now. With Eid now over, it is now upto Iran when and how to respond.

Israel and the USA have been on total alert for the last ten days. The Israeli strike in Gaza on 11 April, the day of Eid, resulting in the deaths of three sons of Hamas leader Ismail Haniyeh may well be the final nail in the coffin.

20

Iran Strikes Israel in 'Self-Defence'

On the night of 13 April, Iran finally struck Israel and fulfilled its promise to its people of a retaliatory response to the earlier Israeli strike in Syria on its consulate in Damascus. As expected, the retaliatory strikes took place after Eid, owing mainly to the religious sensitivities of the people in the Muslim world. The Iranian response came in the form of a collective strike with drones and ballistic missiles, estimated to be more than 200 in number. While most of the drones were intercepted mid-air, some of the missiles found their mark and struck the Israeli Nevatim air base in the Negev desert. Nevatim is from where Israel had launched its F-35 fighters that attacked the Iranian consulate in Damascus.

Act of Self-Defence

Immediately after the strikes, Iran's Permanent Mission to the UN posted an official statement confirming the strikes, stating that they were conducted on the strength of Article 51 of the UN Charter pertaining to legitimate defence. The matter can be deemed concluded. However, should the Israeli regime make another mistake, Iran's response will be considerably more severe. PM Netanyahu too promptly assured his people of the preparedness of the IDF and issued a veiled warning to Iran stating, 'whoever hurts us, we hurt him'.

Despite decades of hostility between Israel and Iran, this is the first time that Iran has launched strikes directly on the former from its territory. In fact, this is the first Iranian attack on Israel as Iran was not part of the Arab coalition which fought the earlier Arab-Israeli wars. The fact that Iran this time resorted to direct strikes clearly indicates that a 'red line' had been crossed when Israel attacked the Iranian consulate in Damascus. Also, the fact that Iran was quick to put out a statement in the UN highlighting Article 51 of the Charter indicates that it has served its purpose of satisfying the demands of its people of exacting revenge and wants no more escalation. Article 51 of the UN Charter states that "Nothing in the present Charter shall impair the inherent right of individual or collective self-defence if an armed attack occurs against a Member of the United Nations".

Reactions

As expected, the USA and the Western countries were quick to condemn Iran's strike. US President Biden reiterated his support to Israel stating that his commitment to Israel's security against threats from Iran and its proxies is ironclad. UN Secretary-General Antonio Guterres condemned the serious escalation represented by the large-scale attack on Israel and called for its immediate cessation. The UK, Canada, Germany, the Netherlands, Norway, the EU and most of the Western countries also promptly condemned Iran for the attack. Within the region, the Saudi foreign ministry issued a statement voicing its concern at the military escalation calling on all parties to exercise restraint. The Palestinians were overjoyed by Iran's strike and came out on the streets of West Bank in celebration. In Gaza too, people celebrated a night with no Israeli strikes, a rare occurrence in the last six months.

What if the Conflict Escalates?

While Iran has made it clear that it considers the 'matter closed', it is not clear whether Israel will actually hold the same view. Netanyahu has been under tremendous pressure in the Gaza war and his right-wing ministers who are part of the coalition may not agree to any plan which indicates reconciliation or 'no action'. Netanyahu has not yet been able to achieve his war objectives in the Gaza war and 'no response' to Iran may make matters worse for him. The 135-odd Israeli hostages in the custody of Hamas have not yet been released, Hamas has not been eliminated, Israeli forces have suffered significant losses in the past six months and there is no clear convergence on how to get a permanent ceasefire or end the war. The economy, which shrunk by almost 20 percent in December 2023 and the closed sea routes to and from Israel are adding to its dilemma.

Israel also faces a completely new war situation. For decades, it has been training, equipping and fighting wars in its neighbourhood. It now faces the prospects of a war with an enemy who is located 1,700 miles away. Iran is also geographically much larger than Israel and therefore has much more capacity to absorb damage. With support across the region through its proxies and militias, it can continue to inflict damage on Israel without involving itself directly. In a manner, therefore, this conflict is unlike any other military conflict where the opposing forces will never face each other, and no tank or artillery battles and no capture of territory is involved. It is a 'stand-off war' which throws up its unique challenges, requirements and dynamics, more so for Israel than Iran. It is therefore a match-up between the military capabilities of a stand-off war involving air strikes, missiles and drones, coupled with non-kinetic means like cyberattacks, closure of sea routes, etc.

How do the Militaries Match-up?

How do Israel and Iran match-up in such a scenario? In terms of aircraft, Israel is definitely far superior to Iran. Its air force comprises the most modern fighter aircraft in the form of F-15s, F-16s and F-35s, with a total of almost 350 aircraft split into 14 squadrons of fighters, 2 squadrons of AH-64 Apache attack helicopters and many other aircraft in different support roles. It has a whole range of armed and unarmed UAVs, including the famous Heron and Hermes 900 armed UAVs. It has a very potent air-defence system in terms of the Patriot System and the Arrow Anti-Missile System. The Patriot is a US system and is perhaps the oldest and well tested air defence system with Israel. It was used during the First Gulf War in 1991 to intercept Scud missiles and shoot down fighter aircraft fired by Iraq, and in recent times it has been used to intercept long-range missiles launched by Houthis from Yemen. The Arrow is a modern anti-missile defence system, developed by the USA, and is designed to intercept long-range missiles, including ballistic. In terms of missile capability, Israel has mostly short-range missiles upto 500-km range which is inadequate to target Iran directly. It however has Jericho-2, a medium range ballistic missile (MRBM), which is a solid-fuelled missile with ranges of 1,500 to 3,000 km and can enter some parts of Iran. Its Jericho-3 is an intermediate range ballistic missile (IRBM) with a range of 4,800 to 6,500 km using inertial guidance with a radar guided warhead. Of course, if required, Israel can always bank upon the USA to provide long-range missiles to target Iran directly.

Iran, on the other hand, has a very poorly equipped and ageing fleet of fighter aircraft in its Air Force, with an assorted array ranging from the US-made F-14, Chinese F-4, F-5 and F-7 along with Russian Sukhois and MiG-29. Most estimates suggest that the total number of such aircraft is around 330-350. However, the Air Force is not Iran's strong point. It is its missile technology that has made its threat more potent than ever. It may be recalled that the USA has been insistent, during talks on Iran's nuclear program, that Iran's ballistic missile program be reined in along with its nuclear program.

Iran's array of missiles is the largest and most diverse in the region. Many Iranian missiles are reported to be inherently capable of carrying nuclear payloads, which has long been an international concern leading to UN Security Council Resolution 2231 which called upon Iran "not to undertake any activity related to ballistic missiles designed to be capable of delivering nuclear weapons". Unlike Israel, which has the constraints of range, Iran has no such problems. Not only does it have an arsenal of medium and long-range ballistic missiles, it also has the luxury of firing these missiles from territories in Syria, Iraq and Lebanon, thus increasing the threat to Israel. In its medium- and long-range category are the Khorramshahr-1, 2, and 3 which are MRBMs with ranges of 2,000 to 3,000 km, Fatah-1 with ranges of 1,400 to 1,700 km and many others like Sejjil (2,000 km), Paveh (1,650 km), etc. It is estimated that Iran used the Khorramshahr missile to target an Israeli base last night. In addition, Iran has developed hypersonic missiles too, which fly at speeds of Mach 5 and above, that is, five times the speed of sound, and are beyond the interception capability of most anti-missile systems. Russia has used such missiles in its war in Ukraine with great success.

In addition to its large arsenal of missiles, Iran possesses a huge variety of drones also, many of which were used in the attack last night. Iran has in fact mastered the art and science of developing low-cost and low-technology drones which are revolutionizing the battlefields. It has been exporting its drones to Russia also where they are being effectively used in Ukraine. Prominent among them is the Shahed category which is basically suicide or Kamakazi drones meant to explode on the targets. A version of these drones, Shahed-101, was reportedly used when three US service personnel were killed and 34 wounded in January 2024 after a drone hit residential quarters at a military outpost in Jordan known as Tower 22 on the border between Iraq and Syria. Shahed-131 was used when the Houthis targeted Saudi oil fields and air fields in 2019; again Iranian made. The Shahed-136 is a long-range drone, having a light carbon fibre airframe and a range of more than 1,500 miles. They can carry 20 to 40kg of explosives, around double that of Shahed-131 and enough to cause significant damage in a non-hardened structure. There are also the Shahed-238 drones which have jet propulsion making them faster and have the capability of carrying a far more payload. There is also the Samad-1, 2, 3 categories of drones which have an effective range of 1,800 km and carry sufficient payload to inflict damage.

The match-up between Israel and Iran is equal although Iran could be said to have the advantage of longer range missiles and a wider variety of drones. Israel has the edge as far as air power is concerned and obviously 'iron clad' support from the USA.

What Next

The ball is now in Israel's court. Iran has made it clear that it considers the matter closed and does not want any escalation. Israel too can get away by saying that it thwarted Iranian strikes and only minor damage to a military airfield was done which is not a major issue. Israel also has the opportunity to use this Iranian strike to turn popular public perception back in its favour, which has taken a severe beating in the past five months due to civilian casualties.

With the suspense of when and how Iranian retaliation is now over, it is time to find an exit option to the ongoing war in Gaza. If Israel however chooses to retaliate, the region could be engulfed in a full-blown conflict.

21

Understanding Iran's Strategic Patience and why it is Now Over

On 13 April, Iran did something which it had not done for decades. It launched a direct military attack from its soil against a nation that is its sworn enemy, Israel, in a massive and simultaneous strike of drones and missiles. It is difficult to say whether Iran was adequately provoked to take this unprecedented action due to the strike on its consulate or whether Iran was patiently waiting for an opportune moment to join the war directly for legitimate reasons. Nonetheless, the retaliatory strike did two things. Firstly, it immediately expanded the scope of the war much beyond Gaza and secondly it signalled to the world that Iran has finally crossed the threshold of patience and that it was no longer willing to fight from the shadows through its proxies in the region.

Iran may have shed its strategic patience by striking Israel directly from its soil. However, the fact that it targeted only military sites clearly indicated a sense of caution, restraint and non-escalation. Before we dwell on the reasons why Iran has finally shed its strategic patience, it may be worthwhile to briefly recap the major provocations in the past and how Iran reacted to better understand this tectonic shift in Iran's policy.

Recap of Major Attacks on Iran

Iran has been in the eye of the storm of the West as well as the Sunni Muslim world in the region for more than two decades. The reasons vary from the threats posed by its nuclear program, its rivalry with Saudi Arabia as also its sworn enmity with Israel. Therefore, the history of most of the previous attacks on Iranian interests is indicative of these factors.

Iran's nuclear program has been repeatedly targeted. In June 2010, the Stuxnet virus attacked the computers at the Bushehr nuclear plant. It soon spread to the Natanz enrichment facility where almost 1,000 out of 9,000 centrifuges were destroyed. Investigations pointed towards Israel and the USA; however, Iran took no overt retaliation. It tightened its cyber security measures and thwarted many later attempts including computer virus attacks like Stars, Duqu, Wiper, Flame, etc. Again, in July 2020 and April 2021, explosions struck the centrifuge production plant at the underground facility at Natanz nuclear plant, the cause of which on both occasions pointed to sabotage.

Iran's nuclear scientists were targeted too. In November 2010, Dr. Majid Shahriari, a professor in nuclear engineering at Shahid Beheshti University in Tehran was killed in a car explosion on his way to work. In November 2020, Mohsen Fakhrizadeh, called the 'Father of the Iranian nuclear weapons program' was killed in a roadside attack outside Tehran. Both these and many other mysterious deaths of nuclear scientists were blamed on Israeli intelligence services.

Among military sites, the Parchin military complex southeast of Tehran was targeted with explosives-laden quadcopter suicide drones in May 2022, killing an engineer and damaging a building. In January 2023, a weapons production factory in Ishafan was struck by drones. Incidentally, this factory is known to produce the Shahed or Kamikaze drones that were being exported to Russia too.

Iran's IRGC too has been repeatedly targeted and its senior commanders assassinated. Qaseem Suleimani, the IRGC commander and considered one of the closest advisers of the Supreme Leader, was killed in a US drone strike in Iraq on 3 January 2020. Seyed Radhi Mousavi, the IRGC's most influential military commander in Levant, was killed in a suspected Israeli airstrike in Damascus on 25 December last year and the most recent strike in Damascus on 1 April killed General Mohammad Reza Zahedi.

Iran's commercial interests too have been targeted. In May 2020, a cyberattack impacted maritime traffic control at Shahid Rajaee port on Iran's southern coast in the Gulf, creating a hold-up of ships waiting to dock. In October 2021, a cyberattack hit the computer systems at over 4,000 gas stations in Iran preventing people from using government-issued cards to purchase fuel at a subsidized rate. In February 2024, Iran's leading south-north gas pipeline was hit by explosions, termed as a 'terrorist act or sabotage'. Once again, the attacks were traced back to Israel.

Despite all such acts of sabotage or attack, Iran maintained restraint and avoided direct military confrontation, opting instead to retaliate in its own way through its proxies in the region. It therefore needs to be examined why Iran had to break its strategic patience this time, after the attack on its consulate in Damascus.

Why the Break from Strategic Patience

There are a number of factors that could have led to this strategic decision.

As regards the ongoing war in Gaza, Iran could have easily continued to hold off Israel through a combination of Hamas, Houthis and Hezbollah and others. With every passing day, Israel was getting impatient and committing mistakes; for example, the attack on three cars of the World Central Kitchen on 1 April, the strike on Iran's consulate, etc. It was also rapidly losing world support due to reckless killing of civilians in Gaza, especially in hospitals, schools and aid convoys. The USA, its principal benefactor, was also losing its patience. Back home in Israel, the continued failure to get back the hostages, mounting casualties among the IDF and the economic downturn was driving Netanyahu's government into a corner with every passing day.

Also, repeated targeting of Iranian assets, IRGC commanders and people in Iran without any direct response was painting a picture of a weak leadership in Iran. The attack on the city of Kermen on 3 January on the death anniversary of IRGC commander Suleimani which killed over a 100 people is a case in point.

With Supreme Leader Khamenei due to turn 85 on 20 April 2024 and no successor appointed, there was also a belief that Iran's policy in the region needed to be set right before it is too late. The poor voter turnout in the parliamentary elections earlier in the year and the protests against the regime in 2021-22 must have also been playing on the minds of the leadership. As Iran has experienced in the past, there is no better method of rallying support for the regime and whipping up national fervour than a strategic game-changing decision like this.

Within the region, the Saudi-Iran peace deal in March 2023 buried decades of hostilities between the two regional rivals. The Gaza war provided an undisputed leadership role in the region to Iran as Saudi Arabia and the UAE took a back seat while Egypt, Turkey and Qatar were busy negotiating a ceasefire.

Its 25-year strategic partnership with China and the increasing cooperation with Russia including supply of drones and missiles for the Ukraine war meant that a very powerful anti-West pole in the form of Russia-Iran-China is challenging the decades-old world order. Plus, Iran's influence across the Levant with President Assad in Syria, Iraq under PM Mohammad Shia al-Sudani and Hezbollah in Lebanon has never been better. Its entry into the BRICS and SCO in 2023 provided Iran added legitimacy in the global discourse.

Quietly and concurrently, Iran's nuclear program is continuing uninhibited after formal talks had broken off last in August 2022. Despite the IAEA finding traces of even 84 percent enrichment in February 2023, there was no punitive action against Iran by the P5–plus-1 or the IAEA and so, Iran continues to enrich and accumulate highly enriched uranium, with the capability of weaponising the program at short notice.

Plus, economically, despite continuing Western sanctions, Iran is doing well. The IMF, in its quarterly report in January 2024, announced that the Iranian economy has outperformed many of the world powers in 2023 with a growth of 5.4 percent. Iran's crude oil export of almost 1.6 million barrels daily is almost back to the pre-May 2018 days when President Trump had pulled out of the Iran nuclear deal and imposed sanctions.

All the above facts cumulatively present a very positive picture of Iran. The only thing required was an opportune moment and the Damascus attack provided it.

What Next

Having tasted success, Iran would be emboldened for the future. Mohammed Jamshidi, Political Advisor to Iran's President, has declared that the "the era of strategic patience is over" and that any Israeli assaults will be met with a 'direct' response. Warning Israel, Iran's President has issued a statement: "If the Zionist regime (Israel) or its supporters demonstrate reckless behaviour, they will receive a decisive and much stronger response".

The Iranian retaliation may have lacked the desired punch in delivery but it has opened up a whole new dimension for consideration in future conflicts in West Asia. If Iran has decided to play on the front foot, it presents a whole new challenge to its adversaries in the region.

22

Israel Strikes Back: Can Israel and Iran Now Call it Quits?

In the early hours of 19 April, Israel's missiles/drones struck Iran, something that PM Netanyahu and his government had promised after the Iranian salvo of over 300 missiles and drones into Israel on 13 April 2024.

Initial inputs on 19 April reported loud explosions in the vicinity of the city of Isfahan. Although some media outlets later presented satellite pictures to show that some part of the air defence battery in Isfahan was damaged, neither Iran, Israel nor the USA are ready to comment on it. The city of Isfahan is important because of the location of critical nuclear plants and air bases of the Iranian Air Force. Iranian media was prompt in dismissing the attempted strike as a complete failure while Israel maintained a stoic silence, neither confirming nor denying the strike. Iran's establishment too dismissed the attacks as ridiculous adding that such failed attempts do not deserve any response. Israel's National Security Minister, Itamar Ben Gvir, was critical of his own government's action, commenting on X with a simple comment 'lame.'

Unlike Iranian strikes on Israel, where several missiles had penetrated through the air defence and caused damage at heavily protected air bases in Nevatim and Ramon, none of the suspected Israel's drones caused any damage in Iran. This may have been a dampener for Israel wanting to cause at least some token damage in Iran, but it sure saved the day for the region as Iran said that there was no need to respond since nothing had happened on Iranian soil. Just a day earlier, Iran's Foreign Minister, Hossein Amir-Abdollahian, told CNN that if Israel again took action against Iran, "the next response from us will be immediate and at a maximum level."

While all this was happening, the UN Security Council was busy voting on the Palestinian request for full UN membership. The USA, showing full allegiance to Israel, vetoed the request almost at the same time that Israel was perhaps launching the strike into Iran.

Will Israel and Iran Call it Quits

Now that Israel has apparently taken its revenge, the world is asking both Iran and Israel to call it even and quit direct targeting to avoid escalating the Gaza conflict into a larger regional war. The question now is whether both will actually heed the advice.

For Iran, there is presently no need to escalate further as its strike on 13 April had found its mark as revenge for the Damascus strike. However, for Israel, it is different. It was attacked by more than 300 aerial military platforms originating from Iran and something which Tehran acknowledged publicly. It took the combined efforts of its entire air and anti-missile defences combined with the efforts of Jordan, the USA, UK and possibly Saudi Arabia to foil it. Yet, some missiles hit its air bases. In return, the Israeli attack on 19 April does not seem to have achieved the desired effect.

For PM Netanyahu, who had promised severe retribution against Iran in the past few weeks, it is difficult to sell it as a successful revenge. He seems to be stuck in a 'no win' situation. In case he does decide to strike harder again, there is a possibility of a severe payback from Iran and its allies (proxies) in the region. Also, it should not be forgotten that the USA has gone on record to state that it won't support Israel in any offensive action against Iran, it won't get into any conflict in the region and it won't seek war with Iran. Without active military support from the USA, Israel does not have the necessary military means to strike and succeed against Iran located 1,700 km away.

On the other hand, Iran is a much larger country and thus has much more capacity to absorb strikes and damage. It also possesses the largest and most potent ballistic missiles program in the region, with ranges that can easily cover Israel. In addition, Iran has developed hypersonic missiles which fly at a speed of Mach 5 and are beyond the interception capability of most anti-missile systems.

Iran also possesses a large variety of drones. It has, in fact, mastered the art and science of developing low-cost and low-technology drones which are revolutionizing battlefields. It has been exporting its drones to Russia where they are being effectively used in Ukraine. Its Shahed missiles, which are 'suicide' or Kamakazi missiles, have been used effectively during the ongoing war.

Ceasefire in Gaza

If Israel and Iran call it quits, at least for the time being, the focus then reverts to continuing efforts to get a permanent ceasefire in Gaza. Despite a UN Security

Council resolution of 25 March calling for an immediate ceasefire and the unconditional release of hostages, no common ground has been found yet between Hamas and Israel. Plus, continued Israeli strikes on Gaza, especially on aid convoys and hospitals, are making matters worse. An Israeli attack in northern Gaza which killed three sons of Hamas chief Ismail Haniyeh on 10 April on the eve of Eid, may also force Hamas to take a hardened position in future negotiations.

Here too, Israel faces an uphill task. Netanyahu has not yet been able to achieve any of his objectives in the Gaza war. The 135 Israeli hostages in the custody of Hamas have not yet been released, Hamas has not been eliminated and Yayha Sinwar, the Hamas leader responsible for the 7 October terror attack, continues to evade Israeli intelligence. On the other hand, Israeli forces have suffered significant losses in the past six months which is now having an effect on the war-fighting capacity of the IDF.

Probably because of this factor, Israel withdrew all its forces (except for one brigade) from Gaza on 7 April, moving most of its formations northwards in anticipation of retaliation by Iran. The Rafah offensive has been put on hold after the USA drew a 'red line' against it. Leaked reports of Israel aiming to build settlements in Gaza after the war, too, do not help in the efforts of seeking a ceasefire. Also, news of Maj. Gen. Aharon Haliva, the head of Israeli military intelligence, resigning on 22 April and taking responsibility for the 7 October Hamas attack, increases the pressure on the IDF.

What Next

The Gaza war is well into its seventh month and has been the longest that Israel has been engaged in ever since it vacated Gaza in 2005. Every day of fighting is dragging Israel down politically and economically. The global narrative too has been pitched strongly against it. The release of hostages should be its top priority and if that means vacating Gaza and agreeing to a ceasefire, it should take it. There will always be another day when Israel can do what it has not been able to do this time. Not all battles are meant to be won, at least not at the cost of larger strategic goals.

SECTION IV

The Rafah Offensive and the Dangerous Escalation

23

Rafah Offensive: Threat of a Dangerous Escalation

It is May 2024 and the war in Gaza has lasted seven months, making it the longest war there since Israel's voluntary vacation of Gaza in 2005. Contrary to expectations, the conflict has not ended swiftly. During this time, however, Israeli strikes have flattened Gaza to the ground, making it completely un-inhabitable, perhaps for decades. The stench of death and decay overwhelms the thin strip straddling the Mediterranean Sea, with estimates of over 34,500 deaths including 13,000 children and over 77,500 injured and maimed for life. Medical aid, food and water have been severely restricted and most international aid agencies including UNRWA as well as WCK (World Central Kitchen) have been targeted and prevented from delivery of life-saving aid.

Despite a UN Security Council resolution of 25 March calling for an immediate ceasefire and unconditional release of hostages, neither of the warring parties has been able to come to a common understanding. In its midst, there was a period of dangerous escalation when Israel and Iran traded aerial strikes in April.

With this threat of escalation over, the focus has now shifted to Gaza and finding means to an early end to the war. As part of the effort, US Secretary of State Blinken was in the region recently to hold talks with Arab leaders. He also stopped over in Israel, meeting PM Netanyahu to deter him from launching a ground offensive in Rafah. Also, if and when the Rafah offensive takes place, what are its implications on ending or escalating the conflict and how would the regional countries react to it, is something to be watched out for.

What is Rafah?

Rafah is a border crossing town in Southern Gaza located on its border with Egypt and is often called the 'lifeline of Gaza' due to the fact that it is one of the main incoming routes for international aid. It is also the opening into the Sinai Peninsula on the Egyptian side. The crossing is manned and controlled by Egypt and Hamas on either side and is the only entry into Gaza not directly under Israeli control. This important crossing was in fact under Israeli control till 2005, when it unilaterally withdrew from Gaza, giving the Palestinians control over a border crossing for the first time. Currently, it is estimated that more than 1.3 million Palestinians are confined in Rafah, driven by Israeli strikes from the northern parts over the past seven months.

Israel's Position on a Rafah Offensive

Netanyahu seems adamant that a ground offensive in Rafah will be the final nail in the coffin of Hamas and irrespective of a deal or not, the planned ground offensive in Rafah would go on. Addressing the nation on 30 April, he said, "We will enter Rafah and we will eliminate the Hamas battalions there – with or without a deal – in order to achieve total victory." Israel's finance minister, Bezalel Smotrich and a member of the right-wing coalition, was more aggressive when he called for annihilating Israel's enemies, saying "there are no half measures. [The Gazan cities of] Rafah, Deir al-Balah, Nuseirat – total annihilation".

Recent developments in the area clearly indicate that the IDF is 'preparing the battlefield' for the Rafah operations. As per reports, two reserve brigades have been called up for duty. Satellite images also show a new city with over 10,000 tents that have come up recently in areas north of Rafah, which can hold thousands of people.

Israel estimates that Hamas' higher leadership and four remaining battalions are entrenched in Rafah. Although Hamas does not possess combat battalions in the conventional sense, Israeli intelligence estimates that most of the remaining Hamas combat cadres are hiding among the Palestinians in Rafah. There has been an intensification of air strikes in Rafah in an attempt to 'soften the target' which has resulted in large civilian casualties in the past few days; 22 killed on 30 April and 13 killed on 2 May. It is estimated that over 250 people have been killed in Israeli airstrikes in Rafah since the start of the holy month of Ramadan in March.

The efficacy and success of an offensive in Rafah to achieve Israel's politico-military objectives is, however, suspect. Best estimates suggest that Israeli operations till now have been able to eliminate 30-35 percent of the Hamas combat cadres and leadership. Can Israel be assured that the remaining Hamas leadership will be taken out in Rafah operations? Can Israel be sure that the military operations will kill the entire military capability of Hamas? Is Israel sure that the remaining weaponry and arsenal are concentrated and hidden in Rafah? Even if Israel kills all the 1.3 million people in Rafah, can it be sure that Hamas has been eliminated from the face of the Earth? Sadly, the answer to most of these questions is 'No'.

Rafah and the Region

Egypt has already lined up tanks and guns along the Rafah border and has clearly spelt out that it is a 'red line' that should not be crossed. Any direct intervention by Egypt not only threatens escalation but could also pose a threat to the 1979 Peace Treaty with Israel.

Turkey too has taken a very hard stand on the issue. Earlier, in March, it had imposed severe restrictions on trade with Israel and on 2 May, it announced suspension of all trade ties with it, owing to its atrocities in Gaza and the West Bank.

Jordan, which could be directly impacted by the influx of refugees in case of an offensive, had made it clear in the very beginning of the war that it is a red line that must not be crossed.

Saudi Arabia is another important regional player. It is also a part of the GCC and in their meeting with Blinken on 30 April, GCC foreign ministers strongly opposed any attempts to displace Palestinians by escalating violence in the West Bank. The Saudi Foreign Minister added that a possible invasion in Rafah will inevitably lead to a humanitarian disaster with severe consequences for the Palestinians and serious repercussions for all parties.

On the other hand, there are contrarian reports that the USA and Saudi Arabia are very close to finalizing a defence pact. Within Saudi Arabia, anti-Israel protests are being dealt with a heavy hand and there are unconfirmed reports that Saudi Arabia had aided Israel and the USA in fending off Iranian missiles during the attack on 13 April. Such inputs and the rather ambivalent position taken by Saudi Arabia raise questions on Saudi Arabia's commitment to the Gaza war.

In case of the Rafah offensive going ahead, there is all likelihood that engagements from Hezbollah into Northern Israel would increase. In the past few weeks, Hezbollah rockets and missiles have successfully targeted Israeli command and communication centres in the North. The Houthis in Yemen continue to disrupt sea trade in the Red Sea and have the ability to up the ante, if required.

The America Factor

The USA is Israel's main benefactor and has assured 'iron clad' support to it. However, it has also repeatedly stressed upon Netanyahu that Rafah is a red line that should not be crossed. Instead, Israel should plan on precise intelligence-based operations to flush out Hamas operatives and leaders. Just a day earlier, on 24 April, the USA had approved US$ 17 billion military aid to Israel as part of an overall package of US$ 94 billion which includes Ukraine and Taiwan. However, its blind support to Israel is causing a severe backlash back home. In the past week or so, there have been massive protests in university and college campuses in the USA where students and faculty have come out in open support for the Palestinians calling out the genocide being committed in Gaza. In an election year, President Biden is caught between two conflicting requirements: the need to support Israel and the pressure to do the right thing. With little time left until July when he and Trump will join the battle directly for the presidency, the USA is left with very few good options, except to prevail upon Netanyahu for an early end to the war.

24

Netanyahu is Trapped in a 'Chakravyuh'

Israel marked Memorial Day on 13 May followed by the 76th Independence Day on 14 May in a rather muted manner, owing to the ongoing war in Gaza. Striking an angry and defiant tone, PM Netanyahu, while addressing the nation, said that Israel would never forget and "will not let anyone else forget" the crimes Hamas had committed on 7 October 2023, making it clear that Israel is in no hurry to end the war until it extracts full revenge from Hamas and 'eliminates it from the face of the Earth'.

In the past few weeks, every passing day has brought more and more negative news for Israel. A brief review of the war over the past seven months clearly reveals that it has so far been a story of missed opportunities, a war fought more on ego than strategy. And Netanyahu, caught in the middle of all this, is finding himself trapped, with walls closing in on him with every passing day.

Missed Opportunities

Israel had vowed revenge after the Hamas terror attack in Israel on 7 October had killed more than 1,100 people, making it the worst single-day attack on it, ever. Its initial war strategy was therefore based solely on revenge and rage. However, after the initial retaliation which led to hundreds of Hamas combat cadres being eliminated and its military potential severely degraded, Israel did not revise its military goals and continued to strike Gaza with the singular aim of 'eliminating Hamas forever'. This was completely unlike the previous wars that Israel had fought in Gaza when Israel, after achieving its military objectives, withdrew its forces from Gaza. However, this time, perhaps Israel decided that 'enough is enough' and Hamas cannot be allowed to mount another attack on Israel. As a result, the war drags on and opportunities to end it have been missed.

The first opportunity came in November 2023, a month after the war started, when a humanitarian truce was agreed to, leading to exchange of hostages, primarily women, children and the elderly. The truce was extended twice before Israel unilaterally resumed its operations on 1 December.

Another opportunity went by in January this year when a ceasefire proposal was presented in Paris on 28 January. The deal proposed a ceasefire of six weeks coupled with the first phase of civilian hostage releases. The ceasefire could be extended for a longer period later.

On 25 March, the United Nations Security Council (UNSC) finally succeeded in getting a resolution passed which demanded an immediate ceasefire and unconditional release of all hostages. Israel was furious at the USA for letting the resolution pass and alleged that it had "abandoned its policy in the UN" and harming the war effort and the measures for the release of Israeli hostages in Hamas's custody. No action has been taken as yet on the resolution.

As recently as 30 April, another deal was presented which involved the release of 33 hostages in the custody of Hamas since the first stage of a 40-day ceasefire. The deal also envisaged a second phase of 40 days when the rest of the hostages, including male civilians and soldiers, as well as the bodies of others would be released in return for the end of hostilities and the return of Palestinian prisoners in Israel. Despite the USA pushing this proposal, PM Netanyahu rejected the deal.

Closing of the Trap

A number of analyses on the war in Gaza have suggested that the terror strike by Hamas on 7 October was a trap that Israel fell into. The initial rage and revenge prevented it from looking at the situation rationally and to use its military superiority to strike hard and end the war swiftly, and on its terms. As a result, with every passing episode in the war, Israel is finding itself getting trapped deeper and deeper in the conflict without any clearly defined exit. A few such events merit attention to highlight this aspect.

One of the major actions that have gone against Israel is the indiscriminate targeting of schools, hospitals, refugee camps and UN compounds leading to global outrage, rapidly shifting the narrative against it and resulting in thousands of deaths.

The Israeli strike on the Iranian Consulate in Damascus 1 April should definitely count as a self-goal. It not only gave the perfect and legitimate opportunity to Iran to strike inside Israel for the first time but also led it to shed its 'strategic patience', signalling dangerous escalation in case of any future provocation.

The withdrawal of all Israeli troops from Gaza (except for one brigade) on 7 April and moving them north has also to be counted as a serious miscalculation. It gave an ideal opportunity for Hamas to return to the vacated areas in Gaza. As a result, the IDF, on its return, is facing renewed battles in Central and Northern Gaza, especially in areas of Gaza city, and Jabilia and Nuseirat camps. The result: not only has its military campaign gone haywire, Israel is being inflicted with major casualties too. Israeli media reports suggest that the IDF has lost more than 20 soldiers in the past three days alone and a major military base close to Tel Aviv has been damaged by a major fire caused by the 'unknown'.

The attack on international aid convoys as well as UN personnel is also causing a severe backlash. As per the UN, more than 190 UN staff members have been killed in the Gaza war till now.

The Rafah offensive will be the final nail. On 6 May, the Israeli military ordered the evacuation of 100,000 Palestinians in eastern Rafah. Israeli tanks entered it in the early hours of 7 May, taking control over the Rafah Crossing on the Palestinian side, opposite Egypt. With over 1.3 million people in Rafah, a full-scale offensive will result in a human massacre of an unprecedented scale.

Almost all the stakeholders including the USA, Egypt, Saudi Arabia, and Turkey have declared that the Rafah offensive is a red line and should not be crossed. The USA has even put its arms shipments to Israel on hold and warned that they could be stopped if there is a full-scale invasion of Rafah. But Israel is not listening and PM Netanyahu has made it clear that whether support or not, Israel will go through with the Rafah operations, stating, "If we need to...we will stand alone. We will fight with our fingernails".

Qatar, the mediator in ceasefire talks, has also termed the Rafah offensive as 'backward'. US National Security Adviser Jake Sullivan has called upon Israel to devise a 'strategic endgame' and a post-war plan. Else, Israel could be mired in a counter-insurgency campaign that would never end.

The Context of 'Chakravyuh'

The context of a 'chakravyuh' (circular military formation) is drawn from the Indian epic, the *Mahabharata,* in which, during the Kurukshetra war, Dronacharya plans a 'chakravyuh' for the Kauravas to trap the Pandavas, especially their main warrior, Arjun. Explaining it, Col. Vivek Chadha (retd.), Senior Fellow at MP-IDSA, said it was a multi-layered dynamic formation set up to surround enemy formations. This extremely complex and deceptive set-up required very high military skills to break through. It was said that only Abhimanyu and Arjuna fighting for the Pandavas could breach it. However, Abhimanyu was not trained to do so. As the story goes, while Arjun was lured to another part of the battlefield, it was left to his son, Abhimanyu, to fight through the 'chakravyuh'. Unfortunately, while Abhimanyu was able to penetrate the various layers of the 'chakravyuh', the other warriors following him were unable to do so, leaving Abhimanyu stranded. Fighting gallantly, he faced insurmountable odds as the inner layers of the formation closed in upon him, until he was eventually brought down by the Kauravas.

However, unlike the *Mahabharata* where Abhimanyu is forced to enter the 'chakravyuh' in his fight for the greater cause and is finally unable to find an exit, in the case of Israel and Netanyahu, they are unwilling to take the many exit routes out of their 'chakravyuh' presented to them from time to time.

Adding to this is another factor. If the USA stops its shipment of offensive military supplies to Israel, Egypt opens a military front across Rafah and Hezbollah ups the ante in the North, the walls of the 'chakravyuh' will start closing in for Netanyahu very soon. Also, the growing opposition at home, especially from the families of hostages, is not making it any easier for him. His own military Chief of Staff, Herzi Halevi, was quoted on 11 May tearing into Netanyahu during security consultations for the failure to develop and declare a so-called 'day after' strategy. There have also been reports of arguments over the war and its end state between Netanyahu and Defence Minister Gallant.

It may therefore be prudent for Netanyahu to review what Israel wants as a definable end state of war soon. Else, the walls of the 'chakravyuh' may keep closing in to an extent where there may not be any viable exit option left.

25

Israeli Strike in Rafah Kills 45: A Tragic Mistake or a Strategic Blunder

On 26 May, in yet another wrongly-targeted airstrike by Israel, seven missiles struck a tented camp in Rafah in the southern Gaza Strip, killing 45 Palestinians. Many more were injured and the ensuing blaze in the camp displaced civilians. The Israel Defence Forces (IDF) initially claimed that it had successfully targeted a Hamas compound and had eliminated two commanders but as videos and the truth of the attack surfaced soon, IDF had to back track. Facing absolute outrage and condemnation, Netanyahu, in his address to the Israeli parliament had to admit that "despite our utmost efforts not to harm innocent civilians, last night there was a tragic mistake." Ironically, the tented camp had been set up in close coordination with Israel and was designated as a humanitarian zone by it itself.

Once again there was strong all-round condemnation and calls for ending the war immediately. Israel has however been dismissive of all such calls in the past and the USA, its prime benefactor, has backed it. This time too it shocked most international observers by stating that Israel has not yet crossed the 'red line'. It would therefore be interesting to see whether this tragic attack can become the catalyst to end the war soon or whether Israel's impunity will continue unabated. Also, with international efforts continually failing to restrain Israel, it also raises questions on how this war will eventually end.

Growing International Pressure

The Rafah offensive has long been declared a 'red line' not only by Egypt, Saudi Arabia and the rest of the regional countries but also by the USA and many Western nations. But PM Netanyahu made it clear that support or no support, Israel will go through with the Rafah operations.

As part of its strategy to eliminate the Hamas leadership and combat cadres from Rafah, the IDF commenced preparations in the first week of May itself. A new city with over 10,000 tents was set up in areas north of Rafah capable of holding thousands of people. Israel followed this by dropping leaflets over Gaza and Rafah asking people to leave Rafah and on 6 May, the IDF issued orders for the evacuation of 100,000 Palestinians in eastern Rafah. Soon, Israeli tanks entered Eastern Rafah in the early hours of 7 May and took control of the Rafah Crossing on the Palestinian side. IDF forces and airstrikes have targeted Rafah ever since on a daily basis. The latest airstrike on the tented camp in Rafah on 26 May is only a continuation in the series of such strikes over the past two weeks.

Surprisingly, and most shockingly, the current strike was launched less than 48 hours after a ruling by the International Court of Justice (ICJ) on 24 May which categorically said that Israel must "immediately halt its military offensive, and any other action in the Rafah Governorate." It also ordered Israel to open the Rafah Crossing for humanitarian aid and also called for the "immediate and unconditional release" of hostages held by Hamas in Gaza. The ICJ is the top court of the UN and its orders are legally binding but, unfortunately, it lacks direct enforcement mechanisms.

The current Rafah strike also comes against the backdrop of three key Western countries joining more than 140 others in recognizing Palestine as a state. In a latest development, Norway, Spain and Ireland announced the formal recognition of Palestine with the Spanish Prime Minister Pedro Sanchez stating that the establishment of a Palestinian state is "the only route to peace" in the Middle East. France and the UK too have hinted on separate occasions that they might recognize Palestine if Israel does not exercise restraint and end the war soon.

On 26 May, Prince Faisal bin Farhan Al Saud, Foreign Minister of the Kingdom of Saudi Arabia, and Espen Barth Eide, Minister of Foreign Affairs of Norway, co-chaired a meeting of Arab and European Foreign Ministers and representatives in Brussels, in coordination with the EU High Representative, Joseph Borrell. The meeting stressed the urgent need for an immediate ceasefire including an end to the attacks on Rafah, release of hostages and ending the war in Gaza. Separately, the Saudi Foreign Minister, in a statement, reiterated that Israel doesn't get to decide whether or not the Palestinians have a right to self-determination. Israel needs to accept that it cannot exist without the existence of a Palestinian state.

In the past 48 hours, there have also been reports of direct face-offs between the Egyptian forces and the IDF. On 27 May, an Egyptian soldier was killed in a clash with Israeli soldiers near the Rafah Border Crossing. Egypt has amassed its troops, tanks and guns across the Rafah border and any escalation could be disastrous not only for the Gaza war but also threaten the four-decade-old peace treaty between the two countries.

Increasing Disillusionment in Israel

Within Israel too, there is growing pressure on Netanyahu to end the war and bring back the hostages. Some of his key ministers in the war cabinet have come out in the open against him in recent weeks. His own military Chief of Staff, Herzi Halevi, and the Defence Minister Yoav Gallant have openly criticized Netanyahu. Speaking to the media on 15 May he said that "the military campaign must end with a diplomatic action. The day after Hamas can only be achieved via elements that would constitute an alternative to Hamas. This is first and foremost an Israeli interest. The key to this goal is military action and the establishment of a governing alternative in Gaza." He added that "delay in decision making will only erode our military achievements and sabotage the chances for the release of hostages." Reacting almost immediately, Netanyahu was emphatic that there will be no discussion on who governs Gaza until Hamas is eliminated, adding that he is "not ready to replace Hamastan with Fatahstan."

Meanwhile, on 18 May, war cabinet minister Benny Gantz issued an ultimatum to Netanyahu demanding an agreed-upon vision for the Gaza conflict that would include stipulating who might rule the territory after Hamas's defeat, and warning that he would quit the coalition if there are no concrete answers by 8 June.

To add to Netanyahu's woes, there is increasing pressure from the families of 130 hostages still held by Hamas. There are reports that some have already died in captivity while some are in a critical condition. Israel's refusal to accept the ceasefire deal repeatedly is adding to the rising discontent with calls for his resignation growing louder.

What Next?

Israel's insistence on continuing with the offensive in Rafah, the errant strike killing 45 people on 26 May and increasing pressure both domestically and internationally, is fast closing the options for Israel. On the military front, the launching of rockets by Hamas from Gaza on Tel Aviv on 26 May is once again a stark reminder that it may not be possible to 'eliminate Hamas from the face of the Earth'. The skirmish with the Egyptian army on the Rafah Crossing does not bode well for the future and it is in the best interests of Israel, Egypt and the region to see that it does not escalate. Hezbollah continues to target Israel in the north effectively and disrupt its communication and surveillance machinery.

In a surprise attack on 16 May, Hezbollah carried out its first ever airstrike on Israel using a kamikaze drone armed with S5 rockets, air-to-surface missiles, to attack the Metula garrison. Reports on 28 May also indicate that Hezbollah has successfully targeted Israeli Meron air-control base with Katyusha rockets, causing heavy damage.

Against the backdrop of the current developments in the Gaza war, the tragic mistake in Rafah on 26 May could not have come at a worse time for Israel.

26

Houthi Missiles Strike Israel, Threaten a Dangerous Escalation

On 19 July 2024, a Houthi drone flew over 2,000 km from Yemen, evaded Israel's air defences and struck an apartment building in Tel Aviv, killing one civilian and injuring at least 10 others. In an immediate retaliation, Israeli fighter aircraft struck the Houthi-controlled port of Hodeidah in Yemen on 20 July, setting a major oil storage dump on fire while killing six people. Houthis too replied by launching a long-range ballistic missile on the Israeli port city of Eilat on 21 July, but it was intercepted by Israeli Air Defence.

This is however not the first time that the Houthis have targeted Israel in the ongoing war in Gaza since 7 October 2023. There have been a number of instances where Houthi-launched missiles and drones have targeted Israel but each time either the strike has landed in a deserted area or has been intercepted.

Immediately after Israel's strike on Hodeidah Port, Israel's Defence Minister Yoav Gallant said that his country aimed to send a clear message to the Houthis, adding that "the fire that is currently burning in Hodeidah, is seen across the Middle East and the significance is clear." In reply, Houthi spokesperson Mohammed Abdulsalam, speaking to *Al Jazeera*, said that Israel "has opened an open-ended war." Hezbollah, which is fighting Israel in the north, released a statement calling the attack "a new and dangerous phase of the extremely important ongoing confrontation."

Who are the Houthis?

The Houthis, also known as Ansar-Allah (supporters of God), is an armed group that emerged in Yemen in the 1990s during the civil war. They have ideological roots in Yemen's ethnic Shia Muslim minorities, the Zaidis. Like other Shiites, Zaidis believe that only descendants of the Prophet Mohammed's cousin and son-in-law, Ali, have the right to lead the Muslim community as imams, who are divinely-appointed successors of the Prophet. Zaidis, also known as 'Fivers,' also believe that Zayd, the great-grandson of Ali, was the rightful fifth imam. Most adherents of Zaydism reside in Yemen. The group owes allegiance to Iran which in turn provides ideological, financial and (military) support to it. The Houthis movement was founded by Hussein al-Houthi and is currently led by his brother, Abdul-Malik-al-Houthi.

In recent times, the group shot into prominence when it overthrew the government in Yemen, following the unrest after the 'Arab Spring' protests of 2010-11. In September 2014, the Houthis took over Yemen's capital, Sana'a, and later placed President Hadi and PM Khaled Bahah (along with the cabinet) under house arrest. President Hadi however escaped to Aden on 21 February 2015 describing the Houthi takeover of Sana'a as a 'coup'. The Houthis took control of Taiz Airport and entered Aden unopposed on 25 March 2015, completing control of the three major cities in the country – Sana'a, Taiz and Aden. Later, President Hadi fled to Riyadh on 25 March 2015.

In response to the Houthi takeover, Saudi Arabia, in coordination with regional Arab allies and the USA, launched airstrikes on Yemen on 26 March, 2015 in an operation codenamed '*Operation Decisive Storm*'. The armed conflict between the Saudi Arabia-led coalition and the Houthis continued till March 2023 when, as a part of the Saudi-Iran peace deal, it was decided that Yemen too will be a part of the peace deal. The internationally recognized government of Yemen, called the 'Presidential Leadership Council' and formed on 7 April 2022, is led by Rashad al-Alimi, but has very limited control over the country while the Houthis currently control mainly the northern and western half of Yemen, including the capital, Sana'a, the port city of Hodeidah and some of the western and northern areas close to Saudi Arabia.

In September 2019 also, the group was in the news when it launched drone strikes against Saudi Arabia. In one such strike on 14 September 2019, Houthi drones struck key oil fields of Abqaiq and Khurais, causing major disruptions in oil production. The fact that the drones managed to penetrate undetected and hit oilfields deep in Saudi territory, more than 500 miles from Yemen, was a surprise for the world at that time.

Later, on 17 January 2022, the Houthis targeted the Abu Dhabi airport in the UAE resulting in three oil tankers being blown off in close vicinity of the main airport and casualties to six persons. This attack came close on the heels of the capture of a UAE ship, *Rawabi,* by the Houthis on 2 January off the coast of Hodeidah in Yemen in the Red Sea.

Houthis in the Gaza War

In the ongoing war in Gaza, the Houthis have offered support to the Palestinian resistance and have taken up the task of not permitting any Israeli-flagged ship or any of the ships of the Western alliance to cross the Red Sea. Despite the USA deploying an aircraft-carrier group in the Red Sea under *'Operation Prosperity Guardian'*, the Houthis have not been deterred. In February 2024, The European Union's Naval Force (EUNAVFOR) too was deployed alongside the US naval fleet under *'Operation Aspides'*, an EU defensive maritime security operation, but that too has not been able to deter the Houthis.

Meanwhile, the Houthis have launched more than 60 attacks on commercial as well as naval warships in the Red Sea over the past nine months of the Gaza war. Their attacks have already resulted in the sinking of two ships; a Liberian-flagged, Greek-owned-and-operated ship *'Tutor'*, sank in the Red Sea in June while a Belize-flagged ship, *'Rubymar'*, sank in the Red Sea in March 2024, both hit by missiles and suicide boats of the Houthis. Earlier, on 15 January, a Houthi missile struck a US-owned ship, '*Gibraltar Eagle*' just off the coast of Yemen in the Gulf of Aden. This was preceded by an anti-ship Cruise missile launched a day earlier on *USS Laboon*, a US destroyer operating as part of the US-led naval operations to safeguard the passage of commercial ships in the Red Sea. In addition, in May 2024, the Houthis claimed to have downed two MQ-9 Reaper drones of the USA too.

A recent report by the US Defence Intelligence Agency acknowledged that container shipping through the Red Sea has declined by 90 per cent since December over the attacks. As much as 15 per cent of the world's maritime traffic flows through that corridor.

Houthis-Military Capability

The military capability of the Houthis is basically centred on two types of weapon platforms; UAVs and ballistic and cruise missiles. Most of the acquisitions and developments in its arsenal have happened after the Houthis took over Yemen's capital, Sanaa', in September 2014, mostly through Iran. Their initial inventory consisted of Russian P-21 and P-22 missiles and Chinese C-801 missiles, both taken from the Yemeni armed forces.

Houthis have the Typhoon missile, which is a rebranded version of the Iranian Qadr with a range of 1,600 to 1,900 km, which was unveiled weeks before the onset of the Gaza war in a military parade. They also possess the Quds-2 cruise missiles with a range of 1,200 km. This missile was earlier used in 2019-20 and 2022 to hit Saudi oil facilities and the UAE airport. They may also possess a version of the Chinese C-802 (YJ-82/CH-SS-N-6 Saccade) anti-ship cruise missile (ASCM) as these missiles were found in a ship smuggling Iranian-made arms to Yemen. The ship had been intercepted by the US Navy's *USS Forest Sherman* (DDG-98) guided missile destroyer in the Arabian Sea, in 2019. As per the Military Balance 2024 report, the Houthis have developed more ASCMs, which were unveiled during military parades in 2023, including two anti-ship versions of the Iranian Quds/351 LACM. One version is allegedly equipped with a radar-homing seeker (Sayyad), and the other has an electro-optical/infrared seeker (Quds Z-0). Both systems could have a range of at least 800 km.

Houthis have also unveiled a variety of anti-ship ballistic missiles (ASBMs) and guided rockets employing Iranian infrared or imaging infrared seeker technology like the 450-km range Asef which appears to be a rebranded ASBM version of Iran's Fateh 313 missile and the Tankil missile which could be a rebranded anti-ship version of the IRGC-developed 500-km-range Zohayr. There are reportedly three smaller ASBMs too; the 140-km-range Faleq, the Mayun and the Bahr al-Ahmar.

As for drones, although the Houthis claim that they manufacture them domestically, most inputs suggest that they are merely assembled in Yemen with smuggled Iranian components. The Houthi drone inventory includes the Iranian Shahed-136 which has a range of about 2,000 kilometres. Even Russia is using these Iranian drones in its war on Ukraine. Houthis also have Iranian-origin Samad-2 and Samad-3 drones which have a range of around 1,500 km and carry a payload of about 20 kg. The drone that was used by Houthis in their attack on Tel Aviv recently is called the 'Yafa' which seems to be an upgraded and locally modified version of the Samad-3, to increase its range and also incorporate features to avoid detection.

All this has propelled the Houthis to prominence in the region as a serious military threat and the successful attack on Tel Aviv in Israel only underscores its potential. It has also helped Iran in its aim to enlarge the scope of its 'Axis of Resistance' not only across the Levant, but across the Arabian Peninsula too. By blocking and restricting sea trade across the Red Sea through the Houthis, another serious dimension of this collective threat has been highlighted.

Can it have a Serious Impact on the Gaza War?

The strikes by Houthis into Israel have opened new possibilities in the ongoing conflict. With the Houthis coming into the picture, the '3H', that is, Hamas, Hezbollah and Houthis, are now actively engaged in the war. However, unlike Hezbollah and Hamas which are fighting Israel across its borders, the Houthis are located 1,800 km away and are unlikely to make any substantial impact on the kinetics of the war. But Israel will now have to be alert and look out for any future drone or missile attack from Yemeni soil. For Iran, which is engaged indirectly in the war through its allies and proxies as a part of the 'Axis of Resistance", this is a great development. Its new president, Masoud Pezeshkian, who was elected recently on 5 July, has already stated his clear intention of supporting the resistance, including Hezbollah.

In the Gaza war, efforts of agreeing on a ceasefire are not yet successful and there are no positive signs on the horizon. Coupled with this, the exchange of fire and missile and rocket strikes between Israel and Hezbollah in the north are increasing by the day. Israel recently ramped up its operations in central Gaza yet again, leading to heavy casualties. Israel's Knesset (parliament) passed a resolution on 18 July that overwhelmingly rejected the establishment of a Palestinian state. All this is only adding fuel to the fire and any mis-step could lead to further conflict escalation.

Houthis, on the other hand, have proved that they are survivors and totally committed to the cause of resistance. The nine-year war with Saudi Arabia and the US-led coalition could not dislodge them nor has any naval force been able to deter their operations in the Red Sea. In such a case, Houthis engaging Israel can only add to the complexities of the conflict which is nearing a year of death and destruction.

27

Hamas Chief Assassinated

On 30 July, when Iran was in a sombre yet celebratory mood as its new president, Masoud Pezeshkian, was being sworn in, little did Iran or the world know that the tempo and tenor of the war was going to turn completely. On the night of 30 July, Hamas political chief, Ismail Haniyeh, was assassinated in a targeted strike on his residence in a closely-guarded area in Tehran. Although he was on the target list of Israel, the sheer audacity of taking out this high-value target in Iran's capital, that too on such an occasion, took the world by surprise.

Night of Chaos in the Region

It was a night of chaos in the region as there were strikes on other capitals in the region too. In Beirut, a precision airstrike took out a senior Hezbollah military commander, Faud Shukra, who Israel had blamed for the missile attack in occupied Golan Heights on 27 July which led to the death of 12 Israeli citizens. Elsewhere, in Baghdad, a missile attack by US forces targeted a base south of the city that was being used by Iraq's Popular Mobilization Forces (PMF), killing four members of the group. As if that was not enough, unconfirmed reports indicate the assassination of Commander Brigadier General Amir Ali Hajizadeh, the commander of the Islamic Revolutionary Guard Corps (IRGC) Aerospace Forces of Iran in Damascus, the same night. If this turns out to be true, it would be a night of four strikes across four capitals in the region, leading to three key assassinations, spectacular in achievement yet hugely escalatory in nature.

Following it up, on 1 August, Israel claimed it had also eliminated Hamas military chief Mohammed Deif in an airstrike carried out in Khan Younis city in Gaza on 13 July. Hamas is yet to confirm his death. A few weeks earlier, Israeli fighter aircraft had struck the Houthi-controlled port of Hodeidah in Yemen on 20 July, setting a major oil storage dump on fire and killing six persons. This effectively means that the three components of '3H' – Hamas, Hezbollah and Houthis – all backed and supported by Iran, have been struck by Israel in the past few days.

The current series of strikes was bound to draw an immediate and sharp response, which was led by Iran. Iran's Supreme Leader, Ayatollah Ali Khamenei, led the charge, outraged that the Hamas Chief could be assassinated in Tehran. His statement was firm and clear about seeking revenge: "The criminal and terrorist Zionist regime martyred our dear guest in our house and made us sad, but it also prepared the ground for a harsh punishment for itself." He added that it was "our duty to seek revenge for his blood as he was martyred in the territory of the Islamic Republic of Iran." Newly-elected president Masoud Pezeshkian too vowed to defend Iran's integrity and make 'terrorist occupiers' regret their actions. The leader of Hezbollah, Hassan Nasrallah, vowed severe retaliation against Israel stating that conflict with it has entered 'a new phase' and that "the enemy, and those who are behind the enemy, must await our inevitable response...You do not know what red lines you have crossed."

What Now?

This series of events has the potential to escalate the conflict across the region. Iran, Hezbollah, Hamas and even Houthis, have vowed to strike back hard. In fact, Iran has even notified the UN that it would carry out a retaliatory attack on Israel in self-defence against violations of its national security and territorial integrity quoting Article 51 of the UN Charter. Iran's Supreme Leader, who convened an emergency meeting of the Supreme National Security Council, has reportedly given clear directions for a direct attack on Israel. Following it up, the Chief of Staff of the Armed Forces of Iran issued a statement: "We are currently studying the response with other resistance groups. Tel Aviv will regret this crime". Iran's new FM has put Qatar and Saudi Arabia on notice that there will soon be a military operation launched against Israel and warned them that their air space was not to be used against Iran.

Earlier, on 13 April 2024, in a similar retaliatory action into Israel, Iran had struck with a collection of drones and ballistic missiles. As per de-classified inputs now available, Iran had forewarned other countries in the region as well as the USA and its Western allies of the impending strike. Thus, most of the projectiles were intercepted.

It is highly unlikely that this time, however, Iran would extend any courtesies of forewarning the USA or anyone of its intentions. Also, this time, the strikes are likely to be more punitive and aimed 'for effect'. With Hezbollah too outraged by the killing of its senior commander, there could be a series of coordinated strikes, along with support from Hamas, Houthis and even the militias of Iraq and Syria to strike Israel from multiple directions.

Anticipating a barrage of missiles and drones targeting Israel this time too, the US Navy has moved at least 12 warships in the region to defend Israel against an Iranian attack, with the *USS Theodore Roosevelt* currently operating in the Persian Gulf. The USA is also bracing up for an attack on its bases and troops deployed in the region. Houthis, who too have vowed to join Iran in its revenge, could launch long-range drones or missiles and even intensify targeting of commercial ships in the region.

There is also the fear that Iran could enforce a blockade in the Persian Gulf, something it has always threatened to do in conflict situations. With almost 21 per cent of global petroleum liquids consumption flowing through it as per the US Energy Information Association, this could be disastrous for the global oil supply and crude oil prices.

Looking Ahead

The multiple strikes and assassinations on 30 July have led to a situation of unprecedented escalation. The USA, which has been pushing for a ceasefire deal since May this year, seems to be getting sucked into another major conflict, forced by its compulsions to support and defend Israel. PM Netanyahu, who addressed the US Congress in Washington DC just a few days ago and who has been fiercely opposed to a ceasefire deal, seems to have got his wish. Gaza is no longer the only focus of war and with more players being dragged in to join it directly, the fears of an escalated and widespread conflict in the region could well come true. As the 'Axis of Resistance' finalises its plans to retaliate, Turkey too has joined in, threatening to strike Israel. As Ismail Haniyah, the assassinated Hamas Chief, is laid to rest in Qatar on Friday, a dangerous weekend awaits the region.

28

Iran's Dilemma: To Exact Revenge, Evade War and Still look Strong

The night of 30 July may have changed the West Asian region forever.

With Israel being blamed for all the strikes, the Gaza war, which has been oscillating between hopes of a ceasefire and continuing deaths and destruction, may have just crossed a critical threshold wherein it may no longer be possible to keep the conflict isolated to Gaza.

It has been over 20 days since the Hamas political chief, Ismail Haniyeh, was assassinated in the early hours of 31 July in Tehran, where he was a state guest for the inauguration of Iran's newly-elected president, Masoud Pezeshkian. On the same night, in Beirut, a precision strike from the air took out a senior Hezbollah military commander, Faud Shukra. In Damascus, Brigadier General Amir Ali Hajizadeh, the Commander of the Islamic Revolutionary Guard Corps (IRGC) Aerospace Forces of Iran, was also eliminated the same night. Three key assassinations across three capitals in the region were hugely escalatory in nature, to say the least, and were bound to draw an immediate and sharp response.

There has been panic in the region, expecting Iran and its allies to unleash a punitive strike into Israel. The USA has appealed to Iran directly and through allies in the region not to undertake any military measures. At the same time, it has rushed naval assets into the region; the *USS Abraham Lincoln* has been rushed in adding to the capabilities already provided by the *USS Theodore Roosevelt* Carrier Strike Group.

Israel too is in a heightened state of alertness, expecting a strike any day. Iran, on the other hand, has been clear and vocal about its options and intentions. At the extraordinary meeting of the Organization of Islamic Countries (OIC), convened at the request of Iran on 7 August, Iran made it clear that the assassination of the Hamas political chief was an attack on its sovereignty and cannot go unanswered.

Iran's Options

Iran is well aware that it is being baited by Israel to join the war. In the earlier instance in April this year when it had retaliated against an Israeli strike on its consulate in Damascus, it was very clear and careful that the strike should be enough to be counted only as retaliation and not as an escalatory action.

This time, however, the situation is different. After the April strikes, Iran had declared that it would no longer exercise 'strategic patience'; and any future strike would be met with an equal and effective counter-strike. The fact that the assassination this time took place in Tehran is an additional embarrassment. Also, Iran has declared that the retaliation would come through a direct strike and not merely through its proxies or allies which too puts additional pressure on it.

What works in favour of Iran is, however, the scope and timing of the attack. There were suggestions that Iran may await the outcome of the ceasefire talks held in Doha earlier this month. The talks have not succeeded as Hamas has rejected the 'bridging proposal' in the ceasefire deal offered by the trio of Egypt-Qatar-USA.

There are also inputs that Iran may wait till 25 August when the 'Arbaeen pilgrimage' which marks the end of the 40-day mourning period for Huseein ibn Ali, the third imam of the Shia Muslims, ends. The pilgrimage takes place across Iraq and Iran with over 22 million people participating. This kind of mass pilgrimage across the region is unparalleled in scale and scope and any threat or attack on it is therefore a major vulnerability for Iran. In case Iran carries out its revenge attack during this pilgrimage, an Israeli retaliation could cause mass casualties among the pilgrims and could be very damaging for Iran's position in the region, especially for Shia Muslims.

The most important factor is however the scope of Iran's retaliation. Iran could decide to strike only at major military sites and commercial infrastructure like ports. Any strike resulting in mass civilian casualties or a strike on sensitive locations like nuclear sites, Parliament, hospitals, etc., would be suicidal and counter-productive. Whatever be the nature of the strikes, Israel is unlikely to keep quiet and is expected to retaliate.

As per some media reports, there are suggestions from within Iran that it should accelerate its nuclear program and declare itself as a nuclear weapon state soon. However, that could prove counter-productive and escalatory as it would give Israel, the USA and others a valid reason to strike Iran hard and deep.

The Wait for Iran's Strike

As the region waits for the Iranian retaliation to take shape, there is no doubt that it, in whatever form it comes, has a huge escalatory risk. The risk of war has also to be taken into account in the context of the size and capacity of each country. Iran with a land area of 1,531,595 sq km is 70 times larger than Israel which has a land area of only 21,671 sq km and thus has more capacity to absorb the shock of military strikes. Most of its important military and nuclear sites are well hidden and dug deep in the mountains making it extremely difficult for the USA or Israel to take them out with missiles and air strikes. Israel, on the other hand, with its small size, is more vulnerable.

In the case of a prolonged war, possible escalation along its borders and support from major military powers would matter a lot too. Here again, Israel faces hostilities across all its borders from Iran's allies. While the USA is bound by its allegiance to support Israel no matter what, it will be interesting to see what role Russia and China play. Both have expressed clear support to Iran in its right to a retaliatory strike. There are reports that Russia has transferred a large number of weapons and equipment to Iran in recent days including Iskander short-range ballistic missile systems and Murmansk-BN electronic warfare systems. The supply of 4.5 generation Sukoi-35 fighter aircraft and S-400 air defence system could also be expedited if the war escalates.

Iran is likely to strike soon and its strikes into Israel will definitely provoke a reaction from it. It has to weigh all its options before acting; how to extract revenge while not giving a full-scale war to Israel and yet look strong in the eyes of its support base and its allies.

29

11 Months On, the War Moves into the West Bank

The conflict in Gaza is completing 11 months of high-intensity war, unprecedented human casualties and mass displacement. The Gaza Strip, bombarded endlessly, has been reduced to rubble and rendered completely uninhabitable. With no ceasefire in sight, this war may well cross the threshold of a year soon.

For Israel, the Gaza war has provided a perfect opportunity to close the debate on the issue of an independent and viable Palestinian state once and for all. Within this, however, it is not only the Gaza Strip that Israel has been targeting but its plans for taking full control over the other part, that is, the West Bank has been put into motion over the last few months.

As part of this strategy, on the night of 27 August, Israel launched a deliberate military operation on the West Bank when Israel Defence Forces (IDF) troops stormed key locations including the city of Jenin, in a bid to 'root out militants'. At least 10 Palestinians were killed on the first night. This incursion is the largest in the West Bank and a grim reminder that the conflict extends far beyond just the Gaza Strip. This move by Israel also raises many key questions. Why now? How does it impact the ongoing efforts to negotiate a ceasefire in the Gaza war?

It may be recalled that prior to 7 October 2023, the West Bank had come under repeated attacks not only by Israeli settlers but also the IDF. In fact, an Israeli raid on Jenin Camp in the West Bank on 3 July 2023 was the fiercest and largest military operation consisting of land as well as air forces in the West Bank in over two decades. Earlier, on 26 January 2023, Israeli forces killed nine Palestinians in a raid in Jenin.

Over the two years preceding the current war in Gaza, there was a drastic escalation in the number of attacks from and into the West Bank. Jenin Camp was in the news for becoming a hotbed of militants and a safe hiding place for them. As a result, the frequency and intensity of engagement by the IDF and police had intensified. Weeks before the onset of the Gaza war, on 25 July, armed terrorists opened fire on the IDF in the Nablus neighbourhood of West Bank. IDF troops fired back, resulting in the death of three Palestinians.

Coming back to the current escalation in the West Bank, there has been a marked increase in violence since October last year. Reports of Israeli settlers targeting Palestinians, including destroying property, have been on the rise. The Israeli Air Force has carried out more than 50 air attacks in the West Bank since the start of the war in Gaza – the majority of them in Tulkarem, Jenin and Nablus. In addition, Israeli settlers have carried out more than 1,300 attacks in the West Bank over this period. At least 680 Palestinians in the West Bank have been killed since October 2023, according to the Palestinian ministry.

Why the West Bank is Important?

The issues in the West Bank go well beyond skirmishes and attacks. One of the major ones is the continuing settlements for Israeli citizens there. Israel captured the West Bank, East Jerusalem and the Gaza Strip in the 1967 war. Over the last 57 years, Israel has built a large number of settlements scattered across the West Bank where more than 700,000 settlers, which is 10 percent of Israel's nearly seven million population live. Despite international condemnation on construction of new settlements, Israel has continued to build them. With each new settlement, the geographical area for a viable two-state solution is steadily decreasing.

Even before the Gaza war, on 26 June 2023, the Israeli Defence Ministry planning committee approved more than 5,000 new housing units in the West Bank. This was over and above the 13,000 units sanctioned by Israel earlier in 2023. Despite being a principal ally of Israel, the USA too has been critical of continued expansion of Israeli settlements in the occupied West Bank and had expressed concern over the announcement of a new settlement in June 2023.

The West Bank also hosts the Al-Aqsa Mosque which has often been a target of violence and vandalism for Israeli settlers. The Al-Aqsa in East Jerusalem, which Israel captured in the 1967 Six-Day War, hosts Islam's third-holiest site, the Al-Aqsa Mosque and the Dome of the Rock, a seventh-century structure believed to be where the Prophet Muhammad ascended to heaven.

A few months before the outbreak of the Gaza war, in the first week of April 2023, there were incidents of unprovoked attacks on Palestinian worshippers at the Al-Aqsa Mosque. Again, on 17 September, Israeli settlers forcibly entered the Mosque complex while Israeli forces attacked Palestinian worshippers at Bab as-

Silsila, one of the main entrances to the Al-Aqsa Mosque compound. Saudi Arabia, the UAE and Egypt were prompt in condemning it with Saudi Arabia's Foreign Ministry even calling it "a provocation to the feelings of Muslims across the world." Again, on 4 October, Israeli Jews entered the Al-Aqsa Mosque complex while the Palestinian worshippers were held back by Israeli forces.

More recently, statements by a far-right Israeli minister, Ben-Gvir, who called for the construction of a synagogue in the Al-Aqsa complex too has led to outrage and condemnation in the West Bank and in the region. Saudi Arabia and countries in the Gulf condemned this proposal with Saudi Arabia categorically rejecting it on 27 August stating that the "extremist and provocative statements" and "the ongoing provocations of Muslims" aroused negative feelings around the world."

Looking Ahead

The military operations by the IDF and the violence by its settlers in the West Bank are not incidents in isolation. With Gaza operations stagnating and pressure increasing to accept a ceasefire deal with Hamas, the West Bank provides the ideal foil for Israel to keep the fire burning. It also helps Israel to keep a strict check on any reconciliation and consolidation taking place within various factions (including Hamas and Fatah) of the Palestinian Authority after they signed a peace deal, brokered by China, in July 2024.

Continuing settlements by Israel and driving away the Palestinian population from its areas in the West Bank also feeds into Israel's strategy of nullifying any possibilities of leaving adequate geographical area in the West Bank for a viable 'Two-State' solution.

There is also the issue of East Jerusalem which is the promised capital for the Palestine State. Israel is not inclined to accept this in any manner. In fact, President Trump, in December 2017, persuaded by Israel, had announced that the USA would recognize Jerusalem as the capital of Israel and move the American embassy there.

The issue of ongoing Israeli operations in the West Bank is therefore a part of a much larger canvas in the overall Israel-Palestine conflict. It is clear that after Gaza it is the West Bank that Israel plans to control and occupy fully, making the prospect of an independent and viable Palestine State an absolute 'no possibility'.

SECTION V

The Demolition of Hezbollah and Ouster of Assad in Syria

30

'Pager' Attacks Target Hezbollah

On 17 September, in another display of how intelligence and technology can be used innovatively on the battlefield, thousands of 'pagers' used by the cadres of Hezbollah exploded mysteriously and almost simultaneously across multiple locations in Lebanon. Initial inputs from the Lebanese health ministry reported that at least nine people were killed and almost 2,750 wounded in these explosions. Iran's ambassador to Lebanon, Mojtaba Amani, too was reported to be injured in the explosions, although it begs a question as to why he was holding a 'Hezbollah pager'. Coming at a time when Israel is shifting the focus of military operations to the North to combat Hezbollah, this attack, both in timing and conduct, has a distinctive signature of a well-planned and orchestrated operation by Israeli intelligence. Hezbollah, taken by surprise, has blamed Israel for the "sinful aggression", saying the country will get its "fair punishment".

What is a Pager? How can it be rigged?

What is a pager? It is a basic communication device which came into being well before modern smart mobile phones and is used to deliver short text messages to the user. Unlike mobile phones, pagers work on specified radio frequencies or groups of frequencies in a network. Also, they have no access to the Internet. As a result, they are harder to monitor and thus are considered safe and useful devices to communicate instructions to cadres of groups like Hezbollah.

A number of theories are being propounded on how so many pagers could be used as weapons to target Hezbollah. One theory suggests that the radio frequency of the Hezbollah pager network was hacked and a sharp signal sent to the pagers which overheated the embedded lithium batteries, exploding the batteries and the pagers. Another theory indicates a deep intelligence operation wherein an entire consignment marked for delivery to Hezbollah was sabotaged, all the pagers rigged with undetectable explosives placed with or within the batteries and thereafter exploded on 17 September through remote activation. There may be several other theories too but the fact that this was such a successful and precise intelligence operation salvages the reputation of Israeli intelligence services to a great extent.

Also, whatever may have been the method of triggering these explosions, this incident has added to the already escalating situation along the Lebanese border where Hezbollah and Israel have been exchanging fire ever since the war broke out in October last year. However, the intensity has increased over the past few months, especially after the assassination of Hezbollah's senior commander, Faud Shukra, in a targeted assassination on 31 July in Beirut.

Hezbollah Attacks in the North

Hezbollah has repeatedly and successfully targeted northern towns and villages in Israel, military communication centres and important places like the northern Israeli town of Kiryat Shmona. In fact, on 25 August, Hezbollah launched hundreds of rockets and drones in one night. While most of the rockets and drones were intercepted by Israeli air defences, some landed in Israel and caused damage to homes in the north. Hezbollah had called the attack a success and a fitting reply for the assassination of its senior military commander, Fuad Shukr.

Iran, which is still to launch its retaliation in response to the assassination of Hamas political chief, Ismail Haniyeh, in Tehran on 31 July, was quick to point out that Israel could not even prevent this limited attack by Hezbollah despite the comprehensive support of the USA and has therefore lost its deterrence power. Its spokesperson added that Israel "now has to defend itself within its occupied territories" and that "strategic balances have undergone fundamental changes" to the detriment of Israel.

Israel too has been wary of repeated rocket attacks from the north by Hezbollah and it realizes that its arsenal of weapons platforms, rockets and drones cannot be destroyed by mere air strikes or artillery assaults. Also, the repeated targeting has resulted in damage and casualties leading to thousands of Israeli settlers being displaced from their homes.

Conscious of this increasing threat, on 16 September, after a meeting of the security cabinet, Israel announced that it has revised its military objectives in the ongoing Gaza war, adding the 'safe return' of northern settlers to their residences as a fourth goal. The previously declared three goals were: completely dismantling the military capabilities of Hamas, ensuring that Gaza does not pose any military threat in the future to Israel and bringing back all the hostages safely. There are also reports of Israel firming up plans for a ground invasion into Lebanon and a number of military formations having been directed towards the north in anticipation.

War in Gaza Continues

Meanwhile, the war in Gaza continues unabated and all attempts at negotiating a ceasefire have failed so far.

The threat from Yemen too remains alive. More recently, on 15 September, the Houthis from Yemen fired a hypersonic ballistic missile at Israel which travelled over 2,000 km in just over 11 minutes, evading all air defences and successfully landing in close proximity to Tel Aviv. Besides this, the Houthis continue to target commercial and military ships of Israel and the Western countries in the Red Sea leading to huge economic losses.

Looking Ahead

As Hezbollah regroups and decides on its response to this 'pager attack', Iran continues to watch from a distance, preparing and waiting for the right opportunity to strike Israel directly, and avenge the assassination of Hamas political chief, Haniyeh. If and when the retaliation takes place, it would definitely force an immediate Israeli counter-strike and, unlike the brief spat in April, this time it could lead to uncontrolled escalation. While the region awaits the inevitable, the latest pager attacks in Lebanon have added a new and dangerous dimension to the conflict, confirming a theory of modern times where technology is all pervasive and, 'what transmits, can be targeted'.

31

War Enters Lebanon

The war in Gaza has taken a dramatic turn over the past few weeks. Israel has rapidly revised its war strategy and despite calls for restraint and ceasefire, the conflict is now poised on a dangerous trajectory of escalation and 'a point of no return'.

It all started with a series of sudden pager explosions on 17 September. A day later, while Hezbollah was still taking stock of the situation, a second wave of remote attacks, this time through remote detonation of thousands of 'walkie-talkie' short-range two-way radio sets held by Hezbollah, shocked them, once again causing heavy casualties and damage. Not finished yet, an airstrike by the Israeli Air Force on 20 September took out Ibrahim Aqil, the head of Hezbollah's military operations and the commander of the elite Radwan Forces. In a matter of four days, Hezbollah's command and communications network had been severely degraded. Earlier on 30 July, Faud Shukra, one of the senior-most military commanders and founding members of Hezbollah, was assassinated by Israel through a targeted airstrike in Beirut.

Hezbollah's Chief, Hasan Nasrallah, has called the pager and walkie-talkie attacks as a 'terrorist acts' and a 'declaration of war' while admitting that they were "unprecedented in the history of the resistance movement in Lebanon" He added that the enemy crossed all boundaries and red lines and that "the enemy will face a severe and fair punishment from where they expect and don't expect".

Hezbollah, which had been engaged in regular rocket and drone attacks into Northern Israel since 8 October last year, retaliated and fired more than 200 rockets and drones into Israel on 18 September, targeting key military sites in Northern Israel. Israel, in turn, conducted punitive air strikes across Southern Lebanon and claimed to have destroyed more than 100 rocket-launchers, as well as other military infrastructure of Hezbollah on 19 September. On 22 September, Hezbollah successfully targeted the Ramat David airbase near Haifa with its new weapons, the Fadi 1 and Fadi 2 missiles. Apart from the town of Haifa, reports indicate that even the city of Nazareth has been targeted by Hezbollah.

On 23 September however, events took a turn for the worse when Israel launched the most massive airstrike in Lebanon till date, resulting in 492 people killed and over 1,645 injured. Israel claimed that the Air Force was targeting homes where 'rockets, drones and missiles' were emplaced by Hezbollah, and urged civilians in Lebanon's Beqaa Valley to leave their homes. Hezbollah too responded and rained over 200 rockets into Israel striking deep, upto the city of Haifa and even some West Bank settlements near Tel Aviv.

What Happens Now?

The last time that Israel and Hezbollah fought a war was the 2006 Lebanon war which lasted over 34 days from 12 July to 14 August. It involved a massive air strike by Israel on 12 and 13 July followed by a ground invasion into Lebanon. Hezbollah, though severely degraded by the airstrikes, had held its ground leading to a stalemate and ceasefire on 14 August. During the war, Israel lost over 120 soldiers whereas more than 1,100 died in Lebanon.

Could the same result be repeated in the current situation? Indications are that Israel has decided to 'take the bull by its horns' and end the menace of rocket attacks and the Hezbollah threat once and for all. The Israeli Defence Minister claimed that Israel is decimating all capabilities built by Hezbollah over the past 18 years and that Hassan Nasrallah will be left alone at the top, with his entire leadership structure wiped out.

Where Does Iran Stand?

While the situation has been escalating in the Gaza war, all eyes have been on Iran, waiting to see how it responds. It may be recalled that Iran had vowed to avenge the assassination of Hamas political chief, Ismail Haniyeh, on 30 July in Tehran. However, weeks and months have passed and Iran's retaliation is still awaited. Reacting to the recent pager attacks on Hezbollah, Iran had vowed revenge with Hossein Salami, the commander of the IRGC, stating that Israel will face "a crushing response from the axis of resistance".

Can Iran Wait any Longer?

Iran has been the main support, ideologically and militarily, behind Hamas as well as Hezbollah. The modern sophisticated drones and missiles with these groups as well as Houthis in Yemen could have come only from Iran.

Iran also realizes that Israel has been baiting it to join the war directly since the beginning and except for a brief spat in April this year, it has so far refrained and exercised caution. The question is how long Iran will wait to take the all-important decision. Also, can it leave Hezbollah and Hamas to fight their own wars while it continues to support them from the back?

As the rapidly evolving situation in South Lebanon indicates, it is not long before Israel and Hezbollah join battle directly on the ground. Going by how the war has progressed in Gaza so far, it is clear that this time Israel is determined to try and end the threat to its borders, people and its security once and for all. Gaza has been completely decimated and the West Bank is being continuously encroached upon. The only remaining threat thereafter is from Hezbollah in the north.

If the situation continues to deteriorate in South Lebanon, Iran may have no option but to join the battle. But will it be too late by then? Would it have lost the initiative and many Hezbollah lives before it steps in?

This war is set to change the political and security landscape of the region forever. The ongoing elections in the USA and the resultant indecisiveness have given Israel a perfect window of a few months to do what it wants to achieve its politico-military objectives. If Iran intends to stop it and retain the strategic advantage that it has so far enjoyed in the Levant, it will have to take quick and big strategic decisions soon, before the situation becomes completely untenable.

32

Israel Eliminates Hezbollah Chief

On 27 September, the unthinkable happened. In one of the most daring and shocking blows in the war yet, an air strike by Israel eliminated Hezbollah Chief Hassan Nasrullah while he was meeting his senior commanders in a bunker deep underground in the suburbs of South Beirut.

Cashing in on the mayhem in the rank-and-file of Hezbollah, Israeli Defence Forces (IDF) commenced limited, localized and targeted ground raids based on precise intelligence against Hezbollah in southern Lebanon on the night of 30 September 2024. Codenamed Operation '*Northern Arrows*', the operations are being backed by precision strikes by the Israeli Air Force and fire support by the artillery. These ground operations, small in scale and scope, are being seen as a precursor to a possible full scale ground offensive into Southern Lebanon later.

The Build-up

Well before commencing this limited ground operations, Israel did what is called in military terminology as the 'preparation of the battlefield' and 'softening of the target'. Commencing with the 'pager attacks' on 17 September in Lebanon, a second wave of remote attacks on 18 September, this time through remote detonation of thousands of 'walkie-talkie' short-range two-way radio sets, stunned Hezbollah. Shortly thereafter, an airstrike by the Israeli Air Force on 20 September took out Ibrahim Aqil, the head of Hezbollah's military operations and the commander of the elite Radwan Forces. Several others were eliminated in the coming days including Nabil Qaouk, member of Hezbollah's Executive Council, Al Karaki, Commander of the Southern Front, Ibrahim Qabisi, Head of Rocket Forces, Mohd Hussein Srour, Head of Aerial Command, etc. However, the biggest and most shocking blow was delivered when an air strike by Israel eliminated Hezbollah Chief Hassan Nasrullah on 27 September, while he was meeting with his senior commanders in a bunker buried deep underground in the suburbs of South Beirut.

Within a span of 10 days, Israeli strikes, helped by precise intelligence, took out the entire leadership structure of Hezbollah and disrupted their entire communication and control network. Israel has also made major gains in successfully targeting weapon depots and rocket and missile launch platforms, severely degrading Hezbollah's fighting potential. As the ground operations now unfold, it is important to examine how the opposing forces match up.

The Asymmetry in the Conflict

The IDF, without doubt, is far superior to Hezbollah or any other fighting group in this conflict. Technologically superior, better equipped and organised and backed by its Western allies, it threatens to overrun any military opposition on the battlefield.

In terms of air power, it has absolute superiority with the most modern fighter aircraft in the form of F-15s, F-16s and F-35s, in its arsenal.

In terms of air defence too, the IDF enjoys unmatched advantage. Its arsenal of air defence and anti-missile systems is led by the short-range Iron Dome (anti-rocket system), duly augmented by David's Sling system, the long-range M901 Patriot PAC-2 system and the Arrow Anti-Missile System. As a result of this superiority, the IDF has been able to strike with its fighter jets with impunity across Lebanese territory while at the same time it has been able to intercept most of the rockets fired by Hezbollah.

In terms of ground forces, IDF has more than 1,000 Merkava main battle tanks (MBT), 1,200 armoured personnel carriers (APC), over 500 artillery guns, including 30 multiple rocket launchers (MRL) and a host of other weapon and surveillance systems. Also, the IDF enjoys direct support from the USA in terms of intelligence, surveillance and strike capabilities.

Hezbollah

Hezbollah or 'The Party of God' is the world's most heavily armed non-state group and has been described as "a militia trained like an army and equipped like a state". This Iran-backed group possesses more than 150,000 missiles and rockets, according to the World Fact Book of the US Central Intelligence Agency, which can hit almost all of Israel. Many of its weapons are Iranian with some being drawn from Russian or Chinese models too. Although Hezbollah leader Sayyed Hassan Nasrallah claims to have 100,000 fighters, most estimates suggest the figure could be about 45,000.

Unguided rockets like the Katyusha missiles with a range of 30 kilometres comprise the bulk of Hezbollah's missile arsenal. It also has Iranian models such as Raad (Arabic for 'thunder'), Fajr ('dawn') and Zilzal ('earthquake') rockets, which have a more powerful payload and longer range than the Katyushas. In the ongoing war in Gaza, Hezbollah has fired Katyushas and Burkan ('volcano') missiles with an explosive payload of 300-500 kg at Israel. It also has Iranian-made Falaq 1 and Falaq 2 rockets. The Qadar-1 ballistic missile is also reported to be in Hezbollah's inventory with a warhead of 500 kg and an extended range and was used by Hezbollah for the first time on 25 September when it targeted Tel Aviv.

Hezbollah uses anti-tank missiles including the Russian-made Kornet which have proved very effective against tanks and armed personnel carriers. It has also reportedly used an Iranian-made guided missile known as 'al-Mas', which can hit targets beyond the line of sight, enabling it to strike from above. Hezbollah successfully used anti-tank missiles during its war with Israel in 2006 when it successfully struck nearly 50 Israeli Merkava tanks.

Although Hezbollah is known to possess Soviet era anti-aircraft gun systems like ZU-23, OSA, Strella, Igla, Pantsyr S-1, etc., it is only during the current Gaza war that it has downed Israeli drones like Hermes 450 and Hermes 900 using surface-to-air missiles.

Hezbollah has also used one-way explosive drones as well as drones that drop bombs and return to Lebanon. These are mostly short range drones supplied by Iran as well as locally-assembled Ayoub and Mersad models, which analysts say are cheap and relatively easy to produce.

However, where Hezbollah has a definite advantage is its well-trained and highly motivated 'Special Forces' who specialise in guerrilla warfare. Having fought Israel in 2006 where they successfully halted Israeli forces before they could reach the Litani River in the north, these are battle hardened and capable of inflicting damage through raids. With the terrain in the area of intended ground operations in Southern Lebanon consisting of rolling hills and defiladed positions, these forces equipped with hand-held and shoulder-fired weapons could pose a huge challenge to Israeli ground operations. Having the ability to operate in small teams, they merge into the folds of the ground, use an intricate tunnel network and unconventional means to close in on the enemy forces undetected. So much so that the IDF calls them the 'ghost soldiers' as they appear out of nowhere and are a major deterrent.

Who holds the Edge?

The IDF certainly seems to hold a disproportionate advantage over Hezbollah. Although some militia groups in Syria and Iraq have pledged support including the option to despatch fighters to fight alongside Hezbollah, it is not likely to make a major dent in current Israeli operations. Iran, despite having pledged to support Hezbollah and extract revenge from Israel, is currently in a total state of chaos and confusion with its proxies facing major losses in recent weeks and is unlikely to be drawn into the war directly.

Israel, on the other hand, buoyed by its recent successes, would want to force home the advantage and secure its objective of safe return of settlers in the north before Hezbollah has the time to regroup and reorganise.

33

Iran Finally Strikes Israel

After a long uncertain period of two months since the assassination of Hamas political chief Ismail Haniyeh in Tehran on 30 July and the assassination of Hezbollah chief Hassan Nasrullah on 27 August, Iran, under tremendous pressure at home and from allies struck Israel directly with a barrage of almost 180-200 missiles on 1 October. Many of these missiles were intercepted but adequate numbers found their mark, not only causing damage in Israel but also delivering a stern message that its methods of provoking escalation through targeted strikes and assassinations will not go unanswered. Israel has, as expected, vowed revenge with PM Netanyahu stating that Iran made a big mistake and Iran will pay a price for its missile barrage.

The Build-up to it

The war in Gaza will complete one year shortly. During this period, Iran has fought effectively through its proxies, the '3Hs' and has prevented Israel from achieving its war objectives through a sustained battle of attrition. However, developments over the past fortnight have delivered huge setbacks to the 'Axis of Resistance'. Hezbollah, in particular, has been the focus of Israeli attacks since 17 September. Unrelenting attacks on it have resulted in complete elimination of its top-level leadership, destruction of its communication network and shattering of confidence in its cadres.

On the Hamas side too, there have been continued losses. Their political chief, Ismail Haniyeh, was assassinated in Tehran on 30 July and his successor and military leader, Yahya Sinwar, too has been missing for the last few weeks. In the West Bank, Israeli operations in Jenin Camp and Nablus since 27 August have inflicted huge losses to Palestinian Islamic Jihad (PIJ) and its allied groups.

As a result, Israel was in a clear state of ascendency while Iran backed groups were in complete disarray and low on confidence.

A Stern Test for the Supreme Leader

It is a well-established fact that Iran's security policies and national strategy are run through the office of the Supreme Leader. Over the past few years, he has however been subjected to setback after setback. When IRGC commander Qaseem Suleimani was assassinated in January 2020, it was a major setback as he was considered a hero in Iran and very close to the Supreme Leader. Iran vowed revenge but did not take any action against the USA that had carried out this attack. The recent killing of the Hezbollah chief is probably the biggest blow to him as he too was a close confidant (some say he was like a son) and the most important key in coordinating Iran's military strategy across the Levant. The unfortunate death of Iran's president, Ebrahim Raisi, in a helicopter crash in May was a huge blow to the Supreme Leader as he was not only being projected as the next Supreme Leader by many but was a key to the success of Iran's strategy in the Gaza war. The presidential elections thereafter threw up a surprise for the regime when the hardliner, Saeed Jalili, was defeated by a reformist Masoud Pezeshkian.

Also, the Supreme Leader has already crossed the age of 85 this year and has not yet appointed a successor. This, coupled with the setbacks in the region, made things only worse for the regime's future in Iran.

Added to this is President Pezeshkian's statement of 29 September stating that "the Western leaders had promised Iran a ceasefire in Gaza in exchange for Iran not attacking Israel over the assassination of Ismail Haniyeh, but they lied" was being seen as lame and weak and one of the key reasons for the killing of the Hezbollah chief. People on the streets were calling for his resignation saying that if Iran had retaliated after Haniyeh's death, Israel would not have dared kill Nasrullah.

Former Iranian President Mahmoud Ahmadinejad's statement that the head of an Iranian secret service unit set up to target Mossad agents turned out to be an Israeli agent himself also caused a huge uproar and further embarrassment.

However, the final trigger for Iran launching the strike was perhaps the directly televised address to the Iranian people by Israel's PM Netanyahu on 30 September in which he called for a regime change, instigating the people of Iran against the leadership. Already under pressure for inaction and looking weak, this address would have been seen as a grave insult by the Iranian leadership.

What Next for Iran?

It is clear that Iran was forced to undertake the strike mission under extreme provocation. In the past few weeks, its cadres and proxies were feeling let down but more importantly Israel was emboldened to expand its war objectives. Israel was keen on taking advantage of the war situation to consolidate its gains and end the threat to its borders from all sides, once and for all.

With Gaza completely decimated and the West Bank almost completely occupied, the only remaining threat to Israel thereafter is from Hezbollah in the north and Israel is keen to push it more northwards of the Litani River to establish a deep buffer zone for the safe return of its settlers in the north. The limited ground operations into Lebanon, launched on 30 September, are aimed at this objective.

By launching a retaliatory strike on 1 October, Iran has definitely put a halt to the free run that Israel has enjoyed in the war over the past two months. It has salvaged a bit of its pride and boosted the confidence of its cadres and proxies in the region, but it has also opened the doors for a huge escalation in the region. Israel has vowed revenge and the US President has pledged support, stating that Israel has a right to respond and that it should be a proportional response. As Israel finalises its options and plans for the counter-retaliation on Iran, the coming days and weeks will tell us whether this episode of retaliatory strikes between Iran and Israel will end after a brief spat like in April, or whether the region will be in the middle of an unprecedented and bloody conflict.

34

Yahya Sinwar Killed

Israel finally gets lucky, eliminates Yahya Sinwar!

On 16 October, Israel continued its run of successful elimination of the top leadership of the opposing forces when it killed the elusive Hamas leader, Yahya Sinwar, in a gun battle in the Gaza Strip. Unlike some of the other successful assassinations of top political and military leaders of Hamas and Hezbollah in the past recent months, this wasn't a planned operation but a gun fight which resulted in the deaths of three Hamas operatives, including Sinwar.

Announcing the news to the world, Israeli Foreign Minister Israel Katz called Sinwar 'a mass murderer who was responsible for the massacre and atrocities of 7 October', adding that it is a military and moral achievement for the Israeli army. Israeli PM Netanyahu, in a televised address, stated that Israeli forces have delivered "a blow to evil" adding that, "while this is not the end of the war in Gaza, it's the beginning of the end". President Biden, congratulated Israel on a very important tactical victory on the battlefield, adding that Sinwar's death marks a moment of relief for Israelis while providing the opportunity for a 'day after' in Gaza without the group in power.

Why is Sinwar's Killing so Important?

Firstly, he is supposed to be the mastermind of the audacious terror attack launched by Hamas on 7 October last year. Secondly, he was the head of Hamas, appointed soon after the assassination of its political chief, Ismail Haniyeh on 30 July in Tehran. Thirdly, he planned and directed the entire military effort of Hamas in Gaza. Even the intricate underground tunnel network running into more than 150 km inside Gaza is supposed to be his brainchild. He also carried immense clout in the highest decision-making set-up in the Hamas and was seen as the main obstacle in Israel getting a ceasefire in Gaza on its own terms.

How can this affect the War in Gaza?

The death of Yahya Sinwar is yet another setback in the top echelons of Hamas. While Ismail Haniyeh's assassination was provocative, to say the least, some other killings in the Hamas leadership too have been significant. On 2 January, Hamas's deputy leader abroad, Saleh al-Arouri, the leader of Hamas's military wing in the West Bank, was killed in an Israeli strike in the Beirut suburb of Dahiyeh. Another top military commander of Hamas, Mohammed Deif, was killed in an Israeli air raid in southern Gaza on 13 July (although Hamas is yet to confirm it). However, for Israel, the prize was always Sinwar who was being hunted for the last 12 months.

For Israel, this lucky break can yield either of two outcomes. Either, it could claim that with the killing of Yahya Sinwar, the main architect of the Gaza war has been removed and therefore it could call it a decisive victory, settle for a ceasefire and seek an honourable exit with momentum on its side. On the other hand, it could take this tactical victory as an opportunity to further intensify its operations against Hamas, hoping to deliver the final death blow to the group.

If it takes the first option, Israel could return to the negotiating table after weeks of stalled ceasefire talks. It may also hope to get more of its terms included in the ceasefire deal, now that Sinwar is no longer there to obstruct it.

However, if Israel decides to press on the throttle in Gaza, the assurance of a clear victory which has eluded it for the last 12 months will continue to be a factor and it would have to then wait either for a clear achievement of its four war objectives or continue this endless war of attrition.

For Hamas and the 'Axis of Resistance', there is no time to mourn the loss, but to regroup and exhibit resilience and resolve. The next level of leadership too has two options. Either, it can 'surrender and lay down arms' as demanded by Israeli PM Netanyahu, in which case the losses and sacrifices over the past one year in the war as also in the struggle over the decades would amount to nothing. Also, it looks quite clear from Israeli statements and resolutions in its parliament that it would also signal the end of hope for a 'Two-State Solution' in the future.

On the other hand, it could take inspiration from the life and death of its leaders and carry on the fight. It has a successful example of Hezbollah to emulate, which even after elimination of the top three layers of its leadership, including its charismatic leader Hassan Nasrallah, is giving an equal fight to Israeli forces in

Southern Lebanon, preventing them from making any major breakthrough, and inflicting heavy losses to personnel and weapon platforms.

The drone video of Sinwar's last moments, released by the Israeli army in exuberance, should count as a tactical error as the Hamas cadres are witnessing their leader going down fighting instead of being hunted down in the tunnels, something which can only inspire new cadres and leaders to fight on. A statement from Iran's permanent mission to the UN stating, "when Muslims look up to the Martyr Sinwar standing on the battlefield, in combat attire and out in the open, not in a hideout, facing the enemy, the spirit of resistance will be strengthened," is clearly indicative of how this killing could be used to its advantage by Iran, Hamas and others.

Looking Ahead: An Opportunity to be Cashed

The ongoing war in Gaza is the longest that Israel and Hamas have ever fought. In past conflicts, Israel undertook swift operations with a clearly defined military objective and ended them on its own terms. This time, however, the outrage and shame of having been outsmarted and outwitted by Hamas, coupled with the huge loss of lives and the taking of hundreds of hostages, has forced Israel to undertake a vastly different approach.

There are very few wars where one party can achieve total victory and annihilate the enemy. In most of the cases, the victor is the one who seizes an opportunity on the battlefield, churns out a suitable narrative hailing it as a major victory and then dictates terms for ending the conflict. Israel has this opportunity now. Yahya Sinwar's killing can be a good enough reason to declare victory and end the war on its own terms.

35

Can Israel Win by Eliminating the Top Leadership of the 'Axis of Resistance'

During the past year of the war and especially since 30 July this year, the killing of a top leader of Hamas or Hezbollah has become a 'go to option' for Israel, not only to relieve pressure back home in Israel but also to put the opposing forces under pressure. The pager and walkie-talkie blasts on Hezbollah in Lebanon on 17-18 September followed by the targeted assassination of Hezbollah Chief Hassan Nasrallah have been key talking points in the war in the past month or so.

However, the targeted killing of top leaders in this war is not a recent phenomenon. As part of its war strategy, Israel has put in huge intelligence resources to track the key leaders of Hamas, Hezbollah and others and take them out at an opportune moment. Three months into the war, on 25 December last year, Seyed Radhi Mousavi, Iran's most influential military commander in the Levant, was killed in a suspected Israeli airstrike in Syria's capital, Damascus. On 2 January, Hamas's deputy leader abroad, Saleh al-Arouri, the leader of Hamas's military wing in the West Bank, was killed in an Israeli strike in Dahiyeh suburb of Beirut. And on 4 January, a suspected US drone attack killed Mushtaq Talib Al-Saidi, deputy commander of operations in the Iraqi capital for the Harakat Al-Nujaba, a pro-Iran militia group.

A few months later, on 1 April, an Israeli air strike targeted the Iranian Consulate in Damascus, resulting in the death of General Mohammad Reza Zahedi, the senior-most IRGC commander in Lebanon and Syria. The biggest blow was the assassination of the Hamas political chief, Ismail Haniyeh on 30 July.

Is the Strategy of Eliminating Top Leadership Working?

There is no doubt that the assassination of a top leader is demoralizing for the cadres. In especially the case of the Hezbollah, the targeted elimination of its entire leadership coupled with the destruction of its communications network through the pager attacks was a severe body blow. Taking advantage of this, Israeli forces decided to launch ground operations into Southern Lebanon to make conditions conducive for Israeli settlers to return to northern Israel. There was a clear understanding in Israel that its forces should drive home the tactical advantage before Hezbollah has time to regroup.

However, as witnessed from the progress of operations in the past few weeks, Israeli forces have not only been halted but have suffered major casualties to personnel and weapon platforms like the famous Merkava armoured tanks. Plus, the ferocity and reach of rocket and missile attacks from Hezbollah has intensified to a large extent, inflicting losses on Israel in the areas of Haifa, Kiryat Shmona, city of Acre, along with other key areas including around Tel Aviv. On the Gaza front too, despite the killing of top leaders, the resistance continues with daily encounters with Israeli forces, inflicting losses with the stated aim of 'eliminating Hamas from the face of the Earth' nowhere in sight.

The targeted killing of top leaders is also working against Israel in other ways. Firstly, it is enabling Iran and its proxies to cry foul and attract the support of additional cadres. Secondly, for Israel, which is already under immense international pressure for indiscriminate killings of civilians in the war, such targeted killings, especially on foreign soil, are pushing more and more countries, including those in the region, vocally against it and reluctantly, in support of Iran and its allies.

Examples from other Wars

The most prominent example has to be Afghanistan. After 'bombing it into the Stone Age' and killing Osama bin Laden through a targeted operation on foreign soil, did the USA succeed in liberating Afghanistan from al-Qaeda and the Taliban? The answer is clearly 'No'. In fact, the USA had to beat a hasty retreat in August 2021, leaving Afghanistan in the hands of the Taliban in a situation worse than what had existed in September 2001, when it had launched the 'Global War on Terror'. Meanwhile, al-Qaeda has spread far and wide into the region and even Africa, mushrooming into different forms and names

The war in Iraq and the subsequent execution of Saddam Hussein has to be another case study in this context. Did the war or the elimination of the top leadership in Iraq result in peace and stability? The answer again is 'No'. In the past two decades since the war, Iraq has not been able to stabilize, has been prone to regular internal and external security threats, including from ISIS, and has become a key ally of Iran, much to the dismay of the USA and Israel.

What about Libya? Did the act of dragging Gaddafi out of a hole in the desert and killing him, help in stabilizing that country? The answer once again is, 'No'. Unlike many other countries in the region which were struck by the 'Arab Spring' protests in 2010-11, Libya continues to remain unstable with no clear leadership and direction.

What should be Done?

Whether against conventional forces or against militias and proxies, war can only be won by clearly stated and achievable military objectives and political goals. Israel, in the past, has been a master of this craft and has successfully fought and ended conflicts in the region, through short and swift wars. However, this time, more out of outrage and embarrassment, the war objectives set out are unrealistic and quite unachievable. In fact, Israel's generals as well as key members of the war cabinet have voiced concerns over them. On 19 June, Israel's Rear Admiral Daniel Hagari told Israel's Channel 13 broadcaster that "this business of destroying Hamas, making Hamas disappear – it's simply throwing sand in the eyes of the public."

Also, against militias and groups like Hamas and Hezbollah who are born out of an ideology based on suppression of people, such assassinations only fuel more anger and hatred and strengthen their collective resolve to fight more fiercely. Remember, these groups and the people they represent are fighting with their backs to the wall in a fight for existence and have therefore nothing to lose. Plus, such incidents give perfect fodder to their mentors like Iran to take the fight one notch further, making the resolution of conflict and ceasefire that much more difficult.

Israel may have to review whether the targeted assassinations are making a meaningful impact towards achievement of their stated war objectives. Yes, every assassination of a top leader of Hamas, Hezbollah and others is seen as a political victory for PM Netanyahu who is fighting a tough battle at home on his war strategy and his inability to bring back the hostages. However, do such assassinations make the task of getting the hostages released easier? Also, in the absence of established and experienced top leadership, the next level of leadership is generally more aggressive and less prone to rational discussions on ending the war and negotiations like the returning of hostages.

Israel may therefore do well to review its war objectives. Targeted killings of top leadership cannot alone win wars. Sometimes, tactical victories like this turn into strategic losses in the long run.

36

As Israel Strikes Iran, it is Time to Quit from a Position of Advantage. Will it?

Israel takes revenge, strikes Iran!

Israel finally struck Iran in the early hours of 26 October when it launched multiple waves of missile strikes into Iran, targeting 'only military targets'. This came about just as the US Secretary of State, Antony Blinken, wound up his visit to the region. He was in Israel and Saudi Arabia on 23 October to discuss modalities and possibilities to end the war in Gaza. This was his 11th visit to the region since the war broke out. On each of the previous visits, he has not only carried messages from the US President but has been at the forefront of the efforts to end the war in Gaza. With the US presidential elections scheduled on 5 November, this was perhaps his last visit to the region before the elections.

Speaking after meeting Prime Minister Netanyahu on 23 October, he stressed the fact that Israel should use its tactical victories against Hamas and Hezbollah in recent times (especially the elimination of their top leadership) and pursue an 'enduring strategic success' in Gaza, adding that "there really are two things left to do: Get the hostages home and bring the war to an end with an understanding of what will follow". He later met Saudi Crown Prince Mohammed bin Salman in Riyadh where again both discussed options and "common efforts to end the conflicts in the region and establish greater peace and security."

The USA, along with Egypt and Qatar, has been at the forefront of ceasefire talks but nothing has come out due to hard positions taken by both Israel and Hamas. The only temporary relief came about in November last year when a seven-day temporary humanitarian truce from 24 to 30 November was observed and some hostages exchanged for Palestinian prisoners in Israeli jails.

In the past few months, Israel has enjoyed the upper hand on most counts on the battlefield. The assassinations of top Hamas and Hezbollah leadership has to be at the top of the success chart. The elimination of Hezbollah Chief Hassan

Nasrallah on 27 September and the killing of Hamas chief and main architect of the 7 October terror attack, Yahya Sinwar, on 16 October have been major setbacks to the 'Axis of Resistance'.

The attack by Iran on 1 October targeting key military sites in Israel was a setback but Israel's retaliation on 26th October successfully targeting three military sites in Iran has levelled the score. On the battlefield too, Israeli defence forces have been mercilessly pounding the Gaza Strip, especially the northern parts, killing and displacing people by hundreds daily. Its operations in the West Bank which were accompanied by the entry of tanks and troops as part of a ground operation on 27 August, have neutralized the resistance there – the focus of the operations being the Jenin camp as well as the areas of Nablus.

On the Lebanon front, Israeli Defence Forces, despite facing stiff resistance, have been able to destroy many rocket launcher sites, weapon depots and even an underground tunnel network. However, stiff battles continue on the ground even as Israel has suffered many tank casualties and a number of its soldiers killed.

As the operations drag on, there are chances that Iran may launch a counter retaliation to Israeli strikes of 26 October. The forthcoming US elections on 5 November would also mean that the window of opportunity that PM Netanyahu had of operating with impunity may close. Media reports indicate that Donald Trump has already told PM Netanyahu to clear up the mess and end the war before his presidency commences (in case he wins).

Review of Israel's War Objectives

A quick review of the war objectives tells us that Israel is still far from achieving its stated objectives. While Hamas has been severely degraded and its top leadership eliminated, it is far from being 'eliminated from the face of the Earth'. Its ability to launch repeated attacks across Gaza continues to irritate Israel and the unprecedented devastation that Israeli strikes are causing, is motivating more and more cadres to join Hamas. As regards Gaza, it has been bombarded like no place ever before. Over 42,500 people have been killed with children and women constituting the majority and over 2 million people internally displaced multiple times. Despite the devastation and the ruin, Gaza being rebuilt and re-used by Hamas or any other group in the future to launch attacks on Israel cannot be ruled out, unless Israel decides to continue its occupation of Gaza forever.

The non-achievement of the third war objective – return of hostages – is the most critical one as far as Israel is concerned. There is mounting pressure on

Netanyahu for his failure to get back the hostages. Meanwhile, the number of hostages remaining alive is reducing with every passing week, due to deaths owing to Israeli action, cross fire or succumbing to ill health or disease. Hamas has made it clear that the remaining hostages can only be released if and when there is a sustainable ceasefire.

The fourth war objective, 'safe return of settlers to the North' too remains elusive. Despite heavy losses, the ability of Hezbollah to launch rocket attacks into Northern Israel cannot be ruled out however deep Israel moves into Lebanon. Even if Israel is able to finally occupy territory upto the Litani River, the attacks by long range rockets could still continue. The advent of armed drones has added to the complexity of the situation.

Where does this leave Israel? Even with many recent tactical successes, its war objectives remain elusive. What can Israel do then, under these circumstances?

Recent Developments

The war is poised delicately with three possible options; drag on endlessly or escalate further; or end with a ceasefire now while Israel still looks the winner.

As regards a ceasefire, there have been multiple efforts towards this. Except for a brief humanitarian truce in November last year, no ceasefire proposal has been accepted by both the warring parties. Most recently, on 21 October, as per media reports, the director of the Egyptian General Intelligence Service presented Israel's Shin Bet chief an idea for a 'small' hostage and ceasefire deal in Gaza. The deal would include the release of a small number of hostages held by Hamas in return for a few days of ceasefire in Gaza. The 'small deal' would then continue with renewed negotiations over a more comprehensive hostage and ceasefire agreement.

On 30 October the new chief of Hezbollah, Naim Qassem, indicated that the group would be open to a ceasefire proposal "according to the conditions that we see as suitable" adding that the group will not beg for it. There are indications that Iran is not very keen to retaliate soon to Israel's attack of 26 October as the Supreme Leader tried to downplay the effect of Israeli strikes when he stated that Israeli attacks should 'neither be downplayed nor exaggerated'. Another important factor is the support from Israel's major benefactor, the USA. With the presidential polls just days away, it is clear that the window where Israel could exert pressure on the USA and act with impunity in Gaza is closing fast.

Looking Ahead

The ball is clearly in Israel's court. It can either pursue its unrealistic and perhaps unachievable war objectives endlessly or think smart and use the opportunity presented on the battlefield to end this war and get its hostages back home. Among all its war objectives, this is without doubt the most important and certainly achievable. It might also stop Iran in its plans for a strong counter retaliation which, as per indications, it is not very keen on, as it would lead to unnecessary escalation.

As time runs out on the current US presidency, unless there is a miraculous development, the war looks destined to drag on for a few more weeks and months. Meanwhile, every day brings news of more and more innocent civilians being killed in Gaza and Lebanon.

37

Netanyahu Fires Defence Minister

On 5 November, while the US electorate was lining up to cast their crucial vote in a bitterly-fought election campaign for the next president, Israeli PM Netanyahu announced that he had fired the country's Defence Minister, Yoav Gallant. Announcing it, Netanyahu said that a 'crisis of trust' led to his decision, adding that Foreign Minister Israel Katz would replace him. Gallant said his removal was due to disagreement on three critical issues; there should be no exceptions for military service, that a national inquiry was needed to learn lessons from 7 October and the hostages should be brought back as soon as possible. He said that he believed it is possible to bring the remaining hostages back from Gaza if Israel makes 'painful concessions' which it 'can bear'.

Previous Disagreements

The disagreements with the defence minister are however not new. It may be recalled that even before the war in Gaza broke out on 7 October last year, Netanyahu had fired Yoav Gallant in March 2023, when he had spoken out against Netanyahu's controversial plans to overhaul the justice system, key among them being the government's decisive control over the committee which appoints judges. Facing tough opposition within the cabinet as also mass protests all over the country, Gallant was reinstated.

Even during the ongoing war in Gaza, disagreements between the two leaders and public statements have been quite evident. In May this year, Defence Minister Yoav Gallant had publicly criticized PM Netanyahu over his indecision on who will govern Gaza after Hamas is defeated. Reacting sharply and almost immediately, Netanyahu had said that there will be no discussion on who governs Gaza before Hamas is completely eliminated, adding that he is "not ready to replace Hamastan with Fatahstan."

Opposition from the War Cabinet and Military

The differences with the defence minister are not isolated as PM Netanyahu has faced repeated opposition against his decisions on handling the war in Gaza and the war objectives, which many within and outside Israel have termed as unrealistic and unachievable. Benny Gantz, a former Chief of Staff of the Israeli Defence Forces and minister in the war cabinet, had first issued an ultimatum to Netanyahu in May asking him to end the war soon. He finally quit the war cabinet on 9 June. Facing tough opposition from another member in the war cabinet, Gadi Eisenkot, and a former chief of staff of the IDF and leader of the National Unity party, who quit, Netanyahu had to disband the war cabinet on 17 June.

Within the military too, Netanyahu has faced stiff opposition. The current IDF Chief of Staff, General Herzi Halevi, was quoted on 11 May as criticizing Netanyahu for the failure to develop and declare a so-called 'day after' strategy. On 19 June, Israeli army spokesperson Brig. Gen. Daniel Hagari in an interview with Channel 13 News in Israel stated that the "idea of destroying Hamas is like throwing sand in the face of the Israeli public."

At Odds with the USA

PM Netanyahu has been at odds even with the USA. Despite many ceasefire deals offered including the 'Biden Plan' which was presented on 31 May and initially agreed to by Israel, Netanyahu has not been keen on any ceasefire proposal. US Secretary of State Blinken, who has been in the region 11 times since the war broke out, has not been able to convince Israel to call off the war. Even after the killing of Hamas Chief and chief architect of the 7 October attack, Yahya Sinwar, on 16 October, Netanyahu is not ready to relent. This, despite Blinken urging Netanyahu during his meeting on 23 October that Israel should use its tactical victories against Hamas and Hezbollah in recent times and pursue an 'enduring strategic success' in Gaza.

Within Europe and many other nations across the world, there is growing disenchantment against Israel, especially with regard to indiscriminate killing of civilians, which has already crossed 43,000 with the majority of them being children and women. Israel's refusal to let critical humanitarian aid enter Gaza and its decision to ban UNRWA, the principal UN agency tasked to distribute aid in Gaza, has also drawn sharp criticism.

The US elections have drawn to a close and therefore the window of opportunity that Israel had of operating with impunity too is fast getting over.

With Donald Trump set to become the US President again, Israel would hope that the kind of support that Trump offered Israel during his first term would be forthcoming. However, with Trump opposed to wars, whether his support this time would include extension of war in the region, is a big question mark. Media reports indicate that Donald Trump has already told PM Netanyahu to clear up the mess and end the war before his presidency commences.

Looking Ahead

PM Netanyahu finds himself in a tight bind, both at home and abroad. The sacking of the defence minister is only a manifestation of the opposition and anger within Israel on his handling of the war, especially the inability to get the hostages back home. He had a clear advantage after the missile strikes on Iran to declare a victory and end the war. His refusal to do so and insistence on carrying on with his 'unrealistic' war objectives has put him in a position where the option of an 'honourable exit' is becoming remote with every passing day.

38

14 Months On, Why the Sum of Tactical Successes on Battlefield have not Delivered a Decisive Strategic Victory for Israel

It is November 2024 and the war in Gaza, unleashed on the region on 7 October 2023, is well into its 14th month with no signs of ending. Along the way, the war has witnessed many twists and turns with each side claiming occasional tactical successes on the battlefield. Obviously, Israel with its far superior military and intelligence capabilities duly backed by 'iron clad support' from the USA, has tasted such successes more often than the 'Axis of Resistance' led by Iran.

However, despite many tactical successes, many of them unique and unprecedented, Israel is still trying to find the right opportunity or decisive victory on the battlefield where it can call it quits. The reasons for this could be many, starting from the war objectives that it defined for itself, the internal political turmoil within Israel or even the dilemma of what is more important, ending the war or getting its hostages back home safely. To better understand this paradox, it is important to list some of the important tactical successes and then examine why and how these victories have not added towards achievement of Israel's strategic objectives.

Important Tactical Successes for Israel

After the initial shock of the terror attack on 7 October, Israel was quick to regroup and launch a massive punitive counter-strike in Gaza. For Israel, the most important and immediate objective was to not only destroy and degrade Hamas's combat capabilities but also deliver a decisive blow to its leadership and command and communications network. Towards this end, an early success in the form of cutting off Northern Gaza from the South by establishing a physical barrier, now called Netzarim Corridor, was an initial success. The focus of operations shifted thereafter to identify the entry and layout of the very complex and intrinsic underground tunnel network of Hamas, called the 'Gaza Metro'. Despite huge condemnation from the international community for targeting hospitals and schools, many of which also served as entry points for these tunnels, Israel persisted in pursuit of this goal and destroyed much of this tunnel network, dealing a severe blow to Hamas.

For Israel, another crucial factor towards ensuring a decisive victory, was to ensure that the Hamas cadres do not get any fresh supply of weapons, ammunition, money and even food, cadres which could increase the cost of victory for Israel. Taking over control of Rafah Crossing was one such requirement. Why is Rafah Crossing so important? It is the most prominent border crossing town in Southern Gaza located on its border with Egypt. The crossing was manned and controlled by Egypt and Hamas on either side, it being the only one into Gaza not directly under Israeli control. In May this year, despite Egypt calling it a 'red line', Israeli forces entered and occupied the crossing and destroyed the tunnels underneath it, an important tactical success.

The string of assassinations of key leaders in Hamas, Hezbollah and Iran has to be counted as not only tactical victories but a huge redemption for Israeli intelligence agencies. The assassination of Iranian General Mohammad Reza Zahedi, the senior-most commander of the Islamic Revolutionary Guard Corps (IRGC) in Lebanon and Syria in an Israeli strike on the Iranian Consulate in Damascus on 1 April was a huge tactical victory.

However, what shook the region and threatened to escalate the conflict drastically were the targeted assassinations in a short period of time which eliminated the entire top leadership of Hamas and Hezbollah including the assassination of Hamas political chief Ismail Haniyeh on 30 July in Tehran.

The pager attacks on 17 September, followed by the successive elimination of almost the entire senior leadership of Hezbollah culminating in the assassination of its leader, Hassan Nasrallah, on 27 September was a huge success for Israel while the killing of architect of the 7 October terror attack, Yahya Sinwar, on 16 October capped this series of successes and acts of redemption for the Israeli intelligence services.

There have been many other tactical successes for Israel. The operations into the West Bank commencing on 27 August when Israel's Defence Forces (IDF) stormed key locations including the city of Jenin in a bid to 'root out militants', dealt a severe blow to the Palestine Islamic Jihad (PIJ) and have virtually eliminated any remaining resistance from the West Bank. The air strikes into Syria targeting pro-Iran militia groups and the severe degradation of the fighting capabilities of Hezbollah in Southern Lebanon through targeted strikes on its leadership, rocket launchers, and weapon depots have also been huge successes.

Why has a Decisive Victory Eluded Israel?

From the long list of military successes on the battlefield, Israel should have declared victory and called back its forces long ago. The sum of these tactical successes has unfortunately not added up to get Israel a decisive victory. Reason? There are many, primary among them being the unrealistic war objectives and the inflexible stand taken by PM Netanyahu.

A quick review of Israel's war objectives is revealing in this aspect.

While Hamas has been severely degraded and its top leadership eliminated, it is far from being 'eliminated from the face of the Earth'. Its ability to launch repeated attacks across Gaza continues to irritate Israel and cause damage and casualties.

As regards Gaza, it has been bombarded like no place ever before and virtually 'flattened to the ground'. Despite this, the possibility of Gaza being rebuilt and re-used by Hamas or any other group in the future to launch attacks on Israel cannot be ruled out, unless Israel decides to continue its occupation of Gaza forever.

The non-achievement of the third war objective – return of hostages – is the most critical one. There is mounting pressure on Netanyahu in Israel on his failure to get back the hostages while the number of those alive is reducing with every passing week.

The 'safe return of setters to the North' too remains elusive. Despite heavy losses, the ability of Hezbollah to launch rocket attacks into Northern Israel cannot be ruled out however deep Israel moves into Lebanon. Attacks from long-range rockets by Hezbollah and the advent of armed drones have added to the complexity of the situation.

The internal political turmoil and disagreements within the Israeli cabinet too have not helped. While Benny Gantz, a former Chief of Staff of the IDF and a minister in the war cabinet, and Gadi Eisenkot, also a former chief of staff of the IDF and leader of the National Unity Party, quit the war cabinet in June this year, the recent sacking of the country's Defence Minister, Yoav Gallant, on 5 November has brought the discontent out in the open.

Looking Ahead

The ongoing war in Gaza has therefore been a study in contrasts. On one hand, there are significant and numerous accounts of tactical successes for Israel over the past year, but on the other hand, it still finds it difficult to 'close it out'.

For Israel, it seems that there is still some ground to be covered and more decisive victories to be achieved. Whether it is lack of clarity on what the end state should look like or a case of huge politico-military overreach or a gross under-estimation of enemy capabilities, is a point of debate. However, evidence from the war till now clearly indicates that the sum of (disjointed) tactical successes has not been able to add up to a decisive victory for Israel in Gaza.

39

Israel's Ceasefire with Hezbollah: More Questions than Answers

After weeks of effort and shuttle diplomacy by Amos Hochstein, President Biden's special envoy, the Israeli cabinet finally 'approved' a ceasefire deal between Israel and Hezbollah on 26 November 2024. The deal which came into effect at 4 a.m. on 27 November, brought cheer to the people in Southern Lebanon who have been bearing the brunt of intense airstrikes for almost two months since Israeli troops invaded Lebanon on 1 October.

The deal agreed upon between Israel and Lebanon comes with assurances from the USA and France on strict implementation and monitoring mechanisms. It is now hoped that Hezbollah too would honour the deal and stop its rocket attacks into Northern and Central Israel which would then pave the way for the 'safe return of settlers' which was one of the four war objectives of Israel. Lebanon's Caretaker Prime Minister, Najib Mikati, welcomed the ceasefire deal, calling it a "fundamental step towards restoring calm and stability" in the country and allowing citizens to return home.

The finer details of the deal however do pose several questions, especially on the timing, the implementation and its effectiveness.

Details of the Deal

As per the deal, the Lebanese army will deploy in southern Lebanon over the next 60 days and take control of the territory presently controlled by Hezbollah. Concurrently, Israel will withdraw its forces over the next 60 days from Southern Lebanon. Hezbollah too would be required to move its forces north of the Litani River, which is about 30 kilometres north of the Israel-Lebanon border. To fill the buffer zone and ensure no future violations take place, additional UN peacekeepers would be deployed. The whole process is to be monitored by an international panel headed by the USA and France. The 60-day truce is designed to lead to a permanent cessation of hostilities in Southern Lebanon and facilitate the safe return of civilians to their respective homes.

Will Hezbollah Abide by It?

Whereas the war was being fought between Israel and Hezbollah, the deal has been agreed upon by Israel and Lebanon. It is a well-known fact that the Lebanese caretaker government does not have much hold over Hezbollah and, therefore, how much and if at all Hezbollah will abide by the deal is a big question mark. To be fair to the Lebanese government, they had interlocutors consulting Hezbollah but the final acceptance is a question mark, especially due to the clause that Israel retains the right to strike back in case of violation and this deal does not specify a permanent end to hostilities. Mahmoud Qamati, deputy chair of Hezbollah's political council, spoke soon after the announcement of the deal and stated that "we want an end to the aggression, of course, but not at the expense of the sovereignty of the state," referring to Israel's demand for freedom of action. He added that "after reviewing the agreement signed by the enemy government, we will see if there is a match between what we stated and what was agreed upon by the Lebanese officials."

How is it Different from UNSC Resolution 1701?

The current ceasefire deal is not new to the Israel-Hezbollah conflict. There is a standing deal endorsed by the UN Security Council on 11 August 2006 which ended the 34-day war between Israel and Hezbollah. Akin to provisions of the current deal, UNSC Resolution 1701 too called for a permanent ceasefire, based on the creation of a buffer zone. It had authorized an increase of force in the UN Interim Force in Lebanon (UNIFIL) to a maximum of 15,000 troops to monitor the cessation of hostilities, ensure that Israel and Hezbollah both withdrew from southern Lebanon and ensure the safe return of displaced persons.

Also, there was to be no sales or supply of arms and related materiel to Lebanon except as authorised by its government. Both parties were required to respect the 'Blue Line' (a temporary 'line of withdrawal' set by the UN in 2000, stretching for 120km along Lebanon's southern frontier and Israel's northern border) and to ensure an area free of any armed personnel, assets and weapons other than those of the Lebanese authorities and UNIFIL between the Blue Line and the Litani River.

Did it succeed? The answer is clearly 'No'. Hezbollah did not vacate but remained in southern Lebanon, well south of the Litani River. The weak Lebanese government could not do much about it and the UN peacekeeping forces had no mandate to evict Hezbollah. Meanwhile, Hezbollah grew stronger, better equipped and better entrenched with time.

Can Israel Ensure that Hezbollah Poses no Future Threat?

Contrary to what Israel would have expected after inflicting huge losses on Hezbollah by taking out its entire top tier leadership with targeted assassinations including Chief Hassan Nasrallah, destroying weapon depots and rocket launchers, destroying underground tunnel network in Southern Lebanon, etc., the group remains very potent and effective. The most recent barrage of around 250 rockets and missiles fired into Northern and Central Israel hitting many locations in key cities of Haifa and Tel Aviv on 24 November is a clear demonstration that Hezbollah is far from being defeated or incapacitated.

Also, even if Hezbollah withdraws to north of the Litani River, its ever-expanding arsenal of rockets and missiles can easily breach the 30-km additional length that would be imposed by the buffer zone. The advent of armed drones adds to the complexity. Also, despite the deal stating that no arms and weapons would be permitted into Lebanon without the government's consent, it is common knowledge that Hezbollah is much more powerful and has a network so complex that it is near impossible to stop the inflow of weaponry. If it was possible, Israel and the USA would have ensured it long ago.

Can the USA Ensure Implementation of the Deal?

The USA has assured Israel and agreed to give assurances that include support for Israeli military action against threats from Lebanese territory "according to international law." However, President Biden has clarified that the assurance does not imply positioning US troops in southern Lebanon, but that the USA and France will provide assistance to implement the agreement. As per the plan, the USA will have senior military officials operating from the embassy in Beirut to monitor the ceasefire in close coordination with UN peacekeepers. How will the USA enforce it by such passive measures is a question mark?

At the end of day, letters of assurances and deals are only good if they are enforceable. The USA is unwilling to put its boots on the ground; UN peacekeepers were already there and will continue to do so; and the Lebanese government or its military is not going to become so strong overnight that it can evict Hezbollah forcibly. How is then any future threat from Hezbollah, whether from north or south of the Litani River, going to be blocked? If Israel, supported by the USA, could not subdue Hezbollah over the past months with its full military might despite the assassination of its entire leadership, how does it hope to ensure it now except through Hezbollah itself honouring the deal!

Why did Israel agree to the Ceasefire?

PM Netanyahu himself outlined three reasons why Israel agreed to the ceasefire. "The first reason is to focus on the Iranian threat," he said. "The second reason is to give our forces a breather and replenish stocks and the third reason is to separate the fronts and isolate Hamas. With Hezbollah out of the picture, Hamas is left on its own. We will increase our pressure on it and that will help us in our sacred mission of releasing our hostages." None of the three reasons indicate a victory over Hezbollah.

The Iran Factor

Iran is Hezbollah's main benefactor and its position on the deal has to be taken note of. Soon after the announcement of the deal, Iran welcomed the end of Israel's 'aggression' in Lebanon and its foreign ministry spokesman, Esmaeil Baghaei, stressed Iran's "firm support for the Lebanese government, nation and resistance". It is unlikely that Iran will take any overt or pro-active action to subvert the deal as it will leave it to the Hezbollah leadership to take a final call.

Looking Ahead

The ceasefire deal between Israel and Hezbollah is a welcome development. However, its success depends on a number of factors, many of which are questionable. The Biden administration has at last got something to take credit for from this war before they make way for Donald Trump. In case it succeeds, it is to their credit; if it falls after 60 days, it will left to Trump to clear the mess – this seems to be the message from Washington. What is however more important is how the deal is implemented and whether it can lead to a similar ceasefire deal in Gaza.

40

Surprise Attack into Syria: More than what Meets the Eye

After a bloody conflict lasting nearly two months, the news of an Israel-Hezbollah ceasefire agreement on 26 November brought a ray of hope for peace and safety for the people returning to their homes on either side of the border in Southern Lebanon. However, on the very next day, a surprise attack by multiple militant groups on northern Syria has once again brought the spectre of war and destruction back to the region. The attack which was launched by a combination of forces led by the Sunni militant group, Hayat Tahrir Al-Sham (HTS), took the Syrian army by surprise and by 29 November, the militant group had captured many areas in the north and northwest, including the important cities of Aleppo and Idlib.

The attack was like a blitz and launched simultaneously along two fronts, that is, Aleppo in the north and Idlib in the northwest. The HTS was supported by two other primary groups; the Syrian National Army (SNA) (it is also known as the Free Syrian Army) which is a Turkey-backed group and the Syrian Democratic Forces (SDF) which is largely made up of Kurdish fighters also known as the Peoples' Protection Units (YPG). The SDF is however considered a terrorist organization by Turkey as it has been fighting along with other Kurdish groups in Southern Turkey.

These rebel groups reportedly formed a loose coalition called the 'Military Operations Command', to launch this offensive into Syria. Over the next few days, the rebel groups encountered almost no resistance from Syrian forces as they took over important highways, airfields and townships. With more splinter groups opposed to the Assad regime and actively funded and supported by the West joining the rebels, the situation threatens to blow out of control in no time and poses the gravest threat in the past five years to the Assad regime.

HTS, which is leading the assault, was formed in 2012 under a different name, al-Nusra Front, and soon aligned with al-Qaeda. Driven by its jihadist ideology, it waged a deadly war in Syria against President Assad till the coalition of Russia-Iran-Syria finally broke the back of the rebels and took over control of most of the territory by the end of 2016. However, after 2016, Al-Nusra broke ties with al-Qaeda and took on the name of Hayat Tahrir al-Sham.

Vowing to crush the rebel attack, Syrian President Bashar Al Assad said "terrorists only know the language of force and it is the language we will crush them with". Iran, equally shocked as Syria if not more by the lightning offensive, was quick to stand in solidarity with its key ally in the region. Its foreign minister, Abbas Araghchi, visited Damascus and met President Assad. Expressing support, he said, "The Islamic Republic of Iran firmly supports the Syrian army and government".

The other key player in this conflict is Turkey, sharing the border along the north with Syria and which has borne the brunt of a refugee crisis from the Syrian civil war since 2011 as also security threats posed to its southern territory by Kurdish rebels operating from Syrian and Iraqi territory. Over the past few years, Turkey has been seeking to normalize ties with Syria. However, President Assad has insisted that Turkey should first withdraw its forces from northern Syria before any talks of normalization can proceed. Speaking on the current attack into Syria, Turkey's Foreign Minister, Hakan Fidan, said, "It would be a mistake at this time to try to explain the events in Syria by any foreign interference" adding that the Syrian government should first "reconcile with its own people and the legitimate opposition".

Why Now?

The attack has come at a time of great flux in the region. The war in Gaza has been going on for over 14 months and shows no signs of ending. Multiple efforts to negotiate a ceasefire have failed to bring an end to Israeli strikes on Gaza. As per official figures, more than 44,300 people have already been killed in Gaza with more than 70 percent of them being women and children. Meanwhile, in October this year, the war got extended to Southern Lebanon when Israeli forces launched a ground offensive in an effort to crush and finish Hezbollah's military capability in Southern Lebanon and push it northwards across the Litani River. Earlier, Israel had been greatly successful in eliminating the entire top leadership of Hamas and Hezbollah through targeted assassinations.

As a result of repeated bombing in Gaza and Southern Lebanon and the assassinations, both Hamas and Hezbollah have been rendered weak and extended. Meanwhile, Iran and Israel too engaged in a direct military conflict for the first time when both targeted each other's territory twice, first in April and thereafter in October. After the last Israeli strike into Iran on 26 October, when it claimed to have caused major damage to one of its nuclear sites also, Iran had vowed to retaliate, but that has still to materialize. The election of Donald Trump as the next president of the USA and its likely effect on the war in Gaza owing to his historically known very strong pro-Israeli stance has forced major recalculations in the region.

Plus, Syria itself is in a weak position, being targeted frequently by Israel and the USA over the past few months. While the USA focused on targeting pro-Iranian groups operating in Syria and launching attacks on US assets in the region, Israel has been bombing targets linked with Iranian support to the war in Gaza. Days before the rebel attack in Syria, on 12 November, the US military carried out strikes against nine targets associated with Iranian groups in Syria, which it claimed were in response to several attacks on US personnel in Syria. Israel, meanwhile, has bombed Syrian territory including Golan Heights with impunity claiming to take out supplies of weapons and material threatening its forces fighting the war in Gaza and Lebanon.

The Syrian armed forces, much weaker in comparison to the military and technological superiority of Israel as also the combined threat posed by rebel groups, has often leaned on its main benefactors, Iran and Russia, to safeguard its territorial integrity. But with Iran and its proxies stretched far in the war in Gaza and Russia having to pull out its troops and assets from Syria to fight the war in Ukraine, it was perhaps only a matter of time before a major threat manifested in Syria.

Why is Syria so Important to Iran?

Iran has been successfully waging a proxy war in the region, especially against Israel, by arming and supporting groups like the Hamas in Gaza, Hezbollah in Lebanon, Houthis in Yemen, Palestine Islamic Jihad in the West Bank and many other smaller groups in Syria and Iraq. It has been able to do so under the umbrella of 'Axis of Resistance' to have an indirect but uninterrupted influence across the Levant, that is, right upto the Mediterranean Sea in the west. Towards this, two countries become vitally important to it – Iraq and Syria.

Iraq has been a very loyal ally of Iran ever since the US war in Iraq ousted the Saddam Hussain regime in 2003 and effectively handed over a weak and unsure nation in Iran's lap. With Iran having a major say in government formation in Iraq, the state has had a Shia prime minister ever since. The current Prime Minister, Engineer Muhammad Shia' al-Sudani, a prominent Shia Iraqi politician, became prime minister in October 2022 after having been nominated by the Iran-backed Shia Coordination Framework, the largest parliamentary block in Iraq. Also, Iran's Islamic Revolutionary Guard Corps (IRGC) has a significant presence in Iraq and has key advisors to its armed forces.

As regards Syria, located closer to Israel and Lebanon, it is an even more vital link for Iran than Iraq. For this very reason, Iran has backed the Assad government to the hilt ever since massive protests broke out in Syria as a part of 'Arab Spring' in March 2011. Along with Russia, Iran ensured that the Assad regime survived and was even able to take back lost territory in Aleppo by the end of 2016.

Syria's contiguity with Lebanon has been the single biggest factor in the emergence of Hezbollah as the biggest military threat to Israel in its proximity. Syrian territory has been effectively used to supply weapons and equipment to Hezbollah over the years. Plus, many pro-Iranian groups have used Syrian territory to launch attacks not only on Israel but also on US assets in the region.

In addition to the military aspects, Syrian ports on the Mediterranean Sea have been used by Iran to export oil, often circumventing Western sanctions. Coupled with the Russian military bases in Syria and the only warm water naval base of Russia at Tartus on the Syrian coast, Syria has been a vital lynchpin in the Russia-Iran military game plan in the region.

Looking Ahead

The current conflict in Syria has come as a shock to Syria as well as Iran and Russia. Syria has faced much larger threats in the past decade but has survived, mainly due to active military support from Russia and Iran.

The situation is however grim for the Assad regime. It took four years of intense military engagement for Syria to take back Aleppo in 2016 but it lost it this time in merely four days. However, after the initial shock, the trio of Syria-Iran-Russia have regrouped quickly and have counter-attacked the rebels. Currently, the rebels have been halted well short of the key city of Hama and fierce battles are on.

China has extended full support to the Syrian regime and the GCC Summit held in Kuwait on 1 December 2024 unanimously pledged support to the Syrian regime. Iran has announced that it will deploy its military forces if required while Iraq has assured military support to crush the rebellion. The current war in Syria may not be the final chapter in the expanding war in the region, but it is definitely one that is of vital importance towards the final end to the war.

41

Assad Ousted in Syria

The story unfolding in Syria looks nothing short of a web thriller series, with every episode coming up with a new and unexpected twist, making it difficult to predict the final outcome. The current season in this thriller announced itself on 27 November when reports of a combined offensive by a group of militant groups moving into Syria from the north and north-west started filtering in. It was nothing new for this country which has been partly occupied by rebels and has been besieged by violence and turbulence for over 13 years. The Syrian army, supported by Iran and Russia, was expected to halt the assault and restore the status quo. However, the blitz-like offensive which was launched by a combination of forces led by the Sunni militant group, Hayat Tahrir Al-Sham (HTS), took the Syrian army by surprise and by 29 November, the militant groups had captured the important cities of Aleppo and Idlib. The Syrian army fought for a while, Russian war planes tried to ward off the dangerous march and the Iranians shared critical intelligence, but all went in vain when the assaulting militants entered Damascus on 8 December and President Bashar al Assad flew off to Russia, having sought asylum.

Why did Damascus Fall So Soon?

The attack caught the Syrian army as well as Iran and Russia by surprise. By the time, the Syrian army could regroup, it was all over. The meek surrender by it and many soldiers abandoning their weapons and running off to Iraq, definitely facilitated the quick demise of the Syrian regime. The role of Turkey in pushing and supporting one of the groups, the Syrian National Army (SNA), which is also known as the Free Syrian Army, was without doubt, a critical factor. Also, the role of Israel and the USA in providing critical intelligence as well as support to the other two major groups in the attack, that is, Syrian Democratic Forces (SDF) and the leader of the pack, Hayat Tahrir Al-Sham (HTS), cannot be understated.

The prevailing situation in the region too greatly helped in the timing and scope of the attack. The fact that it came merely a day after the Israel-Hezbollah ceasefire was announced on 26 November cannot be sheer coincidence.

The Fall was Easy, the Transition Promises to be Difficult

This is not the first time that the Syrian regime was put under this kind of pressure. The anti-regime protests in the form of 'Arab Spring', launched by people frustrated by the dictatorial regimes in the region, found their voice in Syria too when protests broke out in the form of uprisings in the Southern city of Daraa in March 2011. The regime was brutal in suppressing the revolt and the chemical weapons strike in the suburbs of Damascus in August 2013 took the Syrian conflict to yet another level of brutality.

The advent of the Islamic State (IS) in Iraq in 2013 and its subsequent spread into Syria meant that the Assad regime had to face a new and very powerful threat. With the northern areas of Aleppo and Idlib soon under IS control, Assad had to fight a battle for survival. In 2014, when the IS claimed roughly a third of Syrian territory, with Raqqa as its capital, it looked well and truly over for Assad. It took a sustained and intense air campaign by Russia, well supported by Iranian forces, to finally defeat the IS in Syria and help Assad reclaim most of the lost territory.

This time around, however, it seems that Assad has given up hope of recovering from the assault and has sought refuge in Russia. The HTS-led group has appointed Mohammed al-Bashir as a caretaker prime minister on 10 December. Al-Bashir is the head of the HTS-led Syrian Salvation Government (SSG) in the northwest area of Idlib. As per the announcement, he will lead a transitional Syrian government until 1 March 2025, till a more permanent solution is found.

The easy part, the overthrow of Assad, is now over. What is the plan now? With over 50 years of Assad family rule as the sole leader (dictator), no political parties or organizations have survived or evolved. In such a scenario, there are only two possible options for the future of governance in Syria. Either it is a technocratic set-up, with the leader as well as ministers made up of technocrats or the HTS leader Abu Mohammad al Jolani takes over the reins himself. Neither of the options look appealing for the long term.

As regards a technocratic government, it can best be an interim solution. The experiments with interim technocratic governments have not worked in either Libya or Egypt or even Tunisia, all of which bore the brunt of Arab Spring protests and the overthrow of their rulers. The fragmented structure of societies in the region, lack of democratic institutions and each warring group wanting a pie of its own often makes it very difficult for a technocratic government to survive and succeed.

The second option presents an even more dangerous scenario. If Jolani, either independently or in concert with other prominent rebel groups, takes over the country's governance, it is fraught with danger. One has to remember that the HTS is the new avatar of Al Nusra which has roots in the IS and al Qaeda. The IS has vowed to create the Islamic Caliphate and enforce strict implementation of Sharia in the land across Iraq and Syria. Although Jolani has voiced conciliatory notes by announcing that his regime will not enforce any dress or conduct code on women, form an inclusive government for the country and grant amnesty to soldiers who lay down their arms, past precedents in Syria, Iraq, Libya, etc., which were taken over by similar ideologically-driven groups, do not inspire confidence.

Also, Syria, by its character and geography, is a hugely fragmented country, with Sunnis, Alawites, Shias, Christians, Druze and Kurds distributed across different regions, each hugely populated. For over 50 years, the Assad family from the Alawites clan, comprising only 12 percent of the population, had ruled Syria, often through brutal oppression of other demographics. Iran supported the regime not only because it was from the Shia sect of Islam but also because Syria suited it perfectly in its geopolitical designs across the region. Can and will the HTS that is predominantly a Sunni group, be able to bridge the differences between various communities, is a big question.

The role of external players will also be crucial in new Syria. Israel has taken advantage of the chaos and already taken over vast swathes of territory along the demilitarized buffer zone in the Golan Heights in the south in order to create a buffer zone for itself from any future threats. PM Netanyahu has called the ouster of Assad as a 'historic day for the Middle East'. However, he too has cautioned that the 'situation offers great opportunity but is also fraught with significant dangers'. With the HTS ideologically aligned to the cause of independent Palestine, it will be interesting to see how the HTS and Israel face-off shapes up in the future.

Iran is the other principal player in Syria. Despite being at odds with Sunni groups like HTS, IS and Al Nusra, inputs indicate that it has already opened channels of communication with the HTS. If Iran and HTS collaborate, things could shape up very differently in Syria. Remember, even in Afghanistan, Iran is one of the very few countries, which despite being adversely affected by Taliban brutality in the past, had kept the channel of communications open after USA-led forces fled Afghanistan in August 2021.

How Russia plays its cards in the transition will also be equally important to watch. Despite granting asylum to Assad, it is likely that Russia will open some kind of communication with the new regime to retain the right to operate its naval bases in the Tartus and Khmeimim airbase. Both of them are critical for Russian operations in the Mediterranean Sea and the continent of Africa.

The extremely poor economic situation of Syria will be a huge challenge for any future governance structure. As per the World Bank, more than a decade of conflict has worsened Syria's dire economic situation and has led to a dramatic deterioration in the welfare of Syrian households. As per data of 2022, poverty affects 69 per cent of the population and extreme poverty reached 27 per cent, up from a negligible level in 2009. Reliance on food imports, although already an issue prior to 2011, has also intensified with the conflict. In 2023, the Syrian pound depreciated substantially by 141 per cent against the US dollar, while consumer price inflation is estimated to have risen by 93 per cent, exacerbated by government subsidy cuts. With more than a year under conflict due to the ongoing war in Gaza, the real GDP is projected to contract by 1.5 per cent in 2024, extending the 1.2 per cent decline in 2023. All this presents a very grim picture for any future government.

Looking Ahead

The regime change has finally taken place in Syria. People in the streets are rejoicing and hundreds of them living life as refugees are returning home. Assad and his oppressive regime are gone. What is filling the vacuum is however not clear. Despite announcements of its good intentions, an HTS-led government cannot be trusted to heed the voice and needs of the people. Plus, internal pressures from various groups in society, jostling for power between various militant groups and external interests from countries like Iran, Israel and Russia as well as the USA will not let the new regime settle easily and soon.

42

Can HTS and Jolani Prevent the Fragmentation of Syria

The Syrian surprise, the latest episode of the war in Gaza, has now spread its tentacles and its repercussions threaten to alter the landscape of the region forever.

The Assad chapter is over and there is a spontaneous outflow of emotion and cheer on the street, having been freed of the dictator. While there is hope of a better life in the future, there are apprehensions too. The HTS leader Abu Mohammad al Jolani, who is now the de facto ruler of Syria, has a dangerous past, as the HTS is the new avatar of the Al Nusra Front, an offshoot of Islamic State (IS) which was known for its brutality and terror. The IS had vowed to create the Islamic Caliphate and enforce strict implementation of the Sharia in the land across Iraq and Syria although Jolani is trying to project a new and more moderate image by announcing that his regime will not enforce any dress or conduct code on women. It will form an inclusive government for the country and grant amnesty to soldiers who lay down their arms. Yet, past precedents of similar experience in Iraq, Libya, etc., do instil fear and apprehensions.

In the midst of the Assad exit and the HTS takeover in Damascus, what however escaped attention initially is the opportunity that many external players are exploiting to quietly chip away Syria's territory while confusion and chaos still prevails.

Israel Captures Golan, Closes in on Damascus

One of the first to take advantage of the chaos was Israel. It immediately undertook a two-pronged strategy in Syria. On one hand, it sent its forces into the Golan Heights to capture more territory and on the second, it launched over 350 airstrikes across Syria within the first 48 hours, targeting key military bases, airfields and naval vessels. It claims to have destroyed Syria's air force fleet, air defences and the naval fleet completely, while also taking out known weapon depots and suspected chemical weapons storage depots. It also claimed to have destroyed almost 90 per cent of Syria's known surface-to-air missiles, thus ending any threat to the Israeli Air Force in any future engagements. Acknowledging it, Israel's Defence Minister Israel Katz said that the operation to destroy the Syrian fleet had been a 'great success' and added that the IDF was aiming to 'destroy strategic capabilities that threaten the State of Israel'.

On the other hand, Israel, which is already occupying Golan Heights illegally, having annexed it in 1981, for the first time entered even the demilitarized buffer zone in the Golan Heights, a region established after the 1973 Middle East war. The UN immediately called Israel's move into the demilitarized zone a violation of the 1974 disengagement agreement between Israel and Syria. However Israeli officials stated that their incursion was a 'limited and temporary' measure, and described the buffer zone operation as essential to create a 'defence zone free of weapons and terror threats in southern Syria.' However, the most important capture in this operation has to be Syria's highest peak, Mount Hermon, which is the highest place in the region, giving Israel a direct look into Lebanon and Syria. With reports of Israeli forces closing in on areas in the south almost 25 kilometres short of Damascus, Israeli forces would be tempted to retain what has been captured for keeps.

Two statements, both coming from PM Netanyahu's office, spell out clearly Israel's intention – of not vacating what has been captured. The first was the statement that the cabinet had unanimously approved a budget of over 40-million-shekel ($11 million) to encourage demographic growth in the Golan, "out of a desire to double the population of the Golan". This was followed by Prime Minister Benjamin Netanyahu's statement that "strengthening the Golan is strengthening the State of Israel, and it is especially important at this time. We will continue to hold onto it, cause it to blossom, and settle in it". With reports of Druze majority areas in Southern Syria adjoining Golan asking to be 'annexed by Israel', Israel may be further emboldened to hold on to what has been captured.

Turkey Captures 'Buffer Zone' in the North

Turkey, which shares almost 900 km of border along the north with Syria, has borne the maximum brunt of the Syrian civil war since 2011. The influx into Turkey of almost 3 million refugees escaping the civil war as well as the security threats posed to its south by the Kurdish rebels operating from Syria posed a constant threat to it. Turkey considers the Kurdish rebels to be a part of the larger

Kurdish movement and an extension of the Turkey-based separatist Kurdistan Workers' Party (KWP) which has been labelled as a terrorist group by Turkey.

Over the past few years, concerned by these threats originating from Syria, Turkey has been seeking to normalize ties with it. However, President Assad had insisted that Turkey should first withdraw its forces from northern Syria before any talks of normalization can proceed. It is also quite clear that Turkey played a major role in the current rebel offensive which overthrew the Assad regime. The Syrian National Army (SNA), which is backed by Turkey, soon over-ran territory in the north-east including Tal Rifaat town and Manbij city which were previously under the control of Kurdish rebels and the SDF. It has established a significant military foothold in the north, capturing areas such as the city of Afrin and parts of Aleppo. Turkey is keen to retain the captured territory along its south as a buffer zone.

Kurdish Rebels may want to Break Free and Join Kurdistan

The Syrian Democratic Front or the SDF may have aligned with the HTS and SNA to overthrow Assad but it does not fully align with the aims and ideologies of either. It has been fighting the Turkey-backed SNA for years and despite some setbacks in the north, has been able to extend its influence to the south almost upto the Euphrates River, taking the entire Northeast Syria under its control. If the HTS-led government is not able to align with the SDF in the future, the possibility of the SDF breaking free with a large area in the north-east and joining hands with Kurdish forces in Iraq cannot be ruled out.

What About the Alawites?

Alawites, who constitute a mere 12 percent of the population, are concentrated in a small area along the Mediterranean coast in the areas of Tartus and Latakia. With the Assad family belonging to the Alawite clan, they have benefitted the most over the last decades by retaining all important positions in the government and big businesses. With Assad's ouster and the Sunni movement led by the HTS taking over the reins, the possibility of Alawites wanting to break free and forming their own small autonomous enclave, possibly with Russian help, cannot be ruled out.

Iran and Russia Factor

The biggest hit that has been taken due to the sudden collapse of the Assad regime is by Iran and Russia. Iran, already reeling under a series of setbacks in the war in

Gaza due to heavy losses to its proxies, Hamas and Hezbollah, seems to have been delivered a knockout punch with Syria going out of its hands. Similarly, for Russia, the loss of Syria and being forced to vacate its military bases along the Mediterranean coast is a severe blow to its military and geopolitical outreach in the region.

Return of the Islamic State (IS)?

The HTS has its roots in the IS. Already, there are reports of the IS sensing an opportunity, and mustering its cadres in Iraq and Eastern Syria. If the IS and HTS rejoin hands, the whole scenario could turn out differently. A return of the IS in Syria and Iraq would not only be a threat to them but also to the entire region as such, including US assets and bases in Southern Syria and Iraq.

Looking Ahead

The Syrian debacle is yet to fully unfold. A number of external players are pushing to drive home the advantage. If 'winner takes all' is permitted, we might just see a fragmented and unstable Syria and a growing threat of unrest and terror in the region.

Turkey and Israel may rejoice in the short term, having captured major territory as a 'buffer zone'; however, developments in the future may well prove that such encroachments become the fundamental cause for unrest and conflict. In the midst of all this, the greatest challenge for the HTS and Jolani, who are trying to put up a moderate and modern outlook, will be retaining the integrity of Syria.

SECTION VI

Ceasefire Efforts: Failing to Bridge the Trust Gap

43

Seven Months into the War: Ceasefire Continues to Elude Gaza

It is May 2024 and the war in Gaza has completed seven months of hostilities. It has become the longest war in Gaza since Israel vacated Gaza unilaterally in 2005. During this period, Israel has pounded Gaza relentlessly, killing over 34,500 Palestinians including nearly 13,500 children. More than 77,500 have been seriously injured and perhaps maimed for life. Hundreds of bodies remain buried under rubble and with the onset of summer, the stench of death and decay pervades over the area. Medical aid, food and water have been severely restricted and most international aid agencies have been targeted and prevented from delivering life-saving aid. Despite a UN Security Council resolution of 25 March calling for an immediate ceasefire and unconditional release of hostages, neither of the warring parties has been able to come to a common understanding.

The Ceasefire Deal

In the past week or so, there has been hectic activity in an attempt to forge a consensus on a ceasefire deal. US Secretary of State Blinken was on his seventh visit to the region since the onset of the war and held wide-ranging discussions with Arab leaders in Riyadh as well as PM Netanyahu in Israel on 29-30 April. At the end of it, a fresh ceasefire proposal was presented. Hamas agreed to it, much to the surprise of Israel which had hoped that Hamas would reject it standing firm on its stand that there cannot be a ceasefire unless it involves a complete end to hostilities and withdrawal of all IDF troops from Gaza.

The deal presented on 30 April involved the release of 33 hostages by Hamas during the first stage of a 40-day ceasefire. These would include women, female soldiers, elderly hostages and people injured or ill. The deal included the release of thousands of Palestinian prisoners in Israeli jails and the return of displaced Palestinians from the south of the Gaza Strip to the north. The deal also envisaged a second phase of 40 days when the rest of the hostages, including male civilians and soldiers, as well as the bodies of others would be released in return for an end of hostilities and return of Palestinian prisoners in Israel. Hopes were soon dashed when, despite the insistence of Blinken, PM Netanyahu rejected the deal and stated, "We will enter Rafah and will eliminate the Hamas battalions there, with or without a deal, in order to achieve total victory."

As Israel continued its preparations for a ground offensive in Rafah, Egypt, Qatar and the USA came up with another proposal on 6 May which slightly modified the terms of the previous proposal. The proposed deal now comprises three phases of 42 days each. In the first, Hamas would release 33 hostages in return for the release of Palestinians from Israeli jails. Every week, three hostages would be released. This would include the release of women, female soldiers, the elderly and the sick. Moreover, Israel would allow the return of displaced people and permit free movement of Palestinians from south to north Gaza. In the second phase of 42 days, there would be a complete halt to military activity and withdrawal of the IDF from Gaza. In the final phase, there would be an exchange of the remaining hostages and bodies as also a plan for reconstruction of Gaza, to be overseen by international observers.

For the second time in five days, Hamas conveyed its acceptance to the deal leading to celebrations and relief in Rafah and the rest of Gaza. The joy was however short-lived as a statement from PM Netanyahu's office late at night on 6 May stated, "Hamas's latest offer was far from Israel's essential requirements." It added that the war cabinet had decided unanimously to push ahead with an Israel Defence Forces (IDF) operation in Rafah "in order to apply military pressure on Hamas, with the goal of making progress in the freeing of hostages and the other war aims."

US President Joe Biden spoke to Netanyahu over the phone on 6 May and reiterated his strong opposition to an Israeli offensive in Rafah, but Netanyahu doesn't appear to be listening. With this, yet another flicker of hope has been dashed as the 1.3 million people cramped up in Rafah await their fate as Israel ramps up its preparations for a ground offensive there.

Previous Attempts for a Ceasefire

There have been multiple attempts for a ceasefire ever since the onset of the war. The first success came in November 2023 when both the warring parties agreed to a humanitarian truce of four days from 24 November to exchange hostages, primarily women, children and the elderly. As a part of the deal, at least 50 hostages, women and children, were released by Hamas and 150 Palestinian prisoners from Israeli jails. The truce was extended twice before Israel resumed its operations on 1 December.

Another concrete proposal was presented in Paris on 28 January. It proposed a ceasefire of six weeks coupled with the first phase of civilian hostage exchanges, with three Palestinian prisoners held by Israel released for each civilian hostage returned from Gaza. The ceasefire could be extended for a longer period later. Israel, however, voiced concerns over 'some conditions that were not acceptable'. The proposal was offered to Hamas, which came up with its own counter-proposal on 7 February for a ceasefire of 135 days during which all hostages would be set free, Israel would withdraw all its troops from Gaza, and an agreement would eventually be reached on ending the war. Benjamin Netanyahu dismissed it immediately, calling it 'delusional'.

Days before the onset of Ramadan on 11 March, another attempt for a ceasefire was made by the USA, Qatar and Egypt, proposing an agreement in which Hamas would release Israeli captives in return for a six-week ceasefire, the release of some Palestinian prisoners, and more aid to Gaza. Hamas, however, dismissed it stating that it wants a permanent ceasefire instead of a six-week pause and a 'complete withdrawal' of Israeli forces from Gaza, along with the release of Palestinian prisoners in Israeli prisons.

On 25 March, the United Nations Security Council (UNSC) succeeded in getting a resolution passed which demanded an immediate ceasefire between Israel and Hamas and the immediate, unconditional release of all hostages. The USA abstained while the remaining 14 council members voted in favour of the resolution. Israel reacted immediately with PM Netanyahu alleging that the USA had "abandoned its policy in the UN" and was harming the war effort and the measures for the release of Israeli hostages in Hamas's custody. Under Israeli pressure, the USA immediately retracted and came out with a statement that 'the UN Resolution is non-binding' and that Israel can continue what it is doing in Gaza', making a mockery of the whole process in the UNSC.

Previously, the UNSC failed thrice in getting a resolution passed on a ceasefire in the Gaza war. As early as on 18 October, the UNSC failed to pass a resolution even as the humanitarian situation in Gaza was fast deteriorating. The resolution failed as the USA exercised its veto.

Again on 8 December, the USA vetoed a UNSC resolution calling for an immediate ceasefire in the Gaza Strip, arguing that Israel has the right to defend itself against Hamas attacks. The vote was 13 to 1, with Britain abstaining.

On 20 February too, the USA cast its veto for the third time against a UNSC resolution calling for an immediate ceasefire in the Gaza Strip, saying that it feared that a resolution could disrupt hostage negotiations.

Now What?

With this latest ceasefire proposal being snubbed by Israel on 7 May, there is a sense of inevitability about the ground offensive in Rafah. Recent developments in the area clearly indicate that the IDF is back in the area and is 'preparing the battlefield' for the Rafah operations. Israel estimates that Hamas's higher leadership and four remaining battalions are entrenched in Rafah.

On 6 May, the Israeli military issued orders for the evacuation of 100,000 Palestinians in eastern Rafah and there are reports of Israeli tanks entering Eastern Rafah in the early hours of 7 May and taking control of the Rafah Crossing on the Palestinian side, opposite Egypt.

Is There Any Hope for Peace and Ceasefire?

The war in Gaza has undergone a number of ups and downs. The Iran-Israel spat in April almost brought the region to an escalated full-blown conflict. However, both decided to call it quits, at least for the present. However, with Iran shedding its 'strategic patience', any false trigger in the future could lead to massive retaliation.

As for the current situation, the Rafah offensive will be the final nail in the coffin. With Israel moving troops and tanks into Rafah and dismissing the ceasefire proposal, it is a matter of time before a full-scale offensive is launched.

If Egypt retaliates, not only will it jeopardise the 1979 Peace Treaty with Israel, but will make it very difficult for other nations in the region not to act. Till now, except for Egypt, Qatar, Turkey and obviously Iran, other nations including Saudi Arabia and the UAE have maintained a 'stand-off position' on the war.

If the Rafah offensive goes through, three things are certain. Firstly, there will be casualties in thousands, not hundreds. Secondly, Gaza and the 'two-state solution' will be lost for a long time and thirdly, the one thread, 'State of Palestine' which has been a major point of convergence and solidarity in the Muslim world will be lost forever.

44

Eight Months into the War: Biden's Ceasefire Deal Offers Hope

The war in Gaza completed eight months on 7 June and is already the longest conflict in Gaza since Israel's unilateral withdrawal from there in 2005. In these eight months, many red lines have been crossed. In the midst of all this, the people in Gaza have suffered the most, with more than 36,000 killed in Israeli strikes including over 15,000 women and children and over 1.5 million displaced from their homes. Estimates suggest that there might another more than 10,000 dead buried under the rubble of destroyed buildings in Gaza.

Repeated attempts to end the war through a ceasefire have failed except for a brief humanitarian truce in November last year. There is however a fresh glimmer of hope as President Biden announced a comprehensive ceasefire proposal on 31 May, which he said could bring about "the cessation of hostilities permanently" in Gaza.

Biden's Proposal

What is the new proposal and how is it different from the previous ones? The plan proposes a progressive three-phase ceasefire, which Biden said will "bring all the hostages home, ensure Israel's security, create a better day after in Gaza without Hamas in power, and set the stage for a political settlement that provides a better future for Israelis and Palestinians alike." Phase1 of the plan seeks an immediate 'full and complete ceasefire' lasting six weeks. During this period, the IDF will withdraw from all populated areas of Gaza, Hamas will release a number of hostages including women, the elderly, the wounded and several US citizens, in exchange for the release of Palestinian prisoners held in Israel. This phase will continue even if negotiations last longer than the planned six weeks. During this time, humanitarian assistance would surge with 600 trucks carrying aid into Gaza every day.

The second phase calls for the IDF to fully withdraw from Gaza in exchange for the release of all remaining hostages, including male soldiers. The third and final phase is for a major reconstruction of Gaza to include rebuilding its cities, homes, schools and hospitals that were destroyed by war. Regional Arab countries and the international community would contribute and participate in it in a manner that does not allow Hamas to re-arm.

PM Netanyahu's office initially confirmed that the text of Biden's proposal had been accepted by it but the very next day it put out a statement that Israel would not agree to a ceasefire unless Hamas's military and governing capabilities are totally destroyed, all hostages are freed and Gaza no longer poses a threat to Israel.

How is the Biden plan different from the previous ceasefire proposals? On the face of it, it looks quite similar to the previous proposals presented.

The previous plan presented on 30 April also envisioned a truce of six weeks and exchange of hostages. Only, instead of three phases in the current proposal, the previous plan had two phases.

Israel's Conflicting Choices

A number of previous ceasefire proposals as well as the current proposal which was 'offered by Israel' present Israel with two very different and conflicting choices. On one hand, the ceasefire proposals promise the safe return of Israeli hostages in Hamas captivity but, on the other hand, they also present the possibility that Hamas could regroup once the IDF withdraws from Gaza and could therefore pose another terror or military threat in the future.

Within Netanyahu's war cabinet too, there are two camps which seek conflicting outcomes. It is however clear that none of the ceasefire proposals offer what Israel would ideally want – return of all hostages while the IDF continues to hunt down and eliminate Hamas combat capabilities completely. With each passing day, the number of hostages remaining alive in Hamas captivity is reducing. On 4 June, IDF reported that four more Israeli citizens in Hamas captivity had died and now the estimated hostages alive has come down from 132 to 120.

As the war drags on, Netanyahu faces a difficult choice. On one hand, ministers in his cabinet like Finance Minister Bezalel Smotrich and National Security Minister Itamar Ben-Gvir are adamant that the military operations should continue till Hamas threats are completely eliminated. However, on the other hand, Benny

Gantz, minister in the war cabinet, has issued an ultimatum to Netanyahu to end the war soon, demanding an agreed-upon vision for the Gaza conflict that would include stipulating who might rule the territory after Hamas's defeat, and warning that he would quit the coalition if there are no concrete answers by 8 June.

The IDF Chief of Staff, General Herzi Halevi and the Defence Minister Yoav Gallant too have openly criticized Netanyahu over his indecision on who will govern Gaza after Hamas is defeated.

Netanyahu himself is not known to be keen on any ceasefire proposal which leaves the 'job of finishing Hamas incomplete', even if it comes at the cost of the lives of hostages. He perhaps sees this as the only way of remaining in power. Israel's National Security Adviser, Tzachi Hanegbi, reportedly told a group of families of hostages on 30 May that the government wasn't ready to sign a deal to bring all hostages home and there was no Plan B. President Biden too, in an interview on 4 June, hinted that there is "every reason" to think Israeli Prime Minister Benjamin Netanyahu is prolonging Israel's war against Hamas in Gaza for political gain.

Looking Ahead

The current ceasefire proposal announced by President Biden may be consigned to the files like many previous ones, till there is a clear decision that Israel takes on ending the war and getting the hostages back. However, if it chooses the other alternative of chasing the elusive goal of eliminating Hamas from the face of the Earth, the war may drag on, people in Gaza will continue to get killed and there would always be the overhanging threat of the conflict getting out of control should any tactical mistake on the battlefield result in a strategic blunder and draw in more players. There is unfortunately, no third choice.

45

Gaza Braces for a Tough winter as the USA Exercises Veto and Ceasefire Talks Freeze

Donald Trump has been elected US President.

Meanwhile, the war in Gaza, into its 15th month, rages on as repeated attempts to bring about a ceasefire and end the hostilities continue to fail. In the latest such effort through the UN Security Council, a resolution sponsored by the E-10 (elected non-permanent members to the Security Council) on 20 November 2024 failed as the USA vetoed the resolution demanding an 'immediate, unconditional and permanent' ceasefire in the Gaza Strip. While the 14 other members of the Council voted in favour, the veto by the USA meant that yet another resolution failed to pass muster. This is the fourth such veto by the USA in the ongoing war in Gaza, the previous three being drafts presented and debated; drafts S/2023/773 of 18 October 2023, S/2023/970 of 8 December 2023 and S/2024/173 of 20 February 2024.

Besides a call for an immediate ceasefire, the current text also demanded that the parties 'fully, unconditionally, and without delay' implement all the provisions of Security Council Resolution 2735 (2024) of June 2024, in which a three-stage plan for ending hostilities in Gaza had been endorsed. The current text also included the demand for release of hostages, exchange of Palestinian prisoners, the return of the remains of hostages who have been killed, the return of Palestinian civilians to their homes in Gaza – including in the north – and a full withdrawal of Israeli forces from Gaza. The draft also reiterated the primary role of the UN relief agency for Palestine refugees (UNRWA) as the backbone of the humanitarian response in Gaza. Justifying its veto, Robert Wood, the deputy US envoy to the UN said that "we could not support an unconditional ceasefire that failed to release the hostages."

This latest attempt comes in a series of recent setbacks towards securing a ceasefire and ending this bloody conflict which has already resulted in over 43,700 people killed in Gaza, over 3,000 killed in Lebanon and over 2 million people internally displaced multiple times over the past year.

The decision by Qatar to withdraw from the ceasefire talks too has to be counted as a major setback as it was acting as a major interlocutor between Hamas and the West. On 9 November, Qatar announced that it had suspended its mediation efforts between Hamas and Israel until the parties show "their willingness and seriousness" to end the war in Gaza. It was soon followed by reports that Qatar, under pressure from the USA, had also asked Hamas to leave Qatar. Media reports also indicated that Hamas has moved its offices temporarily to Turkey. However on 18 November, Qatar Foreign Ministry clarified that with the negotiations halted, the Hamas leaders had moved to other locations in the region but their office has not yet been permanently closed. The withdrawal of Qatar means that any slim hope of an early ceasefire now looks even more remote as it was mainly Qatar which had direct access to the Hamas leadership during the negotiations.

Independent of the UN Security Council resolutions, the USA too has been actively pursuing an early end to the war. Antony Blinken, the US Secretary of State, has visited the region 11 times to somehow get a consensus on ending the war.

The election of Donald Trump as the next US President too could be a contributing factor in the failing talks and intensifying operations in Gaza. Trump, who is opposed to wars but is very strongly aligned with Israel, has reportedly given a green signal to Israel to 'finish the job' before he assumes the presidency on 20 January 2025. This means that Israel and Prime Minister Netanyahu have got another window of two months to conduct operations and strikes with impunity before Trump takes over and calls it 'over', claiming credit for ending the war. Perhaps endorsing this view, a spokesperson for the Republican Party, Elizabeth Pipko, in a press interaction on 7 November said that President-elect Donald Trump wants to see Israel wrap up its war soon, with decisive victories.

The internal dynamics within Israel too indicate that prospects for an early ceasefire have been buried, at least for some time. The biggest indication towards this is the sacking of the defence minister, Yoav Gallant, on 5 November. Gallant was pushing for a ceasefire deal and bringing the remaining hostages back. Adding fuel to the fire and pushing the ceasefire prospects further back, on 12 November, Israel's Finance Minister Bezalel Smotrich called for an Israeli annexation of the occupied West Bank and added that he has already ordered his department to prepare for this annexation. At a press conference, Smotrich said that "the time has come to apply [Israeli] sovereignty to the settlements in Judea and Samaria (the biblical term by which some Israelis refer to the occupied West Bank)." A day earlier, Israel's newly-appointed Foreign Minister, Gideon Saar, described the demand for a Palestinian state as 'not realistic' shortly after Palestinian president Mahmud Abbas had reiterated his demand for a 'sovereign' country.

Hamas too is unwilling to bow down. Despite heavy losses in the conflict, almost complete blockade of Gaza and losses to its top leadership, it has rejected any proposal for a temporary halt to the war and has reiterated its insistence on a lasting ceasefire. "The idea of a temporary pause in the war, only to resume aggression later, is something we have already expressed our position on. Hamas supports a permanent end to the war, not a temporary one," said a senior Hamas official, Taher al-Nunu, in an interaction with the press recently.

Various ceasefire proposals too have failed to find any traction. The latest, put forth by Egypt last month, proposed a two-day ceasefire to begin with. During this period, four Israeli hostages held by Hamas were proposed to be exchanged for some Palestinian prisoners held in Israeli jails. The temporary truce would allow much-needed humanitarian aid to be delivered to the Gaza Strip and this 'small deal' could then continue with renewed negotiations over a more comprehensive hostage and ceasefire agreement. The proposal however failed to appeal to either Israel or Hamas.

Looking Ahead

The failed UN Security Council resolution is despairing for hundreds and thousands trapped in Gaza who fear death day and night. It also lays bare the futility and absolute helplessness of the international community to bring an end to the war, mostly due to the strong positions taken by one or more of the 'Big Five' at the UN.

As winter sets in, hopes for an early ceasefire are dying. The rare occurrence of snowfall in the Saudi Arabian desert a few days ago and the prospect of the remaining population in Gaza braving the winter in tents and temporary accommodation present a fearful reality. As Israel looks to make use of the window of two months before Trump takes over the presidency, Gaza looks doomed to suffer a stiff and bloody winter.

46

Hamas Needs to Make an Intelligent Choice

It is January 2025 and the Trump era is about to begin!

The West Asian region has been in a fast-forward mode for the past few months. Events and developments that are likely to have a long-term impact on the peace and security of the region have occurred in double quick time. If the rapid fall of the Assad regime in Syria in a matter of 12 days in December 2024 shocked the world, the heavy losses that Iran's proxies in the region have suffered, especially Hamas and Hezbollah, have put Iran on the back foot and have forced it to re-calibrate its regional strategy. Meanwhile, Israel has been on a roll with most of the military threat on its borders eliminated and the vital link between Iran and its proxy, that is, Syria, taken out of Iran's sphere of influence.

Ceasefire Talks in Gaza and Main Sticking Points

Amid all these rapid developments, the war in Gaza, which has triggered these tectonic geopolitical shifts in the region, rages on. Despite numerous attempts to negotiate a ceasefire, it remains elusive, with Hamas and Israel sticking to their 'non-negotiable' issues. Meanwhile, Donald Trump, who is set to take over as US President on 20 January, has made it very clear that the ceasefire should be negotiated before he takes office. In a press interaction on 7 January, he said, "If those hostages aren't back by the time I get into office, all hell will break out in the Middle East. And it will not be good for Hamas. And it will not be good, frankly, for anyone. All hell will break out."

In the hope of a timely deal, the negotiations in Doha continue. US Secretary of State Anthony Blinken is hopeful that the US-Qatar-Egypt trio will be able to clinch the deal as the Biden Administration's last hurrah. On 6 January, Hamas released a list of 34 hostages that it offered to free in the first lot as part of a ceasefire deal. The list included 10 women and 11 men between the ages of 55 and 80, as well as two children and 11 other ailing male hostages. Israel was quick to dismiss the list, saying there was nothing new in it and that Hamas had failed to include details of the living or dead in it.

In addition, there are significant gaps yet to be bridged. Among the most significant differences are how the war is proposed to be ended and the withdrawal of Israeli Defence Forces (IDF) from Gaza. While Hamas is insisting that the ceasefire deal should end the war and should be accompanied by the complete withdrawal of the IDF from the Gaza Strip, Israel is thinking differently. For Israel, getting back all its hostages is of primary importance in any deal, while it should retain some of its forces in the Gaza Strip. As per inputs, Israel has offered to vacate the Rafah Crossing and the Philadelphi Corridor as part of the deal but is not ready to vacate the deployment of forces in the Netzarim Corridor, which is a kilometre-wide line running across the Gaza Strip, dividing North and South Gaza. The IDF has also strengthened its presence in the corridor over the past few months, expanded the buffer zone around it, and constructed concrete outposts for soldiers, a clear sign that the IDF presence there will last for a long time. There are also differences in the timelines of the ceasefire, monitoring mechanisms as well as details of Palestinian prisoners to be freed.

What are Hamas's Options?

With Southern Lebanon, West Bank, and Syria sorted, Israel is clearly in an ascendant position. In recent weeks, it has intensified its military strikes in Gaza to put more pressure on Hamas. On the other hand, Hamas is now fighting the war alone as opposition to Israel from all the other sides is virtually eliminated. Plus, with the ouster of the Syrian regime, the vital link between Iran and Hamas too is broken, which makes it harder for Iran to replenish supplies to Hamas.

In such a situation, Hamas would do well to consider the following issues while negotiating a ceasefire deal:

- How long can Hamas keep fighting Israel in the ongoing war, keeping in mind the heavy losses that its cadres have suffered, as well as mounting civilian casualties? Plus, with most of its senior leadership eliminated, can it risk fighting to the last man?
- With every passing day and week, the number of hostages alive will keep reducing, with many succumbing to ill health or cross-fire. Once the number of hostages reduces significantly, the only bargaining chip with Hamas would go.
- Iran is no longer in a position to support Hamas militarily or financially.
- Trump 2.0 is likely to support Israel in all its moves in the war, and a free hand to Israel could spell further trouble for Hamas.

- Israel has made it clear that the IDF will not vacate the Gaza Strip, and Hamas does not have the capacity to ensure anything contrary to it.
- There is little support for the continuation of the war in Gaza in the Arab world.
- Hezbollah, a key ally of Hamas, was supporting the war and fighting Israel in the north. In November last year, it however, was offered the Hezbollah-Israel ceasefire on terms ultimately favouring Israel, and yet it agreed to it.
- The most critical issue that triggered the Gaza war, that is, the Palestine issue, looks dead and buried, at least in the current times. Hamas and other groups have done what could be done to bring the issue back to the front page over the past year. Beyond this, it is not a fight that Hamas can fight alone.

Hamas, therefore, does not have much leverage left to negotiate with Israel in this war. Even on the hostage issue, PM Netanyahu has repeatedly made it clear that it cannot be a restricting factor in Israel achieving its military goals in Gaza.

Looking Ahead

The ceasefire deal is bound to come about sooner than later. Hamas has to choose between accepting a deal when all is almost lost and when it can tactically withdraw and live to fight another day. Hezbollah was under a similar situation, having lost all its top leadership and most of its military capabilities. It was offered a harsh deal, yet it agreed to it. Almost two months down the line in Lebanon, the fragile ceasefire holds although Israel has not shown any indications of pulling out its forces from Southern Lebanon yet. Hezbollah meanwhile, has withdrawn to the North and is trying to regroup and rebuild.

Hamas in the Gaza Strip is in a similar situation. A ceasefire deal now, even under unfavourable conditions, may look like a defeat, but it would give it space and time to regroup and plan for the future. In the long run, it could well turn out to be an intelligent choice.

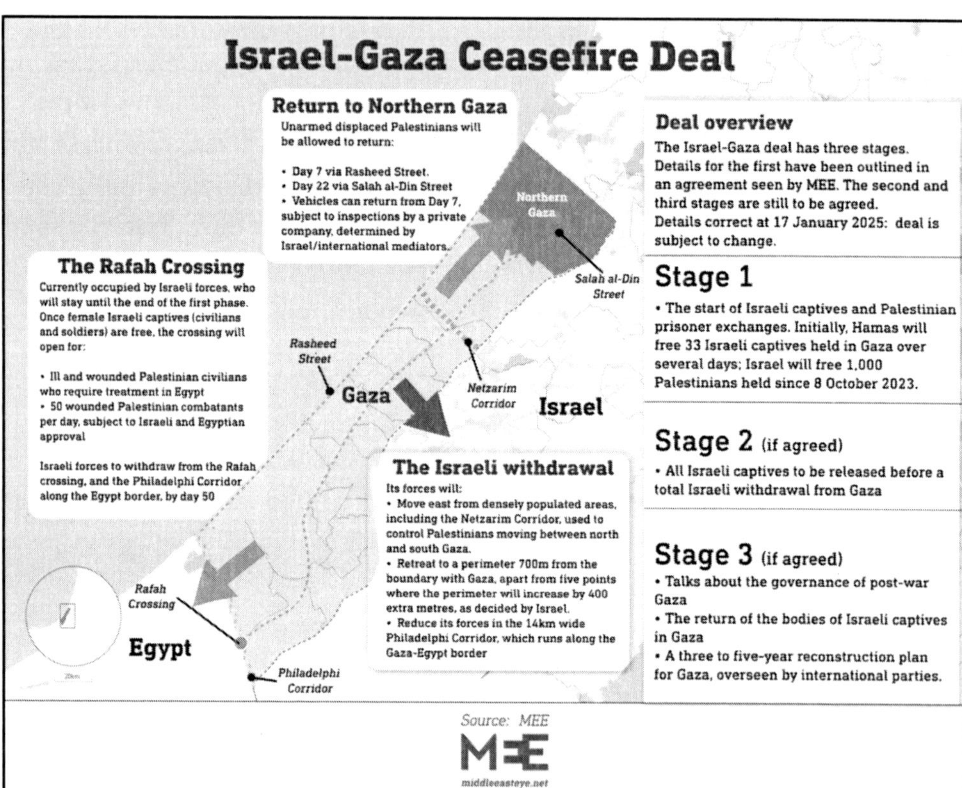

Map of Ceasefire Deal January 2025 - Middle East Eye

47

Ceasefire in Gaza, Finally

After weeks and months of hectic parleys and negotiations, the ceasefire deal in Gaza was finally announced on 15 January 2025. The official announcement by the Qatari Foreign Ministry late at night sparked immediate celebrations across Gaza and the Arab world. This deal, coming after 15 months of intense fighting, has already resulted in over 46,000 Palestinians killed in Gaza (many more as per unofficial counts), most of them women and children. The Gaza Strip has been flattened, more than two million people have been displaced internally and most critical infrastructure like hospitals, water supply, and schools have been completely destroyed.

Confirming the agreement and explaining the deal, Qatar's Prime Minister and Minister of Foreign Affairs, Sheikh Mohammed bin Abdul Rahman Al Thani, spoke to the media, stating that "with faith and commitment, we have reached this moment. Together with our partners, we will ensure the implementation of this agreement. A joint follow-up mechanism between Qatar, Egypt, and the USA will monitor progress to safeguard the deal and bring lasting peace".

As the deal takes shape from the morning of 19 January, Sunday, the question on everyone's mind is why now and what made it possible?

The Deal

The ceasefire deal includes three stages. The first stage, which lasts for 42 days, includes a ceasefire, withdrawal, and redeployment of Israeli Defence Forces (IDF) outside densely-populated areas, the release of hostages and exchange of prisoners, and the return of internally displaced persons to their places of residence in the Gaza Strip.

Hamas would release 33 hostages in the first phase of the deal, including women, children, and men over the age of 50, and those under it who are wounded and sick. This spans the entire 42 days of phase 1, starting with the release of three hostages on day 1. For every hostage released, Israel would release 30 Palestinian prisoners.

During the critical first phase, the IDF would gradually withdraw from Gaza towards a buffer zone in the east, near the border with Israel. In addition, the IDF will vacate the Netzarim corridor, which is a kilometre-deep line running across the Gaza Strip, dividing North and South Gaza. The IDF will also gradually withdraw from the Philadelphi corridor on the border between Gaza and Egypt. Incidentally, these two withdrawals were the main sticking points in earlier negotiations.

Talks on conditions and implementation of the second phase are to commence on the 16th day of the first phase. Phase 2 will end on Day 84 with the complete withdrawal of IDF forces from the Gaza Strip and a permanent ceasefire. It will also include the release of all the hostages, including the dead still held by Hamas.

The third phase is all about reconstruction and rehabilitation of the Gaza Strip, in which the Arab countries will be the major stakeholders. There is also talk of an international monitoring force to be deployed to prevent any future agreement violations, but those details are still in the discussion stage.

The first stage, however, is most critical as it would not only lead to the silencing of the guns and airstrikes for the first time in 15 months but will also set the stage for the future peace process. Apart from the ceasefire, compelling and urgent humanitarian aid delivery aspects are also critical. Accordingly, the first phase also includes intensifying the safe and effective entry and distribution of humanitarian aid on a large scale throughout the Gaza Strip, rehabilitating hospitals, and health centres, bringing in civil defence supplies, fuel, etc. As per the deal, 600 trucks carrying critical supplies would be permitted daily into Gaza.

Given the atmosphere of hostility and mistrust between Hamas and Israel, the deal has proposed that Qatar, Egypt and the USA act as guarantors of the agreement to ensure that all three of its stages are fully implemented by both parties.

Why Now?

All sides have welcomed the deal. However, the question is, how was the deal clinched and why now? Remember, the deal that has been agreed upon is the mirror image of the 'Biden Plan', presented in May 2024 which had the same three phases of 42 days each and similar conditions. The UN Security Council endorsed it on 10 June 2024, and Hamas publicly accepted it. Israel initially concurred but the very next day, rejected it.

So why now? There is a lot in the media that says that Donald Trump is the main factor that changed or instead forced Israel to change its mind. The visit of Trump's newly-appointed Middle East Envoy, Steve Witkoff, to Israel and his meeting with PM Netanyahu on 10 January, where he is supposed to have delivered a 'stern message', seems to have tipped the scales in favour of the deal.

Given Trump's history as the most ardent and staunch supporter of Israel, this pressure tactic may come as a surprise. In his first term, Trump had done for Israel what no other US president had dared. He had recognized Jerusalem as Israel's capital in December 2017 and had moved the US Embassy to Jerusalem. He had orchestrated the signing of the Abraham Accords in September 2020, which set the road map for normalization of Israel's relations with the Arab world. And he unilaterally revoked the Iran Nuclear deal in May 2018, much to the delight of Israel, further adding his 'maximum pressure' policy on Iran, throttling its funds and economy like never before.

So why did he pressurize Israel now? The answer is twofold.

For Trump, resolving the Gaza conflict aligns with his broader strategic goals, including countering Iran and fostering normalization between Israel and Saudi Arabia. Trump has also made it clear that he does not endorse wars.

Secondly, Trump would have conveyed to PM Netanyahu that there is a more significant battle to be fought and won than the war in Gaza. This war is with Iran, the common enemy for both Israel and the USA. After 15 months of fighting, there is not much left to achieve in Gaza. Also, most of the threat to Israel on its borders has already been eliminated, with Hezbollah demolished in the North and the West Bank well under the control of the IDF. To add to Israel's comfort, the ouster of the Assad regime in Syria has broken the vital link between Iran and its proxies, delivering a fatal blow to Iran's strategy in the region.

From an Israeli perspective, most of the military goals in the Gaza war had been achieved. Also, fighting over 15 months, mostly with reservists, had led to injuries and casualties as well as war fatigue. The Israeli economy too had been set back considerably over this period. Plus, getting back the hostages would be a win for PM Netanyahu any day. Thus, this would have been a good time to get the deal done even at the cost of looking compromised and pressurized.

48

A Fragile Ceasefire

The ceasefire in Gaza came into effect on 19 January after months of contested negotiations and delays. Facing death and destruction from continuing strikes from the Israeli forces as well as from increasing starvation and disease, it has come about as a major relief to thousands of Palestinians. While the cessation of hostilities has brought momentary relief, the underlying tensions remain unresolved. Key developments, such as Israel's refusal to vacate the Netzarim Corridor, the resignation of the Israeli Defence Forces (IDF) Chief, internal political dynamics in Israel, statements coming out of Washington on emptying Gaza of people and delivery of 2,000-lb bombs to Israel, are raising questions on the continuity of the ceasefire and the long-term peace process.

The Netzarim and Rafah Corridors: Critical Flashpoints

One of the most contentious issues threatening the ceasefire is Israel's occupation of the Netzarim Corridor. This thin strip of land, which divides the Gaza Strip into two halves, North and South, is critical for the displaced Palestinians to return. Israeli forces were to permit safe return of Palestinians to Northern Gaza on 26 January after the second exchange of hostages, but in an unexpected twist, they have refused it, saying that Hamas should have released a 29-year-old civilian woman, Arbel Yehud, on 25 January as part of the second set of hostage release. It was only after intervention and mediation by Qatar that an agreement was reached. Hamas promised to release her by Friday, 31 January, and Israel, in turn, permitted Palestinians to cross over to the North. Earlier, thousands of Palestinians attempting to return to their homes in the North on 26 January were fired upon by Israeli forces in a clear violation of the ceasefire.

In the South, Israel has declared that it will maintain control over the Rafah border crossing, the key passage between Egypt and the Gaza Strip, throughout the first phase of the ceasefire. It has also denied claims that the Palestinian Authority was to oversee operations at the crossing. The crossing is crucial as it is the only one through which critical humanitarian aid is to flow in.

As per the ceasefire deal, the IDF has to vacate the Netzarim corridor, as well as the Philadelphi corridor (on the border between Gaza and Egypt) by the end of Phase 1. However, it is not clear whether the IDF would stick to this. Both these standoffs could increase the trust deficit between the parties and fuel fears of renewed violence.

Spate of Resignations in Israel

Adding to the complexity is the resignation of the IDF Chief, a move that has sent shockwaves throughout Israeli political and military circles. Although Lieutenant General Herzi Halevi, in his resignation letter, said that he was resigning "due to my acknowledgment of responsibility for the (military's) failure on 7 October', inputs suggest that the resignation is tied to disagreements over the handling of the Gaza conflict and the ceasefire terms. Reports also indicate that the IDF Chief was at odds with the government's approach, particularly concerning the Netzarim Corridor and the scale of military operations in Gaza. Along with him, Major General Yaron Finkelman, the head of Israel's southern military command, which is responsible for Gaza, also resigned.

Separately and before the ceasefire, Ben Gvir, the Minister for National Security from the far-right coalition, had resigned from the cabinet, expressing his disapproval of the ceasefire. Another far-right minister, Smotrich, who is the Finance Minister, has also threatened to resign if Israel does not re-commence the war after Phase 1.

The change in military leadership, leading from disagreements with the political bosses, raises questions about the direction of Israeli military strategy moving forward. Also, political discontent and pressure from coalition members in the government adds to the fear that PM Netanyahu may buckle under pressure and resume military operations in Gaza at the first opportunity.

America's Role is Creating Doubts

The role of the USA has also come under scrutiny. President Donald Trump, who took the credit for getting the ceasefire implemented under threat of 'all hell will break loose', is himself having doubts on the continuity of the deal. Just after his inauguration, while speaking to reporters, he said that he is "not confident" that the ceasefire will hold. He added that the ongoing conflict is not of direct concern to the USA and "that's not our war, it's their war." On 25 January, he added more fuel to the fire, and perhaps tested a 'red line' in the region, stating that he would like to see Jordan, Egypt and other Arab nations increase the number of Palestinian refugees they are accepting from the Gaza Strip, suggesting that the 1.5 million population in Gaza should vacate the area to "just clean out" the war-torn area. It not only drew instant criticism, but Egypt and Jordan promptly rejected the idea. He also informed the media that he has cleared the obstacles for the delivery of 2,000-lb bombs to Israel, something that was stopped by the previous Biden administration, fearing mass casualties through its use in Gaza.

These statements and intentions from the USA embolden hardline elements within Israel and can prove counter-productive to the continuation of the ceasefire. It may also force Hamas to harden its stance when further talks are held on Phase 2 of the ceasefire.

Hamas: Re-emerging from the Shadows

On the ground, Hamas appears to be consolidating its control in Gaza. The group has taken charge of public aid distribution, leveraging this role to strengthen its support base among the civilian population. Images of Hamas operatives coordinating relief efforts and ensuring the delivery of essential supplies have bolstered their narrative as defenders of Palestinian interests. By positioning itself as a governance entity capable of addressing civilian needs, Hamas is reshaping its role in Gaza, undermining repeated calls by Israel to ensure that Hamas does not have any say in the future governance of Gaza.

Also, there are inputs to suggest that Hamas has been able to recruit nearly15,000 new cadres, thus recouping most of its losses. These developments also give fodder to the far right in Israel who are advocating resumption of the war as Hamas is yet to be completely eliminated.

Israeli Operations Continue

As the Gaza ceasefire went into effect, Israel has shifted its focus to the West Bank. It launched a 'large-scale military operation' in the city of Jenin to 'eradicate terrorism in Jenin,' as per a statement from Prime Minister Benjamin Netanyahu's office. On the first day itself, 10 Palestinians were killed leading to massive protests and calls by Hamas and other groups to wage a war of resistance.

A statement from Elise Stefanik, the US ambassador to the UN, stating that Israel has a biblical right over the whole of West Bank does not inspire any confidence in cessation of hostilities. In fact, coupled with Trump's move to recognize Jerusalem as the capital of Israel in December 2017, in his first term, it only adds to speculation of continued Israeli operations in the occupied West Bank.

On the Lebanon front, Israel has refused to vacate Southern Lebanon and fired at the residents who were attempting to return to their homes on 25 January, the designated day for complete withdrawal of Israeli forces from Lebanon. Such actions clearly undermine the spirit of the ceasefire in the Gaza war. Succumbing to pressure from the USA, the Lebanese government has agreed to extend the ceasefire terms till 18 February, but is likely that the IDF may still refuse to vacate the space then too.

Will the Ceasefire Hold?

The pictures and videos of people returning to their homes in Gaza, crossing the Netzarim Corridor on 27 January, have brought cheer in the region and would have definitely boosted the morale of the 'Resistance'. Similar stories of defiance and resilience are emerging from Southern Lebanon too. It begs the question if Israel and its allies have succeeded in their war objectives with regard to the complete elimination of Hamas and Hezbollah and obliteration of Gaza. Hopefully, it will force the 'powers to be' to sit back and think on the futility of war and the loss of human lives as also a long-term solution to the problem.

As regards the ceasefire in Gaza, the sustainability will depend on several factors, including the resolution of key flashpoints like the Netzarim Corridor, control of the Rafah border crossing, the intent of Israeli leadership, and the role of international actors. Refusal to address the root causes of the conflict – such as the Israeli occupation, blockade of Gaza, and lack of a viable political solution towards a viable and independent state of Palestine – means that tensions will simmer and a conflict could resurface. Also, how the talks on Phase 2 of the ceasefire progress after 3 February will be key to hopes of a permanent end to the war. However, the dynamics within Israel and the developments on the ground so far only indicate that the truce is fragile and could break at the smallest provocation.

Without significant concessions from both sides and sustained international pressure, the ceasefire risks being another temporary reprieve in a long cycle of violence. The international community must act decisively to address the root causes of the conflict, prioritize humanitarian relief, and hold all parties accountable. Only then can the fragile truce in Gaza evolve into a foundation for lasting peace.

49

Ceasefire under Threat

Gaza is under a complete clampdown after talks on a ceasefire continue to falter. Phase 1 of the ceasefire ended on 1 March, and with no agreement on either Phase 2 or continuation of Phase 1, there is an air of uncertainty and fear among the people of Gaza. Meanwhile, Israel has been progressively tightening the screws on humanitarian aid and critical supplies into the Strip. For the people in Gaza hoping to gather pieces of their shattered lives and return to their destroyed homes, these developments, coupled with threats from Israel that it could resume military operations into Gaza anytime, are bringing back the horrible memories of death and destruction caused by over 16 months of devastating war.

Developments So Far

Phase 1 of the ceasefire ended on 1 March and all the conditions for it were met including the withdrawal of the IDF from the Netzarim Corridor. However, Phase 2 talks which were to begin on 16 February, never got off to a serious start with both Hamas and Israel trading allegations of ceasefire violations. While Hamas accused the IDF of not vacating the Netzarim Corridor and continuing to conduct sporadic military operations in Gaza, Israel threatened to walk out of the deal, accusing Hamas of disrespecting the dead hostages by making a public spectacle of their return. It took urgent and serious intervention from the regional interlocutors and the USA to see that all the terms of Phase 1 were implemented.

As regards Phase 2, while Hamas is ready and has offered to release all the remaining hostages in one go, it is clear that Israel is not at all keen on progressing talks on a ceasefire till its war objectives are fully realised. The USA too seems to be dithering in its commitment to end the war, and to let Israel do what it deems proper to fulfil its war objectives.

Committed to ending the war as a part of his election promise, President Trump gave hints of this U-turn as early as on his inauguration day when he said in his first interaction with reporters that he is 'not confident' that the ceasefire will hold. And during PM Netanyahu's visit to the White House on 4 February, he again shocked the world by saying that the USA will 'take over' and 'own' Gaza after resettling Palestinians elsewhere under a plan that would turn Gaza Strip into 'the Riviera of the Middle East'. The proposal of cleaning out Gaza was promptly dismissed by the regional countries and has forced them to look at alternative options to end the war in Gaza.

Meanwhile, with talks on Phase 2 of the ceasefire faltering, the USA came up with a bridging proposal regarding the ceasefire which stated that Phase 1 of the ceasefire could be extended for another 60 days to tide over the holy period of Ramadan, which began on 1 March and runs until 29 March and the Jewish Passover holiday on 19 April. During this period, Hamas would release half the hostages on Day 1 and the remaining on the last day if a permanent end to the war is agreed upon. As per estimates, 58 Israeli hostages remain in Hamas custody, including 34 who Israel says are dead. However, during this extended period, the IDF will continue to stay in positions in Gaza, which are the Rafah Crossing and the Philadelphi corridor. While Israel welcomed the proposal, it was promptly rejected by Hamas, claiming that instead of an extension of Phase 1, the talks on ending the war in Phase 2, as a part of an agreed deal, should be pursued.

The Clampdown

Reacting to Hamas's rejection of the extension offer, Israel immediately ordered a total stoppage of the humanitarian aid convoys into Gaza Strip on 2 March, stating that there will be consequences for Hamas if the temporary truce extension is not agreed upon. Hamas termed it as "cheap blackmail, a war crime and a blatant coup against the (ceasefire) agreement." Israel's decision also drew instant condemnation from all countries in the region. In an attempt to add more pressure on Hamas and Gaza, Israel announced cutting off electricity supply to Gaza on 9 March, piling more misery on the people. With the only two functioning desalination plants working in Gaza forced to shut down due to lack of electricity supply and diesel, this is also a significant health hazard looming in Gaza. Meanwhile, the USA has concurrently sanctioned and released additional military aid including supply of the 2,000-lb bombs to Israel, previously halted by the Biden administration due to concerns over civilian casualties, further exacerbating tensions and undermining Trump's claim to ending wars.

Egyptian Plan for Gaza

Forced by the threats of the 'taking over' of Gaza by Trump and the clampdown by Israel, the regional countries have been forced to come up with their own solutions. Egypt presented its plan for the reconstruction of Gaza at the Arab Summit on 4 March, putting forth a plan to rebuild Gaza at a cost of US$ 53 billion. Egyptian President Al Sisi pitched it as "a plan that aims for a comprehensive and just settlement of the Palestinian issue, ends the root causes of the Israeli Palestinian conflict, guarantees the security and stability of the peoples of the region and establishes the Palestinian State."

The Egyptian plan envisages rebuilding Gaza by 2030 without removing its population. The first phase calls for starting the removal of unexploded ordnance and clearing more than 50 million tons of rubble created by Israel's bombardment and military offensives. Thousands of temporary housing units would be set up for Gaza's population while reconstruction takes place. The plan envisages completely reshaping the Strip and building 'sustainable, green and walkable' housing and urban areas with renewable energy in the later phase. It renovates agricultural lands and creates industrial zones and large park areas. It also calls for opening an airport, a fishing port and a commercial port. Hamas would cede power to an interim administration of political independents until a reformed Palestinian Authority assumes control.

Israel dismissed the proposal and has ruled out any role for the Palestinian Authority in Gaza, and concurrently seeks complete disarmament of Hamas. Meanwhile, true to its unpredictable nature in conducting business, the Trump Administration announced on 5 March that it has been holding direct talks with Hamas to end the war and release of American hostages held in Gaza. The talks, held by the US presidential envoy for hostage affairs, Adam Boehler, are unprecedented as the USA has never engaged directly with Hamas. To add to the mystery, Israel claimed no knowledge of the talks and that it had been kept in the dark.

Looking Ahead

The failure to move onto Phase 2 of the Gaza ceasefire deal and the complete blockade enforced by Israel is undermining the prospects of peace and ending the war in Gaza. The stoppage of critical humanitarian aid and the lack of clean drinking water are adding to the misery of its people. Israel is hoping that Hamas would relent under pressure from people in Gaza to extend Phase 1 of the truce.

What is not, however, clear is what Israel and the USA aim to achieve by extending the ceasefire by 60 days without an explicit 'day after plan' in mind.

Also, how Israel wants to achieve its war objectives, especially concerning complete elimination of Hamas from the Gaza Strip, is unclear, even to most in the Israeli establishment. Hamas, despite suffering huge losses, especially to its leadership, is not down and out. In fact, as per admissions by the previous Secretary of State of the USA, Anthony Blinken, Hamas has recruited over 15,000 combat cadres over the past year, recouping significant losses. Also, the continuing ceasefire or lack of military engagement is only giving Hamas additional time and space to regroup. With UNRWA banned by Israel from operating in Gaza, Hamas has also emerged as the major agency for distribution of humanitarian aid to the people in Gaza. The return of hundreds of Palestinians from Israeli jails, primarily due to the exchange deal, has led to people in Gaza hero-worshipping Hamas. As a result, its status, instead of being diminished, is improving by the day.

Therefore, there are important questions that need to be answered. However, the clampdown and blockade of Gaza do not seem to point towards any of those or even resolution of this conflict. Unless there is a clear plan, agreed upon by both warring parties, and has the endorsement of major regional stakeholders as well as the USA, the prospects for lasting peace and solution to this conflict will continue to look dim. Amid this deadlock, the suffering unfortunately has to be borne by the people in Gaza.

50

Ceasefire in Flames as Israeli Forces Re-launch Ground Offensive

"If those hostages aren't back by the time I get into office, all hell will break out in the Middle East", roared Donald Trump during a press interaction on 7 January, weeks before he was to assume office as the 47th President of the USA. Well, hell was averted then as a ceasefire deal was soon agreed upon between Israel and Hamas on 16 January, bringing a temporary halt to the endless bombardment and killings in the Gaza Strip.

The ceasefire deal was to finally result in a long-lasting solution to the conflict but it soon became clear that it was agreed upon only for the Trump administration to take the credit and not to really end the war. While the 42 days of Phase 1 of the ceasefire, which ended on 1 March, was largely complied with, there is no agreement on subsequent phases. Despite US Special Envoy Steve Witkoff visiting Israel more than once in search of a negotiated settlement, Israel stood firm that there is going to be no more ceasefire. The lull was finally broken when Israel initiated air strikes into Gaza on 18 March, and with the ground forces moving into Gaza on 20 March, it seems that people in Gaza are in again for a long period of uncertainty and fear coupled with devastation and death.

What has Happened since 1 March

Phase 1 of the ceasefire ended on 1 March. With the talks on Phase 2 of the ceasefire not progressing well, Israel ordered a clampdown on Gaza and stopped the entry of the humanitarian aid convoys into Gaza Strip on 2 March.

With the humanitarian situation worsening by the day, the USA came up with yet another bridging proposal on 13 March: to extend Phase1 of the ceasefire upto 20 April, stipulating that Hamas should release 5 living and 9 dead hostages on the first day of the extended ceasefire. The proposal was rejected by Hamas which continued its insistence on upholding the original terms of the ceasefire deal.

The signs turned ominous when news of an Israeli airstrike on 15 March filtered in, reporting the deaths of nine humanitarian workers in the strike in the town of Beit Lahia in Gaza. And finally, any hopes of continuing the truce were shattered when Israel formally re-launched its military campaign into Gaza on 18 March with a series of airstrikes across the Gaza Strip, killing more than 400 people overnight, which is being termed as the deadliest single day strike since the war broke out. Israel's Defence Minister Israel Katz made it clear by stating, "Tonight we returned to fighting in Gaza", adding that "the residents of Gaza will pay the full price if Israeli hostages are not returned and Hamas remains able to govern in the Strip".

Ground forces re-entered Gaza on 20 March, re-occupying the Netzarim Corridor and once again cutting off the Gaza Strip into North and South. On the first night itself, Israeli forces killed over 59 people as fear of death and displacement returned to Gaza

What is Behind the 'Second Strike'

Israel has claimed that Hamas is responsible for forcing its hand by repeatedly refusing the American proposal to extend the ceasefire and return the hostages. However, a few other developments, especially inside Israel, may give a better insight into the reasons behind the resumption of war.

Ben Gvir, the Security Minister in PM Netanyahu's cabinet and a very powerful member of the Far Right Party, had quit the government when the ceasefire was agreed upon. Plus, Finance Minister Smotrich also threatened to leave the government if Israel moved to Phase 2 of the ceasefire deal. Both these ministers and the other members of the Far Right are critically important right now as the annual budget, which the Cabinet approved in November 2024, is supposed to be passed by the end of March 2025 or the government would automatically fall, triggering early elections.

The recent case for dismissing Shin Bet chief Ronen Bar over issues of mistrust and questions on loyalty was also bringing a lot of heat on the government. PM Netanyahu's announcement of his dismissal on 16 March had sparked a nationwide protest and the resumption of conflict was a good option to deflect attention.

Also, PM Netanyahu was to appear in court on 18 March in the cases of corruption against him. The hearings obviously got postponed due to national security requirements, owing to the resumption of hostilities.

The US factor too is important here. The very close rapport between President

Trump and PM Netanyahu is no secret to anyone. For Trump, his responsibility towards Gaza was over the day Netanyahu obliged Trump by agreeing to a ceasefire in January, before Trump took office. Trump made it clear on the first day itself on 20 January that he was not confident that the ceasefire would last.

The next is the Iran factor. The USA, after imposing Maximum Pressure 2.0 on Iran and repeated threats of military action in case support to its proxies was not reined in and the nuclear program curtailed, shot off a letter to the Supreme Leader in Iran on 12 March, asking Iran to join talks on the nuclear program failing which there could be a possibility of military strikes on Iran's nuclear facilities. As expected, Iran dismissed any suggestions of talks under threat.

Concurrently, the USA launched airstrikes against Houthis in Yemen on 15 March, accusing them of obstructing the passage of ships through the Red Sea. Trump also threatened Iran by stating that any strike from Houthis would be considered a strike by Iran and that it would be held responsible.

Thus, as far as the USA and Donald Trump are concerned, having fulfilled the initial promise to obtain a ceasefire and the attempt to extend it with a bridging proposal, the Gaza problem was easily left to PM Netanyahu 'to sort out'. Also, recent developments towards negotiating a ceasefire in the Russia-Ukraine war, the strikes on Houthis and the engagement with Iran only help in deflecting the focus from Gaza.

What Lies Ahead?

The resumption of fighting in Gaza does not bode well for the future peace and security in the region. Israel has said that this time it will continue the military operations for 'as long as it takes' to achieve the military objectives. Having witnessed the re-emergence of thousands of Hamas cadres during the ceasefire and the huge public support for them, especially during the release of Palestinian prisoners and distribution of aid, Israel is not likely to take any more chances. The question is, how and when will Israel be able to achieve its military objective of complete elimination of Hamas? Also, with no plan for 'day after' clear yet, at what stage will Israel call off military operations eventually? And, after that, how does the situation evolve? Will there be any future discussion on a two-state solution or governance of Gaza?

It is clear that none of the parties involved in the conflict, especially Israel, has any clear answers to these questions. While the resumption of war may have come as a relief to PM Netanyahu domestically, for the people of Gaza, it marks yet another phase of continued death and destruction.

51

Another Ceasefire Proposal Goes Down

It has been more than two months since Israel revoked the brief period of peace in Gaza by launching airstrikes on 18 March 2025.

On 26 May, yet another attempt at a ceasefire in Gaza ended abruptly after Israel and Hamas refused to accept a deal that could have ended the misery of the people in Gaza, even if temporarily, and would have ushered in critical food, water, and medical aid for the starving and dying population. Steve Witkoff, the US Envoy for the Middle East, was reported to have outlined the offer which stated that "Israel will agree to a temporary ceasefire that would see half of the living and deceased hostages return and lead to substantive negotiations to find a path to a permanent ceasefire, which I agreed to preside over." The deal would see around 10 living hostages and 10 bodies of hostages, along with hundreds of Palestinian security prisoners, released in two stages during a roughly two-month ceasefire. During that time, Israel and Hamas would have held negotiations on the terms of a permanent truce. The offer, one of many in the recent past, however, found no takers.

Meanwhile, death and misery in Gaza continue. In a fresh push towards eliminating the threat of Hamas from Gaza, Israel launched a new military campaign on 16 May, called 'Gideon's Chariots,' a reference to a biblical warrior. The campaign aims "to achieve all the goals of the war in Gaza, including the release of the hostages and the defeat of Hamas." Following it, on 18 May, over 100 people were killed in Gaza in one night alone in an extensive ground operation coupled with an intense air campaign.

As per Gaza's Health Ministry, 3,785 people have been killed since Israel ended a ceasefire in March, bringing the total killed to at least 53,900 Palestinians and over 122,500 wounded. As per estimates, over 70 percent of these are women and children, including infants, leading to an outcry in the international community and humanitarian groups. On the other hand, of the 251 Israeli hostages taken on 7 October 2023, Hamas is still holding 58 hostages. These include the bodies of at least 35 confirmed dead by Israel, and at least 20 believed to be alive.

Israel's Dilemma: Hostages or Hamas

As the fresh offensive of Israel takes shape, the deteriorating condition of the remaining hostages is causing concern. At home, PM Netanyahu is facing increasing pressure from the families of the hostages with every passing day. Hamas has repeatedly refused to release any more hostages until Israel agrees to a permanent end to the war and withdraws its forces from Gaza. Israel, on the other hand, is insisting on the complete surrender of Hamas, including the demilitarization of Gaza and the removal of Hamas from any future governance structure there.

As Israeli forces continue their hunt for Hamas, they scored a major tactical victory on 13 May when they eliminated Muhammad Sinwar, the de facto chief of Hamas in Gaza and brother of Yahya Sinwar, the Hamas Military Chief who was killed by Israeli forces in October last year. However, despite repeated military successes, Israel is nowhere near achieving its military goals. Reports of Hamas recruiting fresh cadres in hundreds and re-arming them are also a matter of concern. With Hamas not relenting and the number of hostages still alive shrinking day by day, Israel is facing a huge dilemma; to choose between getting the remaining hostages at the earliest or risk their lives while it continues to work on finishing Hamas completely, forever. Meanwhile, with increasing reports of starvation and mass killings in Gaza, there is an increasing pressure on Israel to call off the war at the earliest.

Increasing International Pressure on Israel

On 4 May, Israel's security cabinet approved a plan to expand military operations in Gaza, including the 'conquest' of the Palestinian territory and a new push for its residents to leave Gaza Strip forever, and the launching of 'Operation Gideon's Chariots' on 16 May. Following this offensive, Israel is facing unprecedented pressure from its allies. The UK, Canada and France have threatened sanctions. On 19 May, UK's Keir Starmer, France's Emmanuel Macron, and Canada's Mark Carney, issued a joint statement condemning Israel's handling of the humanitarian situation in Gaza and called on Israel to immediately halt military action in the enclave and allow in more aid, threatening "further concrete actions in response" if Israel refuses. PM Netanyahu was quick to state that the three countries are 'on the wrong side of history'. The European Union, Israel's biggest trade partner, too is reviewing its landmark Association Agreement with Israel.

Spain too, which has been vocal in its opposition to Israel's military campaign in Gaza, held the fifth official meeting of what is known as 'The Madrid Group' on 25 May, a group of key European and Arab nations. A statement at the end of the meeting called on the international community to impose sanctions on Israel to force it to stop its war in Gaza.

However, it is the support from its key ally, the USA, which is starting to become a concern for Israel. Its alliance with the USA, which has always stood strong, is on shaky ground in the light of the increasing casualties and continuing deaths due to starvation, especially those of children. The fact that Donald Trump visited the West Asian region earlier this month on his first foreign visit after taking over as President and did not include Israel, is a statement in itself. The ongoing US-Iran nuclear talks, despite strong opposition from Israel, are also a sign of discord. There have also been media reports of verbal spats between Trump and Netanyahu over the Iran nuclear deal. Although the USA continues its support to Israel by supplying military aid, increasing international opposition to its military operations in Gaza means that Israel is largely left to fight this battle against Hamas on its own.

Looking Ahead

The war in Gaza has been going on for 20 months and shows no signs of relenting. While Hamas has been severely degraded, it has not yet been completely ousted. Despite launching a concentrated ground offensive, it is not clear how and when Israel would be able to declare the achievement of its military objectives. Meanwhile, the number of living hostages is coming down with every passing week.

SECTION VII

Trump and the Gaza War

52

The Root Causes for the Gaza War Lie in Trump's First Presidency

It is May 2024 and the war in Gaza is at a critical inflection point, having just completed seven months.

Except for a brief humanitarian truce of a week in November last year, when 50 Israeli hostages, mainly women and children, were released in exchange for the release of 150 Palestinian prisoners from Israeli jails, there has been no ceasefire. While the region and the world wait in hope for an early cessation of hostilities, it may be worthwhile to identify a very crucial element in policy decision making by the USA in the region, which set off events and developments leading to the trigger to the current war. Some of them point directly to President Trump's policies during his presidency of 2017-21.

Trump's Iran Policy

Trump's Iran policy was based fundamentally on whatever Israel thought of Iran, that is, Iran is enemy No.1. Flowing from it, two important policy decisions were taken during Trump's first presidency which specifically affected the West Asian region. These were the pull-out from the Iran nuclear deal and the signing of the Abraham Accords. As we will see in subsequent paragraphs, these two short-sighted policy decisions resulted in re-arming of Iran as well as swelling of frustration among the Palestinian groups which felt abandoned and left out.

Revoking the Iran Nuclear Deal

The Iran nuclear deal was signed in July 2015, which PM Netanyahu had immediately called a historical blunder. During Trump's election campaign in 2016, revoking the Iran nuclear deal became a critical election promise and a major rallying point for Jewish votes. After taking over the presidency in January 2017, therefore, he immediately set out to see how the Iran nuclear deal could be revoked.

Delivering on his election promise, Trump pulled out of the Iran nuclear deal on 8 May 2018 terming it a "horrible one-sided deal that should have never ever been made". Following it up, the US Secretary of State, Mike Pompeo, announced a list of 12 demands, fulfilment of which would be a must for any future deal with Iran. Some of these issues were not even part of the nuclear deal like putting severe restrictions on Iran's ballistic missiles program, stopping enrichment of plutonium reprocessing, closing its heavy water reactor, and ending support to Middle East 'terrorist' groups, including Hezbollah, Hamas, Islamic Jihad, Houthis, etc. Despite pressure from other members of P5 plus1, the UN and the IAEA, Trump did not relent, pushing Iran back into a strict sanctions regime. Barack Obama, whose administration had negotiated the deal, condemned Trump and said that without the nuclear deal, the USA could eventually be left with a losing choice between a nuclear-armed Iran and another war in the Middle East.

How did it affect Iran? In most ways, it unshackled Iran. It was no longer obliged to accept very strict 'anytime anywhere' inspections and scrutiny in its nuclear program. It was put under sanctions, which was nothing new as it had been enduring punitive sanctions by the USA and other Western countries for decades. In April 2019, after the USA designated the Islamic Revolutionary Guard Corps (IRGC) of Iran as a 'Foreign Terrorist Organization', Iran decided to break free from the nuclear deal and decided to install a cascade of 20 IR-6 centrifuges at Natanz nuclear plant. Soon, Iran was enriching uranium at 20 percent which was further increased to 60 percent in April 2021. And now, as per the IAEA quarterly report of February 2024, Iran's total enriched uranium stockpile is at 5,525 kilograms, including 121.5 kilograms of uranium enriched up to 60 per cent purity. By the IAEA's own theoretical definition, around 42 kg of uranium enriched to 60 per cent is required for making a nuclear bomb.

Did the USA gain anything out of it? Nothing, except to deliver on an election promise. Today, Iran's nuclear program is a real threat and neither the USA nor the IAEA have any control, observation or oversight on it. Meanwhile, Iran is merrily enriching uranium and building its options.

The Abraham Accords

The second issue was the Abraham Accords which were primarily aimed at creating a US-Israeli-led bloc with Arab countries against the 'Axis of Resistance' comprising Iran and allies in Yemen, Iraq, Syria and Lebanon. The accords were signed between

Israel and the UAE in September 2020, merely months before the US presidential elections which Trump was projected to lose. Some other nations like Bahrain, Morocco and Sudan followed shortly thereafter in joining the Accords.

How did the Abraham Accords come about? Again, it was born out of perceived threats from enemy No.1, Iran. There was a clear belief that Iran had to be reined in and Israel had to be mainstreamed with the Arab nations for the region to be safe from Iran's military threats. This time however, it was not only the USA and Israel but some Arab countries too that were on board, owing mainly to the military threats which were posed by the Iran-backed Houthis in the ongoing war in Yemen in 2019-2020.

What were these threats? In 2019, there was a sudden spurt in attacks by Iran-backed Houthis involving attacks on oil tankers in the Strait of Hormuz as well as missile attacks on Saudi airports and oil pipelines. Most of the strikes were through drones or missiles which originated from Yemen but bore clear signatures of having been supplied by Iran. On 12 May, four ships, including three oil tankers, were damaged in an attack off the coast of the UAE. On 14 May, Saudi Arabia reported armed drone attacks on the East-West pipeline of its national oil company, Aramco. Soon thereafter, there were reports of missile attacks, twice, on Abha International Airport in Saudi Arabia on 12 and 23 June 2019. Earlier, on 25 March 2019, Saudi Arabia had reported seven missiles launched from Yemen towards its cities of Riyadh, Jazan, Khamis Mushait and Nazran. All the missiles were intercepted and destroyed. The downing of a US drone by Iran flying over its airspace on 20 June 2019 was however the final straw and evoked an immediate and strong response from the USA. Reports suggested the US President Trump had ordered retaliatory military strikes against Iran, to be executed at dawn on 21 June, before changing his mind at the last moment. All this caused serious alarm in Arab capitals and brought the region closer to the threat of a military conflict between the USA and Iran than it had been in the recent past.

This was therefore the perfect opportunity to integrate Israel closer with the region and the Abraham Accords were the result of this sustained effort, which was clearly aimed at exploiting the narrative of Iran being the common enemy of the region. However, it deliberately and perhaps conveniently overlooked the most fundamental issue of friction and discord between Israel and the Arab region, that is, the Palestine issue. Although the text of the Abraham Accords signed with the UAE stated, "Committing to continuing their efforts to achieve a just, comprehensive, realistic and enduring solution to the Israeli-Palestinian conflict", nothing moved forward. So, when news started filtering in in the second half of 2023 about Saudi-Israel normalization, as a follow-up to the Abraham Accords, there was an absolute sense of abandonment and loss of hope among the Palestinian groups.

How was the Policy Flawed?

The Iran Nuclear Deal was the result of very sustained and successful negotiations which would have kept Iran's nuclear program always in check and therefore eliminate any threat of a 'nuclear weapons program'. When seen in the context of the threats from Iran to the Arab countries, this was the most prominent one and, if it was contained, the region was safer. Revoking it without any consideration of the consequences was a death blow to prospects of peace in the region.

Economic sanctions too have not worked on Iran. The IMF, in its quarterly report in January 2024, announced that the Iranian economy has outperformed many of the world powers in 2023 with a growth rate of 5.4 per cent. Iran's crude oil exports of almost 1.6 million barrels per day are almost back to pre-May 2018 days, when President Trump pulled out of the Iran nuclear deal and imposed sanctions.

Within the region too, things have never been better for Iran. The Saudi-Iran peace deal in March 2023 buried decades of hostilities between the two regional rivals. Soon thereafter, Syria was re-admitted to the Arab League. Reconciliation with countries like Egypt, the UAE, and Turkey is proceeding well. It has become a full-fledged member of SCO and was admitted in the BRICS in July 2023. The Gaza war provided Iran with an undisputed leadership role in the region, as Saudi Arabia and the UAE took a back seat. Plus, its military strikes into Israel have not only shattered the invincibility of Israel's defence systems but has provided a glimpse of Iran's huge military potential to the world.

Looking Ahead

Trump's policy gives three important lessons for the future. One, if it isn't broken, why fix it? Pulling out of the Iran nuclear deal was clearly that and the outcomes clearly prove it. Secondly, any imposition from the outside never works if it does not recognize local realities. Efforts to impose a Western style of democracy did not work after 'Arab Spring' in 2011-12, the Gulf War of 2003 in Iraq did not get the regime change that the USA wanted and the Abraham Accords too could not have succeeded by ignoring local realities. Thirdly, regional peace and security decisions have to be based on an historical perspective and a clear understanding of core issues, especially in a turbulent region like West Asia. Here too, the Abraham Accords failed, especially with reference to the Palestine issue. When the possibility of Saudi-Israel normalization and consequent abandonment of the Palestinian dream dawned upon the people in Gaza and West Bank, they had no choice but to throw themselves into the war, knowing full well that Israeli retaliation will destroy their homes and their lives.

53

Trump 2.0 and the Gaza War

The US elections are finally over and Donald Trump emerged as the winner and took over as the President for the second time on 20 January 2025.

While the US elections were closely monitored all over the globe, the two regions where it was perhaps most closely followed were probably the West Asian region and Europe-Russia, for obvious reasons, due to the ongoing wars. The Russia-Ukraine war would be at the threshold of completing three years while the war in Gaza would have completed 16 months of death, devastation, and misery by the time Trump takes over office. With the Biden administration having failed miserably to halt either of the wars, there is hope that Donald Trump would weave some magic and bring peace to both the regions. The hope also stems from the fact that Trump is averse to wars and even in his victory speech, he clearly stated that he is here not to start any war but end the wars.

Trump 1.0 and the Israel-Palestine Issue

After taking over office in January 2017, the Trump Administration put the Israel-Palestine issue on priority. It was therefore not a surprise that the White House hosted the Palestine Authority (PA) President, Mahmoud Abbas, as early as in May 2017. During the meeting, the US President "stressed that he is personally committed to helping Israelis and Palestinians achieve a comprehensive peace, and that any peace settlement can only be the product of direct negotiations between the Israelis and Palestinians." He was however also critical of the Palestinians when he told President Mahmoud Abbas to stop incitement and crack down on terrorism.

President Trump, however, took the world totally by surprise when, on 6 December 2017, in a press conference, he announced his twin decisions to formally recognize Jerusalem as the capital of Israel and to move the US Embassy there from Tel Aviv. Calling his decision a "new approach to the conflict", he added that it was long-overdue and a "necessary step" to enhance the peace process. Obviously, it invited immediate and severe criticism from West Asia, especially Palestine.

It was soon followed by reports of the Trump Peace Plan, reported first in

February 2018 following a meeting of Arab and European Foreign Ministers in Brussels. It indicated that the USA as well as the international community would grant recognition of a Palestinian state and acceptance of East Jerusalem as its capital. The plan also called for placing the Old City of Jerusalem under 'international protection' while Israel would continue to have its capital in Jerusalem.

The Trump Administration called the proposed plan the 'deal of the century', while the Palestinian Authority denounced it as a conspiracy aimed to liquidate the Palestinian cause. The plan was however withheld until it was finally presented by President Trump on 20 January 2020. Calling it 'Peace to Prosperity', he unveiled the 181-page plan, standing side by side with Israeli PM Netanyahu, announcing that "My vision presents a win-win opportunity for both sides, a realistic two-state solution that resolves the risk of Palestinian statehood to Israel's security."

The plan even included a conceptual map of a two-state solution. Key proposals included US recognition of Israeli sovereignty over territory that the plan envisages being part of Israel. Trump boasted that the plan would "more than double the Palestinian territory and provide a Palestinian capital in eastern Jerusalem." He added that no Palestinians or Israelis will be uprooted from their homes, suggesting that existing Jewish settlements in the Israeli-occupied West-Bank will remain. The plan was promptly dismissed by the Palestinians, calling it a conspiracy and a one-sided deal.

The Abraham Accords has to be the next and most significant step in Trump 1.0. Signed after hectic parleys over months, the accords had twin aims; firstly to bring about broad-based acceptance and reconciliation of Israel with the Arab world. Secondly, it singled out, without specifying, Iran as enemy No.1. In the subtext of the Accords was also implanted the Palestinian issue subtly, however, giving no assurances or timelines.

Trump 2.0 and Options to End the War in Gaza

In the ongoing war in Gaza, Trump has, more than once, supported Israel's right to defence. He has been in close touch with PM Netanyahu all along and in an interview to an Israeli media house in April this year, he said that Israel needs to "finish what they started" and "get it over with fast," adding that Israel was "losing the PR war" because of the visuals coming out of Gaza.

Even before the elections, media reports indicated that Trump had told PM Netanyahu to clear up the mess and end the war before his presidency commences. Immediately after his victory in the recent elections, he has clearly hinted at pushing for an early end to the war. A spokesperson for the Republican Party, Elizabeth Pipko, in a press interaction on 7 November said that President-elect Donald Trump wants to see Israel wrap up its wars soon, with decisive victories.

What are therefore the options to end the war in Gaza?

The Trump presidency does not start till 20 January 2025. Intense bombardment being carried out by Israel in Gaza and Southern Lebanon since 7 November indicates that Israel has got itself time for another two months to achieve its war objectives. The announcement by the Israel Defence Forces on 6 November that Israeli ground forces are getting closer to 'the complete evacuation' of northern Gaza and that residents will not be allowed to return home in Northern Gaza, clearly indicates that Israel wants to go full throttle for the next two months.

It is therefore very likely that Trump and Netanyahu have decided to give Israel another window to 'finish the job' and thereafter agree to end the war or even announce a unilateral ceasefire, something that Israel has done in the past conflicts in Gaza. They might also accept the broad terms of the 'ceasefire plan' proposed in May 2024, which was duly endorsed by the UN Security Council, as a way to end the war and which has been accepted by Hamas also. This would be the perfect kick-start to his presidency in Trump 2.0, making him the peacemaker that he claims to be and successfully 'ending the war'.

Coupled with the above reasoning, it is also very unlikely that Israel would yield now, more for political reasons than anything else. Israel would achieve little, especially for the future, by giving the Biden presidency the credit for ending the war. The only big question is whether Netanyahu will even agree for a ceasefire in January. The Trump Administration would bank upon his past deliveries for Israel in Trump 1.0 to persuade Israel to end the war. A promise of a possible Abraham Accords 2.0, taking in more countries like Saudi Arabia to align with Israel, could also add to the effect. Also, Trump is known for a clear transactional relationship even with close allies like Israel and with elections now over, it will be difficult for Netanyahu to say 'No' to President Trump, especially if the USA threatens to put a stop on critical military aid.

Looking Ahead

From the experience of Trump 1.0, it is clear that his policies in the region will continue to heavily favour Israel and that he will use this ploy with Israel to end the war soon after taking over. Meanwhile, Israel will use this window of two months to 'finish the job' till Donald Trump takes over as the president on 20 January.

54

Trump Proposes 'Take Over' of Gaza

In a statement that shocked the world, Trump, with Israeli Prime Minister Benjamin Netanyahu beside him, said on 4 February that the USA will 'take over' and 'own' Gaza after resettling Palestinians elsewhere under a plan that would turn the Gaza Strip into 'the Riviera of the Middle East'.

It drew instant condemnation across the globe, with many calling it bizarre, ridiculous, unbelievable, etc. Even British Prime Minister Keir Starmer, the staunchest ally of the USA, refused to support it stating, "They [Palestinians] must be allowed home; they must be allowed to rebuild, and we should be with them in that rebuilding on the way to a two-state solution." As expected, Hamas condemned it outrightly stating: "We consider [the plan] a recipe for generating chaos and tension in the region because the people of Gaza will not allow such plans to pass."

This proclamation has also threatened the fragile ceasefire in Gaza, which commenced on 19 January 2025. Over the past 15 months of intensive bombardment, over 80 per cent of Gaza's infrastructure has been destroyed and the war has resulted in the deaths of more than 47,500 Palestinians. Some estimates suggest that more than 76,000 tonnes of TNT have already been dropped over the Gaza Strip, more than the combined TNT dropped over London, Dresden, and Hamburg in World War II. By enforcing a complete blockade across the Strip, the population was deprived of life-saving medicines, food, and clean drinking water, leading to worldwide condemnation, with some states even accusing Israel of committing genocide in Gaza.

Despite minor violations, the truce has facilitated four successful rounds of hostage exchanges so far. By 1 March 2025, 33 Israeli hostages are expected to be released in exchange for hundreds of Palestinian prisoners. As discussions on Phase 2 of the ceasefire commence in Doha, the stakes are high, with potential implications for a permanent cessation of hostilities.

Gaza is gradually witnessing the return of displaced residents. The influx of international aid, although limited, brings a glimmer of hope for the reconstruction of lives and infrastructure. However, statements from Israeli and US officials underscore the fragility of the ceasefire and the uncertainty surrounding the peace process. Hundreds of thousands of displaced individuals are returning to their homes, including those in Northern Gaza, previously depopulated by Israeli Defence Forces (IDF) operations. Humanitarian convoys are delivering approximately 600 truckloads of food and medicine, and 50 trucks of fuel daily. Additionally, 50 critically ill Palestinians, primarily children, have been permitted to cross into Egypt for medical treatment since 1 February, offering a semblance of hope to the affected families.

Calls to 'Clean Out' Gaza

It is now a well-established fact that it was Donald Trump who, through his Middle East Envoy, Steve Witkoff, prevailed upon PM Netanyahu to agree to a ceasefire deal before he assumed the office of the US President on 20 January. Having got the deal, Trump is no longer sure of its longevity or future. On 25 January, he added more fuel to the fire by calling Gaza a 'demolition site' that should be vacated. He called upon Jordan, Egypt and other Arab nations to increase the number of Palestinian refugees they are accepting from the Gaza Strip, suggesting that the 1.5 million population in Gaza should vacate the area to 'just clean out' the war-torn area. It drew instant criticism from the region, followed by prompt rejection of the idea by Egypt and Jordan.

Meanwhile, PM Netanyahu became the first foreign dignitary to be hosted by President Trump when he was invited to visit Washington on 3 February. Netanyahu, who agreed to the ceasefire deal under immense pressure from Donald Trump, is expecting a significant return to his loyalty, key being his right to resume the war after Phase 1 ends on 3 March. Domestically, Netanyahu faces significant opposition from far-right factions within his coalition. National Security Minister Ben Gvir has resigned in protest against the ceasefire, while Finance Minister Bezalel Smotrich has threatened to follow suit if hostilities do not recommence after the end of Phase 1 of the ceasefire. The resignations of IDF Chief, Lieutenant General Herzi Halevi, and Major General Yaron Finkelman, head of Israel's southern command, further complicate the political landscape.

Palestinians in Gaza too have vocally opposed the proposed displacement, asserting their determination to rebuild their lives in their homeland. A Palestinian was quoted to have said, "The Israeli army killed us but we remain in our destroyed houses. We don't need life outside our land and will not move one metre away from it so he can say whatever he wants – he can't beat us." Another old lady, standing in front of the ruins of her home in Northern Gaza, rebuked Trump, saying, "I am waiting to rebuild our house and live in it, and neither Trump nor anybody else matters to us." Hamas, too, was prompt in calling out the statement as irresponsible, adding, "We call on the American administration and President Trump to walk back from these irresponsible remarks that contradict international law and the basic rights of our Palestinian people on their land."

Trump's authorization for the delivery of 2,000-lb bombs to Israel, further exacerbates tensions and undermines confidence in the peace process.

The Road Ahead: Phase 2 of the Ceasefire

Negotiations on Phase 2 of the ceasefire are underway, with critical stipulations including the complete withdrawal of IDF forces from Gaza, including the Netzarim corridor, which bisects the Strip, and the Philadelphi corridor along the Egypt-Gaza border. The release of all remaining hostages by Hamas, both living and deceased, is also part of the deal. However, the political rhetoric emanating from Washington and Tel Aviv raises doubts on the ceasefire's durability. Netanyahu's domestic challenges and Trump's obligation to reciprocate Israel's compliance with the ceasefire have created an environment of uncertainty.

Resilience of Gaza

Despite the geopolitical complexities, the people of Gaza are demonstrating remarkable resilience. An estimated 600,000 individuals are projected to return to Northern Gaza by the end of Phase 1, with many others resettling across the Strip. Efforts to rebuild hospitals and restore essential services are underway, supported by the gradual influx of humanitarian aid.

Regional actors, including Egypt and Jordan, have steadfastly refused to accept additional Palestinian refugees, reinforcing the right of the Palestinians to remain in their homeland. Saudi Arabia's insistence on resolving the Palestinian issue as a precondition for normalization with Israel further highlights regional solidarity with Gaza's populace.

Looking Ahead

Gaza and its people, who have been witness to many wars, are once again proving the futility of war in solving the issue. Their collective defiance to any proposals of vacating Gaza permanently and the firm resolve to rebuild their lives on the ruins of their homes and the deaths of their loved ones, shines well above the continued threats of war and displacement. Also, any attempt to resume military operations will require a big enough violation or provocation from Hamas, which is unlikely as it is in the process of regrouping and rebuilding. Any military operation against over 600,000 people who are now returning to Northern Gaza will not only be difficult but may well put a permanent end to hopes of a conflict resolution.

For President Trump, the legacy of owning a renewed conflict in Gaza would be a considerable political liability. For PM Netanyahu, the outcome of the conflict and ceasefire may well define his political future. The path forward hinges on sustained diplomatic engagement and a commitment to address the underlying causes of the conflict.

SECTION VIII

The '12-Day War'

55

Israel Attacks Iran, Threatens All-out Regional Conflict

Israel strikes Iran, launches "Operation Rising Lion".

In a surprise but not unexpected move, Israel launched unilateral and unprovoked air and missile strikes deep into Iranian territory in the early hours of 13 June 2025. In a televised address to the nation, Prime Minister Netanyahu called it a necessary move to ensure Israel's survival. Alleging that Iran had developed enough fissile material in the past few months to build up to nine nuclear bombs, he said that waiting was no longer an option and Israel was compelled to launch 'Operation Rising Lion', a targeted military operation, to roll back the Iranian threat to Israel's very existence. Around 200 Israeli Air Force fighter jets struck more than 100 nuclear, military and infrastructure targets across Iran in one night.

The initial wave of the Israeli strikes on 13 June was precise and backed by real-time intelligence. It not only successfully struck the most critical nuclear enrichment facility at Natanz, around 200 km from Tehran, but also did a repeat of what Mossad did in Lebanon in September 2024, when it took out the entire top leadership of Hezbollah, including Hasan Nasrallah, in targeted strikes and assassinations. This time too, the Israeli intelligence took out the central military leadership and nuclear scientists of Iran in one night of spectacular intelligence-based operations. Among those killed were Islamic Revolutionary Guards Corps (IRGC) chief, Maj. Gen. Hossein Salami; Armed Forces chief, Maj. Gen. Mohammad Bagheri; Emergency Command head, Maj. Gen. Gholam Ali Rashid; and Brig. Gen. Amir Ali Hajizadeh, commander of the IRGC Aerospace Force.

Israel also claimed it had eliminated Gholam-Reza Marhabi, head of the Iranian Armed Forces intelligence. Adding to Iran's misery was the death of Ali Shamkhani, who was the top adviser to Iran's Supreme Leader, Ayatollah Ali Khamenei. Also killed were six nuclear scientists who were key figures in Iran's nuclear program. They included Mohammad Mehdi Tehranchi and Fereydoun

Abbasi. Tehranchi was a theoretical physicist and the president of Islamic Azad University of Iran, while Abbasi was a nuclear physicist and the former head of the Atomic Energy Organization of Iran. The Israeli strikes also took out many key air defence assets of Iran, drastically reducing Iran's military capability to counter or stop further aerial strikes by Israel.

To add to the confusion and chaos in Iran, Israeli intelligence claimed it had launched armed drones from within Iran to target some critical targets in Iran, as well as to intercept Iranian missiles in the launch phase itself. The fact that Israel could smuggle in material and set up a drone base inside Iran was a reminder of yet another spectacular intelligence operation carried out by Ukraine inside Russia, in which it smuggled drones inside Russia and launched them, taking out critical aerial assets of Russia in an operation code-named 'Operation Spider Web'.

Iran was quick to respond and struck at the heart of Tel Aviv in Israel on 14 June. In a major missile strike, it struck many areas in Tel Aviv, including a direct strike on Israel's Military HQ building, 'Kirya', which is often called 'Israel's Pentagon'.

With the strikes continuing, both sides are claiming major successes. Israel, after having destroyed most of Iran's air defence network, is claiming 'air superiority' over Iranian skies. Israel struck the oil depot in the vicinity of Tehran on 15 June, which resulted in a major fire. Although Iran claimed to have doused the fire, further attacks on Iran's energy infrastructure are likely to continue. Iran, on the other hand, struck the critical port of Haifa in Israel on 15 June, which has reportedly caused significant damage not only to the port infrastructure but also to the oil refinery in its close vicinity.

With both sides hardening their positions, it is unlikely that the conflict will end soon. The big question is whether the conflict can remain contained to the territories of Israel and Iran or whether it could spiral out of control, engulfing not only the region but threatening a conflict that could have global ramifications.

Can the Conflict Remain Contained?

Israel started this war on the pretext of neutralizing any attempts by Iran to get a nuclear weapon. Having already conducted strikes over Natanz and Fordow, it is clear that Israel is likely to follow up on its stated objective. Within this is also the understated objective of forcing a regime change in Iran. By taking out the top military leadership in Iran and threatening deep strikes into Iran, Israel is hoping that many people in Iran who have often tried to revolt against the Islamic regime will be able to mobilize enough support and momentum to topple it.

For Iran, this war is about survival as well as prestige. It has made it very clear that the nuclear enrichment program is its sovereign right and that it will not give it up. It has often been stated that there is no plan to convert this nuclear program into a weapons program. As recently as 25 March 2025, an intelligence assessment by Tulsi Gabbard, Director of National Intelligence of the USA, stated, "The intelligence community continues to assess that Iran is not building a nuclear weapon".

In fact, Iran and the USA were scheduled for their fifth round of talks on a possible nuclear deal on 15 June, which has since been called off after Israel undertook this unilateral military action. Iran, therefore, feels cheated and sabotaged, while Israel feels it is now or never to subjugate Iran into submission and possibly overthrow the regime.

In such a scenario, the possibility of the conflict spiralling out of control is large. It may be recalled that a few days before the conflict broke out, Iran had declared that it had in its possession documents which not only clearly proved Israel's nuclear weapons program (an open secret that Israel has neither confirmed nor denied earlier), but also critical information on Israel's key nuclear facility at Dimona. Iran further had threatened that it will strike Dimona if its nuclear infrastructure is threatened. Having suffered strikes on Natanz and Fordow already, will Iran strike Dimona, is a big question. Also, if Dimona is struck, will it lead to a nuclear radiation risk? Will it force Israel to nuke Iran, is another big question.

Iran has also threatened that any nation that actively assists Israel in the war is likely to be targeted by it, either by attacking its assets in the region or through its proxy groups worldwide. Examples of Western embassies being targeted by terrorist groups, often traced back to Iran, is not uncommon. Plus, the USA and UK have a wide presence in the Gulf region in the form of military bases and assets that could come under direct Iranian threat if the situation escalates. In such a scenario, countries like the USA and UK could get involved directly in the conflict, endangering the region. With Russia and China having condemned Israeli strikes and committing to support Iran, this could well spiral out of control in no time.

However, from a global perspective, the biggest threat is from Iran threatening to close the Strait of Hormuz. Some reports indicate that the Iranian Parliament has already indicated that Iran is seriously looking at closing it, if it faces continued threats. If this happens, it could have a devastating effect on the global economy. The Strait is the only sea exit from the Persian Gulf to the Gulf of Oman and the Arabian Sea in the Indian Ocean. According to the US Energy Information Administration, about 20 percent of global oil consumption flows through the Strait, and is described as the 'world's most important oil transit chokepoint'. At its narrowest point, it is 33 km (21 miles) wide, but shipping lanes in the waterway are even narrower, making them vulnerable to attacks and threats of being shut down. Almost 18-20 million barrels of crude oil flow through it every day with major oil-exporting countries like Saudi Arabia, Iran, the UAE, Kuwait, Iraq, and Qatar relying heavily on the Strait to transport their oil to international markets. It also handles large quantities of liquefied natural gas (LNG) exports, especially from Qatar, the world's second-largest LNG exporter.

Major energy-importing nations like India, China, Japan, South Korea, and European countries rely on oil imports from the region and any closure or disruption could lead to inflation, supply chain disruptions, and recessionary pressures in multiple economies. Some estimates suggest that crude oil prices could shoot up from the current level of US$ 72-75 to anything up-to US$ 110-120 per barrel. Given the past threats of closure of the Strait of Hormuz and the criticality of oil supply lines, some alternative pipelines, like the East-West Pipeline (Saudi Arabia), from the Persian Gulf to the Red Sea and the UAE's Habshan-Fujairah pipeline, bypassing the Strait, have been built but they are nowhere of the scale required to replace the shipping across the Strait of Hormuz. Plus, the threat of Houthis in Yemen blocking any ships across Bab-al-Mandeb in the Red Sea, in solidarity with Iran, adds to the complications.

In any case of oil supply disruption, the USA is likely to be forced to join the battle directly. The US Fifth Fleet in Bahrain could get involved soon. China, which is the largest oil importer, is also likely to assist Iran more directly, more through military supplies and satellite imagery. Russia, having signed a 10-year 'comprehensive strategic partnership treaty' with Iran in January 2025, is likely to step in too. Having already committed modern weapon platforms to Iran after Iran's October 2024 brief military spat with Israel, any delivery of S-400 air defence systems or modern fighter aircraft from Russia could not only escalate the conflict but also add to the military muscle of Iran.

In any of the above cases, the role of key Arab nations in the region would be critical too. If the USA or any Western asset in any of the regional countries are attacked, how will they react? Also, any disruptions in oil supplies will be a critical decision point in their calculus.

Looking Ahead

It is often said that it is easy to initiate a conflict but very difficult to call it off. In the case of the Israel-Iran conflict, the added risk of it spiralling out of control and engulfing the entire region makes it even more dangerous. Israel may have initiated the conflict based on an unsubstantiated threat, but as it is finding out very early into the war, Iran is a formidable adversary and stand-off weapon platforms and intelligence-based assassinations cannot roll over Iran.

56

USA Strikes Iran Nuclear Sites

USA joins the war, bombs Iranian nuclear sites!

On 22 June, American B-2 bombers bombed Iran's most secure nuclear enrichment site at Fordow, bringing an end to a week of speculation whether the USA will relent to Israel's request. With 30 Tomahawk missiles striking the other two prominent nuclear sites at Isfahan and Natanz simultaneously, the USA has severely damaged, if not destroyed, Iran's nuclear program for a long time if not forever. However, what it has perhaps unleashed is an all-out conflict in West Asia, which may not be restricted to only Iran and Israel now. Initial reactions from Iran suggest that the Strait of Hormuz will be closed and many Western and American assets in West Asia could now be targeted by Iran and its proxies in the region. How Russia, China and other Arab nations will react is yet to unfold but one thing is clear, all shackles are off now and the world is at war!

In an era which Prime Minister Modi has forcefully advocated for the last three years that "this is not an era of war", the world seems to be moving in a totally opposite direction. India was itself involved in a sharp but brief conflict with Pakistan following a dastardly terror attack in Kashmir on 22 April, killing 26 innocent tourists. 'Operation Sindoor', launched by India, struck deep into Pakistan, causing unprecedented damage to the terror infrastructure as well as Pakistan's air and air defence capabilities. Although the conflict was called off after 96 hours after Pakistan pleaded for an immediate ceasefire, tensions continue to simmer.

Elsewhere in the globe, the situation is no better. The Russia-Ukraine war has completed three years since Russia launched 'Special Military Operations' in February 2022. Despite tall claims by US President Trump that he would end the war soon after taking over the presidency, the conflict has become bitterer in the past few weeks. The daring 'Operation Spider Web' launched by Ukraine on 1 June, through smuggled drones into Russia, destroyed more than 40 combat aircraft of Russia, including strategic bombers and surveillance planes. Russia, in turn, has intensified ground as well as air operations in Ukraine, targeting key assets including the capital city of Kyiv. In addition, Russia has warned European countries that any direct military aid to Ukraine may draw them into the conflict as well, forcing the EU as well as other major countries in Europe to take urgent measures to upgrade their defence preparedness as well as increase their defence budgets exponentially.

In West Asia, the most conflict-ridden region since the end of World War II, the war in Gaza continues unabated. Every day brings reports of Israeli strikes resulting in more deaths and destruction. Latest official figures indicate that the death toll in Gaza has crossed 57,000, of which 70 percent are women and children.

Although there is no active conflict presently in neighbouring Lebanon and Syria, the undercurrent of unease and tensions continues. While the Lebanese army has assured Israel that it will keep Hezbollah on a leash, the possibility of Hezbollah's resurgence, primarily to support Iran in the future, cannot be ruled out. In Syria, although a swift military operation ousted the Assad regime in December 2024, the new government under Al Sharaa is still finding its feet, and reports of skirmishes continue.

However, the most worrisome conflict is the Israel-Iran conflict. Initiated by Israel on 13 June, unilaterally and unprovoked, Israeli strikes targeted and damaged Iran's nuclear enrichment sites in Natanz, Fordow, and Isfahan. In addition, Israel has eliminated almost 20 of Iran's top military leadership and nuclear scientists. Iran's retaliation through missile strikes has also made a significant impact in Israel by causing substantial damage in the cities of Tel Aviv and Jerusalem, Israel's Military HQ, Haifa port city, and the Soroka hospital in Southern Israel. But the strikes by B-2 bombers delivering GBU-57 deep penetration bombs may have upstaged everything that has happened so far.

Despite threats from the USA of direct military intervention in Iran and demands that it surrender, Iran has refused to bow down. In turn, Iran has threatened to strike US military assets spread across more than 19 locations across West Asia. Also, the threat of closure of the Strait of Hormuz, the thin lifeline of crude oil and gas flow to the world, has caused panic and alarm across the globe as any such disruption could cause a spike in crude oil prices, adding to the inflationary trends across the world. In addition, any strikes on US assets in the region would draw in the regional Arab neighbours directly or indirectly into the conflict, something that countries like Saudi Arabia, and the UAE have successfully avoided since 7 October 2023.

Towards the Indo-Pacific, China is quietly upping the ante. Over the past year, tensions between China and Japan soared after near-continuous deployment of Chinese advanced surveillance naval vessels in Japan's contiguous zone. Recently, Japan reported a near collision when a Chinese fighter jet from the aircraft carrier *Shandong* made 'abnormal approaches' to a Japanese patrol aircraft over the Pacific Ocean. Also, conflicting claims and disputes over islands and maritime assets around the South China Sea as well as China's claims over Taiwan are a recipe for conflict, even through an unintended trigger.

Other regions like the Pakistan-Afghanistan border continue to remain conflict-prone, with frequent reports of cross-border skirmishes. Africa has its own share of conflicts and destruction though terror. In one recent incident, more than 150 people were killed in Nigeria's Yelewata community on 13 June, when unknown assailants opened fire on villagers who were asleep.

Looking Ahead

The increasing range of conflicts in the world reflects the breakdown of the global order established after World War II. The emerging global powers like China and resurgent powers like Russia, are challenging the space being ceded by the declining supremacy of the superpowers of the Cold War era.

Meanwhile, the West Asian region is looking at uncertain times. The strikes on Iran nuclear sites could unleash a region-wide conflict or it could also be the end-game for Iran.

57

'Off Ramp' Achieved: Will the Ceasefire Last?

Iran gets its revenge, bombs an American military base in Doha, Qatar.

A week is a long time in geopolitics and in West Asia, one night can be enough. Overnight, the region oscillated between the threats of an all-out conflict as Iran fired missiles at the American military base in Qatar, to a sudden sense of hope and peace when President Donald Trump announced on his X handle late in the evening on 23 June that a ceasefire had been agreed to by Israel and Iran!

However, for this ceasefire to happen, a face-saving and acceptable 'off ramp' was required for all the three parties in the conflict, that is, the USA, Israel and Iran. While the USA claimed that its B-2 bombers delivering the deep penetration GBU-57 bombs had inflicted massive damage to the Fordow nuclear enrichment site in Iran, Israel claimed victory by pushing back Iran's nuclear program sufficiently with strikes on its nuclear facilities at Natanz, Isfahan and Arak. This, combined with the targeted assassination of top military leadership in Iran and many key nuclear scientists, gave them a perfect 'off ramp'.

Perhaps, the most difficult part was for Iran. Aerial and missile strikes from Israel for over 10 days, huge losses to its air force and air defence, many missile launchers and depots destroyed, oil depots burnt, key military leadership eliminated and, most importantly, the US strikes on Fordow, all made it very difficult for Iran to agree to a ceasefire. However, stage managed and well-orchestrated strikes on the Al Udeid base of the US military in Qatar on 23 June, combined with one last salvo of missiles into Israel in the early hours of 24 June, gave something that Iran could sell as a victory back home. Also, Iran had consistently stated that the war was initiated by Israel on 13 June and that it would cease firing if Israel also did so.

Now that a ceasefire has been achieved, there are many questions to be answered and mysteries to be unravelled. The biggest question is whether the ceasefire will hold. In an explosive and fragile politico-military situation that exists between Israel and Iran, nothing can be said for sure and the smallest of triggers can unleash a fresh wave of strikes. It is very unlikely that Iran would initiate any fresh strikes given the weak military position it finds itself in, but with Israel and PM Netanyahu, one can never be sure. He can manufacture any fresh reason to strike, even if his own intelligence agencies don't stand by the threat projections.

The second big question is tied to the reason for the commencement of the current conflict – the rapidly developing threat of Iran developing nuclear weapons. The key military objective emerging from it was complete destruction of the nuclear capability of Iran. Despite the US intelligence agencies and the International Atomic Energy Agency (IAEA), both clearly stating that Iran was nowhere near developing a nuclear weapon, Israel went ahead and bombed the nuclear sites and other infrastructure in Iran on 13 June.

Israel inflicted significant damage at Natanz, Isfahan and Arak putting them out of service for a long time, if not permanently. However, the enrichment plant at Fordow, buried 270-300 feet underground in a rocky mountainous area, was beyond the military capabilities of Israel. Having shaped the battlefield favourably and achieved complete air dominance, Israel sought American help. The USA finally obliged when its B-2 bombers delivered their payloads on 22 June. Trump claimed absolute obliteration of the Fordow plant but the satellite imagery released later tells a different story.

The success of the US bombing was based on an assumption that two or more GBU-57 bombs would create a crater deep enough to reach the plant depth at 270-300 feet and then explode. This is due to the fact that a GBU-57 bomb can penetrate upto 200 feet of earth, and drill a pinhole about 32 inches wide (the diameter of the bomb) before exploding and creating a crater. Thus, to achieve the desired effect, two or more bombs would have to go with precise accuracy through the same pinhole to reach a depth of 300 feet, technically an (almost) impossible task. Satellite imagery clearly showed two groups of three pinhole craters, each separated by a few feet atleast. This implies that each bomb had individually drilled a hole, probably upto a maximum depth of 200 feet and then exploded. The rocky mountainous terrain would have made the task only harder. Resultantly, whether the combined effort of six GBU-57 bombs could reach the required depth of 270-300 feet is a big question.

Satellite imagery also showed a long line of trucks leaving Fordow on 19 and 20 June, evacuating key equipment and enriched uranium. Plus, the entry and exits to the plant were sealed, well before the bombs were dropped. Even initial reactions and assessments by the US and Israeli intelligence agencies indicated modest damage while Iran claimed that the bombs failed to achieve any effect.

If Fordow has survived and the nuclear material is safe somewhere, can it be claimed that the nuclear threat from Iran has been eliminated? At best, it has been pushed back a few years. Plus, now it gives Iran legitimate reasons to not only withdraw from the Nuclear Non-Proliferation Treaty (NPT) but also weaponise its nuclear program.

The second and implied objective of the conflict was the toppling of the Iranian regime. That too has not happened. In fact, the entire nation which has been bitterly divided over regime policies, is rallying together behind it. Also, Khamenei has reportedly nominated three clerics as his potential successors to ensure continuity.

The next big questions go back to the root cause of the ongoing conflict in the region, the Gaza War. Will this ceasefire lead to a ceasefire in Gaza? Will Israel end its military campaign and withdraw its forces from Gaza? Where does it leave Israel's unfinished business of completely eliminating Hamas? And, of course, the mother of all questions, what about the future course of the Palestine issue? If none of these questions are answered, the region is back to 12 June, a day before Israel launched its pre-emptive strikes in Iran.

The Israel-Iran conflict may have ended for now, but deep fissures in the relationship remain. Iran has been badly hit but its missiles striking deep into Israel have shocked Israel and the world. A fragile peace may prevail, but the nuclear weapons race may have just got heated up, leading to a question of not 'if' but 'when' will Iran develop a nuclear weapon.

SECTION IX

Israel ups the Ante, Qatar Strike and the '20 Point Trump Peace Plan'

58

An Indefinite War Looms Ahead as Israel Moves in to 'Occupy Gaza'

The war in Gaza took an ugly turn on 7 August 2025 when the Security Cabinet in Israel approved a new war plan proposed by PM Netanyahu to occupy Gaza. The plan is anchored on five principles which include disarming of Hamas, return of all hostages (living and dead) and complete demilitarization of Gaza as the primary objectives, while the remaining two follow-on objectives are complete Israeli security control in Gaza after the war and establishment of a civil administration that is neither Hamas nor the Palestinian Authority. Speaking to the media later, PM Netanyahu added that "we intend to control all of Gaza. We don't want to keep Gaza. We want a security perimeter. We want to hand Gaza over to Arab forces that will govern Gaza properly." The plan was approved despite major reservations on its execution and chances of success by Israeli Defence Forces (IDF) Chief of Staff, Lt Gen Eyal Zamir who argued that such an operation, apart from slim chances of success, would endanger the hostages and could lead to Israeli military rule in Gaza with full responsibility over two million Palestinians.

In a war that has been dragging on for almost two years, its cost has reached unprecedented proportions in the modern era. Over 61,000 civilians have been killed in Israeli strikes (the figures could be much larger once the thousands of missing are accounted for later) and a population of over two million displaced internally multiple times. To add to the misery, a food crisis is now adding deaths due to starvation, a fact acknowledged by the Israeli government too, albeit reluctantly.

What is New about 'Occupy Gaza'?

On the face of it, the new plan only looks to reinforce the current Israeli occupation in Gaza and further intensification of military operations. As a result, it reduces any chance of an early ceasefire or an end to the war. More importantly, from an Israeli people's perspective, it puts the lives of the remaining hostages in Hamas custody in grave danger. It may be recalled that of the 251 hostages initially taken by Hamas, 50 are still in their custody of which 20 are expected to be alive.

The new plan envisages expansion of ground operations to take over Gaza City completely. The operations would be expanded into the 'central camps' and beyond, the city of Deir al-Balah and the tented camps in Muwasi, a vast cluster of displacement camps along the coast. The IDF has identified them as Hamas strongholds. These are also areas where Hamas may be holding hostages in tunnels or other secret locations.

In view of the new plan, the ongoing military operation in Gaza, 'Operation Gideon's Chariots' has been wound up. 'Operation Gideon's Chariots' was launched on 16 May this year, well before the Israel-Iran '12-day war', and was aimed to destroy Hamas's military and administrative infrastructure in Gaza, and to rescue the Israeli hostages held in Gaza. Over the next three months the number of civilians killed in Gaza due to IDF operations dramatically rose from 53,500 (in April) to more than 61,000 at the beginning of August, more than 6,500 killed in merely three months. Of these, more than 1,500 have been killed at food collection points established by Gaza Humanitarian Foundation (GHF), a joint initiative by Israel and the USA to provide food aid to people in Gaza. This initiative has failed miserably in its aim to deliver food to the starving population, mostly due to inability to manage the huge surge of crowds coming for food and the allegations by the IDF that Hamas cadres have tried to sabotage food delivery efforts.

Also, 'Operation Gideon's Chariots' failed to achieve its stated objectives. As a result, Hamas continues to inflict casualties on the IDF. Nearly 895 soldiers of the IDF have already lost their lives in the war with more than 48 killed since the launch of the operation. Adding to the misery is the fact that the IDF is no closer to complete destruction of Hamas than it was in May this year. The hostages continue to be in Hamas custody and all attempts at getting them back through a ceasefire deal have failed.

Is there an End State?

Israel's insistence on a military solution which aims at complete annihilation of Hamas poses serious questions. Hamas, despite being battered, remains effective in Gaza. Over the past 22 months, most estimates suggest that almost 12,000 to 15,000 Hamas cadres have been eliminated although the IDF estimates are higher at almost 23,000. But the worrying fact for Israel is that thousands of cadres have been recruited afresh and that there is yet no alternative to Hamas in Gaza.

The new plan also risks threats to lives of thousands of people living in concentrated areas of cities and camps in Gaza. Refusal to allow international agencies to distribute aid and failure of the GHF to deliver food to the starving population is adding to the pressure, including that from the USA, Israel's principal benefactor. The decision by many within the international community including countries like France, UK, Australia, etc., to recognise the state of Palestine too is adding to the pressure on Israel.

Within Israel too, the refusal by Israel to accept any end state unless Hamas is completely eliminated even at the cost of the lives of the remaining hostages is causing widespread protests and opposition. More than a dozen retired senior officials in Israel, including IDF chiefs of staff, intelligence chiefs, Shin Bet and Mossad directors, and police commissioners issued a joint video message on 10 August calling for an end to the war, arguing that Israel has racked up more losses than victories and that the fighting has dragged on for political reasons rather than strategic military need. Families of hostages are out on the streets protesting against the grave danger their loved ones would face once IDF launches new operations.

Without a complete victory in Gaza, there is no scenario of a 'Day After' as admitted by many senior Israeli officials who, in the same breath, also acknowledge the improbability of achieving this aim. The war in Gaza is therefore doomed to carry on, motivated more by political greed than military logic. The people in Gaza meanwhile face another long scary period of starvation, death, destruction and relocation.

59

Israel Targets Qatar, Crosses Yet another Red Line

It is 9 September 2025 and the Gaza war has exploded; a red-line has been crossed yet again.

While the world was watching the shocking images coming out of Nepal where the youth, frustrated with the government, had taken the law into their own hands, another shock was in the offing later in the evening on 9 September. Out of nowhere, unprovoked, and many would say uncalled for, Israeli fighter jets launched missiles into Doha and Qatar, targeting a building where senior Hamas officials had gathered to discuss and consider the latest ceasefire proposal mooted by the USA, just a day earlier. Initial reports indicated that the Israeli strike had succeeded in taking out the senior leadership of Hamas including Palestinian chief negotiator, Khalil Al-Hayya. However, it was later confirmed that although six Hamas people were killed, most of the senior leadership escaped unhurt as they were not present in the building when the missiles struck. PM Netanyahu was quick to issue a statement that the strike was "a wholly independent Israeli operation. Israel initiated it, Israel conducted it, and Israel takes full responsibility". The statement was issued almost too quickly as if to shield the USA and President Trump from the aftershocks of the strike, which has been condemned almost universally across the globe.

The failed attack however, raises serious questions on the global order (which already is in a state of total collapse), sanctity of international borders, territorial integrity and nation's sovereignty, dangers of being a mediator in a regional/global conflict as Qatar is realising now, the gains or futility of such attacks in ending prolonged wars and perhaps, most of all, whether 'might is right' and 'winner takes all' will be the new norm, going forward in world affairs. While this may not be the last that the world has heard of Israel violating global norms and striking inside sovereign nations at will, there are a few important threads to be considered.

The Complicity of the USA

It is no secret that the USA and especially President Donald Trump have vowed unequivocal support to Israel in the Gaza war right from the start. It is also not a secret that Israel will not be able to continue the war if the USA withdraws its material and moral support. However, it is the deceit and duplicity that is more enraging than the support itself.

The USA presented a new ceasefire plan to Hamas and Israel on 7-8 September, giving the Hamas leadership 48 hours to agree to it, as a final warning. The Hamas leadership was convened to discuss the proposal on 9 September when Israel struck. Sounds as familiar as an earlier script? The same script was in play in June too when the USA announced that it and Iran would be holding the fifth and perhaps conclusive talks on the Iran nuclear deal on 15 June. Lulled into complacency perhaps and lured into the trap, Iran was struck by Israel on 13 June, sabotaging chances of any fruitful talks or any deal. The USA, instead of rebuking Israel, was complicit enough to assist Israeli jets in their continued strikes over the next 12 days, intercepted incoming missiles from Iran and on 24 June, even obliged Israel by dropping GBU-57, deep penetrating bunker-bursting bombs on the Fordow nuclear plant in Iran.

Coming to the attack in Qatar on 9 September, the USA pleaded that it came to know of the Israeli attack merely 10 minutes before the missiles struck. The Al Udeid air base in Doha is the largest American military base in the region and serves as the forward headquarters for US Central Command, also known as CENTCOM, which controls US military operations in the entire region. One of the key functions of this base is its self-defence, and in the larger security umbrella across the region, is surveillance and air defence. Both these functions are 24x7, 365 days a year. Plus, they have the most modern systems, to say the least. To imagine that such systems would require a phone call to know of an incoming missile is embarrassing to say the least. Also, the Israeli jets flew more than 1,500 km to Qatar to fire the missiles which would have entailed air-to-air refuelling which again only the USA provides. Is it then the case that the USA air-defence and surveillance systems require a phone call to be activated and that its refuellers refuel Israeli jets in international air space just for fun?

What Should the Regional Countries Do?

It is not only Qatar but the entire region which is in a state of shock. Violating Iranian territory in June 2025 may have been a different case as Iran and Israel had been exchanging blows earlier too. But Qatar, which has been mediating the ceasefire deal and hosting rival delegations over the past two years, being targeted, is shocking. Also, the statement from Israel's Knesset Speaker that this strike is a message to the entire region which was soon followed by PM Netanyahu threatening Qatar and any other country with more strikes (if required) is a chilling reminder to the regional countries of what can await them too.

The futility of American security guarantees too has been brutally exposed, not for the first time either. It may be recalled that the Houthis from Yemen had successfully fired missiles and drones into Saudi Arabian oil fields in September 2019 and the Abu Dhabi airport in January 2022. Even in the ongoing Gaza conflict, when the Houthis blocked the passage of ships across the Red Sea, the entire American naval might was unable to dislodge the threat. On top of it, is the American policy since the mid-2010s, pronounced during President Obama's term, of disengagement from the region and not putting any American boots on the ground in a regional conflict, actually working?

Two lessons are clear therefore to the regional countries, especially Saudi Arabia, the UAE, Jordan and Egypt. Firstly, if the red lines that are drawn are not acted upon when violated, then a future catastrophe is waiting round the corner. It may be recalled that Jordan had drawn a red line at the start of the Gaza War with regard to violation of its air space and pushing of refugees into Jordan. Similarly, Egypt had announced that taking over Rafah was a red line which could invite reaction. Israel has violated both these and many more red lines with impunity without any fear of reprisal. Similarly, both Saudi Arabia and the UAE have maintained an ambivalent position in the Gaza war and have in fact assisted Israel in moving cargo and goods and even use of air space to its fighters, in the hope and expectation that the war in Gaza will end soon and that the normalisation with Israel could then progress. However, the visit of the UAE president to Qatar on 10 September to express solidarity and the strong statement from Saudi Arabia expressing full solidarity and support to Qatar, placing all its capabilities at its disposal, are an indication that the reality of the situation is perhaps dawning onto them now.

What can they do? A unified military action akin to the 1973 Yom Kippur war is most unlikely, given the almost non-existent security forces in these countries, having purchased their sovereign security through (non-existent) American guarantees. It is also clear that the promise of normalisation which was the whole purpose of the Abraham Accords, signed five years ago in September 2020, too has been deeply subverted by Israel. What can however act as a telling deterrent is collective economic and diplomatic action to isolate Israel in the region. The regional countries have to also collectively think hard and long on the utility or futility of the American military presence in the region if, at the end of the day, what they are going to get as a safety net is no safety at all.

The Indian Predicament

India too finds itself in a very delicate predicament as it enjoys a very close and strategic partnership with Israel on multiple fronts, especially security and modern technology. Just a day prior to the attack in Qatar, India and Israel had successfully concluded a bilateral investment treaty (BIT).

Having championed the cause for a stable and rule-based world order, India cannot condone Israeli action in Qatar. However, its close ties with Israel also inhibit it from condemning it outrightly unlike many other Western countries like the UK, France, and Spain who have outrightly condemned Israel. It was perhaps due to this that the initial statement from the Ministry of External Affairs expressed 'concern' while a later tweet from PM Modi 'condemned the violation of sovereignty of the brotherly state of Qatar', without however naming Israel.

It may be recalled that earlier too, India has been caught in a similar bind with respect to Israel. On 14 June, when the SCO initially issued a statement condemning Israel for its attack in Iran, India distanced itself from it, but was a signatory to the joint statement issued at the SCO Summit on 31 August in Tianjin, China, where the SCO clearly condemned the USA and Israel for its attacks on Iran.

Where Does it leave the Gaza War?

The war in Gaza meanwhile drags on. Israel has intensified its operations in Gaza city, bringing down huge buildings in precision air strikes. With blockade continuing, the state of starvation and deaths is becoming critical with each passing day. Already, more than 64,000 people have died in Gaza due to Israeli operations while 20 living Israeli hostages in Hamas captivity look at an uncertain future due to the absence of a ceasefire deal. Reports of unarmed civilians being shot while collecting food are adding to the allegations of a planned genocide in Gaza.

On the other hand, ceasefire efforts are not bearing any results. Any hopes of an early ceasefire have now evaporated with Qatar being targeted as it is most unlikely to host any such talks soon while the Hamas obviously will not trust the USA or Israel anytime soon.

Going Forward

Prime Minister Netanyahu has vowed to pursue the enemies of Israel anywhere, anytime, akin to what the USA did after 9/11. However, there are a few things that Israel may do well to consider. The USA was in Afghanistan for 20 years and yet did not achieve any decisive victory. At the end of it, it had to withdraw in August 2021 in a very embarrassing situation, leaving the Taliban back in power. Curiously, Qatar had hosted the Taliban too, where the US-Taliban peace deal was made in February 2020. Is Israel also looking at an unending and prolonged war in Gaza lasting for years? Does it have the stamina or resources for it? Is it ready for a scenario where, at the end of it all, Hamas (like Taliban) will be back in power?

The missile attack on Qatar has raised many critical questions. While Israel has the right to seek justice for the 7 October terror attack, such attacks violating the territorial integrity of sovereign countries is unacceptable. Instead of continuing the war without a realistic end-goal in mind, it may be worthwhile to consider a solution that brings its hostages back home while instituting measures in conjunction with the regional and global players to ensure security and co-existence in the future.

60

Trump Announces a 20-Point Peace Plan

Another plan, another attempt at ceasing hostilities in Gaza! Will it end the misery this time?

Amid this continuing conflict and resultant deaths and destruction in Gaza, the USA announced a '20-Point Trump Peace Plan' on 29 September 2025 that offers an ambitious roadmap towards finding a lasting solution to the conflict, starting with an early ceasefire and an immediate return of hostages. With Israel already having endorsed the plan and Hamas too agreeing to a few of the main points, there is hope as mediators conduct detailed negotiations in Cairo to finalise the details to execute this plan. Meanwhile, the war has completed two years and the people in Gaza, exhausted and helpless, wait and pray for this misery to finally end.

There are however multiple questions to be answered before peace can finally return to Gaza. Some of the more important ones are: Can this plan deliver lasting peace? What is the assurance that Israel will not revoke this ceasefire, like in March 2025, and re-launch military operations again? With Hamas agreeing to the plan partially (primarily on issues of return of hostages), how will Israel seek to fulfil its military objectives, one of which is the complete elimination of Hamas? And most importantly, despite the insertion of a "credible pathway to Palestinian self-determination and statehood, which we recognise as the aspiration of the Palestinian people", can this plan lead to the elusive Two-State Solution, leading to an independent and sovereign state of Palestine, coexisting with Israel? The answers to most of them are ambiguous at best and seem to be heavily loaded in favour of Israel.

How is the 20-Point Plan Different?

While the current 20-point proposal looks positive and ambitious, it is not much different from various proposals mooted earlier. Most of the previous ceasefire proposals including the 'Biden Plan' of May 2024 and the later plans presented jointly by Qatar, Egypt and the USA had similar pointers like in the 20-Point Plan, emphasising on the return of the hostages, withdrawal of Israeli forces from Gaza and a joint plan for rebuilding it in a 'day after' scenario.

The 20-Point Plan, however, has few distinguishing features which are different from previous proposals, most of which target Hamas and its future existence. The most important is point no. 4 which states that "within 72 hours of Israel publicly accepting this agreement, all hostages, alive and deceased, will be returned". This is starkly different from previous proposals as Hamas had previously insisted that the final return of hostages has to be in sync with the complete withdrawal of Israeli forces.

The next is point no. 9 which states that Gaza will be governed under the temporary transitional governance of a technocratic, apolitical committee, made up of qualified Palestinians and international experts, with oversight and supervision by a new international transitional body, the 'Board of Peace,' which will be chaired by President Donald J. Trump. This is again a new insertion as there was no clear mention of such an arrangement in any of the previous ceasefire proposals. The fact that the US President is to lead the overarching body of governance in Gaza is new, aimed perhaps to keep Israel more in control than Hamas.

Complete demilitarization of Gaza and Hamas at point no. 13 is yet another different one as the earlier proposals had no mention of demilitarisation of Hamas or Gaza. The formulation of an International Stabilisation Force (ISF) with Arab and international partners to be immediately deployed in Gaza at point no. 15 is also new. Previously, the Arab countries were not at all ready to deploy boots on the ground in Gaza.

Curiously, the Israeli forces seem to have been given a free hand to decide when, if and how to disengage from Gaza. Point no. 16 states the Israel Defence Forces (IDF) will withdraw based on standards, milestones, and timeframes linked to demilitarization that will be agreed upon between the IDF, ISF, the guarantors, and the USA, with the objective of a secure Gaza that no longer poses a threat to Israel, Egypt, or its citizens. This implies that the IDF will retain the authority to decide if and when to withdraw, what constitutes a violation of the ceasefire and upto what line it should withdraw, with almost no oversight.

ISRAEL'S WAR ON GAZA

Israel's withdrawal to the 'yellow line'

In the first phase of the Gaza ceasefire plan, Israel is set to withdraw its troops to the agreed 'yellow line' within 24 hours, after which a 72-hour period will begin for the handover of Israeli captives.

Gaza Map as per Trump's 20 Point Peace Plan - Al Jazeera 9 October 2025

Looking Ahead

Two years into the war, people in Gaza are exhausted and desperate. Hamas has been battered and requires time to regroup and think about its future. Israel too is not in a good position with many prominent countries including France, UK, and Australia according recognition to Palestine in the recent UN General Assembly session. The Israeli missile strike into Qatar on 9 September not only brought the entire region to stand together against Israel but also brought upon the ire of the USA and President Trump, especially on Israeli PM Netanyahu. Plus, there is continuing pressure for the safe return of hostages in Israel.

This plan therefore offers relief and a chance for off-ramp to each of the stakeholders. To the USA, it offers an opportunity to reclaim its leadership role and trust it had lost in the region, especially after the Qatar missile incident. The forced apology from PM Netanyahu to the Qatari Emir, in the presence of Donald Trump, followed by a public statement of apology were no mean achievements, even for Donald Trump.

How the plan unfolds in the coming weeks and days is most crucial. Hamas, having agreed to release all the hostages, dead or living, is likely to go through with it. This would not only help Israel tick one of its critical war objectives, but will also give Hamas the higher moral ground in case Israel continues its military operations thereafter. The entry of critical humanitarian supplies too is likely to commence once the hostages are released, bringing in vital relief to the starving population in Gaza.

It is however beyond this that the plan could face hurdles. An apolitical transitional government and the formation of ISF are not easy and may take months if not longer to happen. Similarly, demilitarisation of Gaza and Hamas is easier said than done. Hamas, like Hezbollah, while signing a ceasefire deal with Israel in November 2024, may agree to the terms but could retain some weaponry, cadres and capability as insurance. The (deliberate) omission of what happens in the West Bank concurrently as also an ambiguous mention of a "credible pathway to Palestinian self-determination and statehood" leaves the question of Palestinian statehood largely unanswered.

As the peace deal takes shape, there is hope that the saga of death and destruction in Gaza will finally come to an end, at least for a foreseeable future.

61

Gaza Ceasefire Holds on, Enters Crucial Phase

It is December 2025 and the fragile peace in Gaza is holding.

The ceasefire in Gaza, which came into effect on 10 October as a result of the '20-Point Peace Plan', has been largely successful till now, as it moves into its third month. Most of the easily achievable objectives have been achieved and there is a sense of respite and relief across both sides after more than two years of war in Gaza, which, more than once, threatened to engulf the entire region.

As an immediate result of the ceasefire, Israeli forces have ceased operations and have pulled back to a designated 'Yellow Line' in Gaza. The 20 living hostages have safely returned to Israel while the bodies of 27 out of 28 dead hostages have been returned to Israel. Plus, critical humanitarian aid has started trickling into Gaza.

The Ceasefire So Far

This was however the more visible and easily achievable part of the deal. The prospects of the fragile ceasefire converting into a lasting peace, however, face daunting challenges as many issues in Phase 2 of the ceasefire still need to be agreed upon and executed. Phase 2 hinges on three vital components. The first is the establishment and positioning of the International Stabilisation Force (ISF); second is the disarming of Hamas and demilitarisation of Gaza; and thirdly, the governance of Gaza by a technocratic, apolitical committee made up of qualified Palestinians and international experts, with oversight and supervision by an international transitional body, the 'Board of Peace,' to be headed by President Donald Trump.

Each of these is a challenge in itself but, for the peace plan to have any chance of success, they have to be implemented. Hamas, for its part, has stated that details of Phase 2 are yet to be discussed and that there is no question of it agreeing to complete disarming and surrendering although some inputs in the past few days suggest that it may be willing to put its weapons in 'freeze' if it remains a part of the future governance of Gaza. Israel is, however, adamant on disarming Hamas and that it can play no further role in the future of Gaza.

Phase 2

Among the issues critical to Phase 2 is the deployment of the ISF which will act as the line of separation between Hamas to the west and Israeli Defence Forces (IDF) to the east. As part of the process, the US Central Command is hosting an international conference in Doha on 16 December with partner nations to plan the International Stabilization Force for Gaza. More than 25 countries are expected to send representatives to the conference, which will include discussions on troop contributions, command structures, rules of engagement, areas of deployment, regulatory and dispute resolution mechanisms, etc. Among the countries willing to participate in the ISF, Indonesia has indicated its intention to provide up to 20,000 troops while some reports suggest that Pakistan too has expressed its willingness to participate. Whether the meeting on 16 December will provide concrete answers for a framework of the ISF will have to be seen. Later, Israeli PM Netanyahu is scheduled to meet President Trump on 29 December in Washington, before a final go ahead is given for the assembly and deployment of the ISF, early next year. Also, the ISF alone is not the key to the 'Gaza Peace' riddle as there are many other key impediments that would need to be overcome before there can be any hope for a lasting peace in Gaza.

Key Impediments to Lasting Peace

The ISF is perhaps the starting point of Phase 2. In it, there are key questions to be answered before it takes shape and becomes effective. The number of troops required for an effective 'peace enforcement' mission is the start point. Having identified the numbers and type of troops, countries have to volunteer to contribute troops. In a line of separation extending 40-45 km across the length of Gaza which includes many key crossings and built-up areas, the number of troops is the key. Command structure is the next important issue. Indications are that an American or a European General may be designated as the Force Commander. This, however, may be detrimental to confidence building as the USA is seen as a party to the conflict in Gaza. A General from the region or Indonesia (likely to be the largest troop contributor) may be more apt. What about India? As a nation which is trusted by both the warring parties and has more experience in UN peace-keeping missions than most countries, India may be the best suited to provide the leadership role in it.

The line of deployment and mandate given to ISF is the next important question. Clearly, if the IDF stays along the 'Yellow Line', then it would continue to hold more than 50 percent of the Gaza Strip and, more importantly, control over a crucial crossing on the Gaza-Egypt border, the Rafah Crossing. Egypt has time and again stressed on the fact that its right to coordinate two-way movement across the Rafah Crossing is important and perhaps a 'Red Line' while discussing plans for long-term peace. Therefore, the pull back of the IDF to a 'Green Line' as the ISF deploys could be an important factor for the success of the ISF. The third crucial element of the ISF is the mandate. Will it be mandated to fight Hamas in Gaza or will it, like many UN peace operations, be limited to maintaining peace across the line of ceasefire? If the mandate includes fighting Hamas, it may limit not only the number of nations contributing troops but also the long-term prospects of peace.

Demilitarisation and disarming of Hamas is definitely the next big question. While Hamas has ruled out disarming and surrendering, it may be more willing to participate in a 'military freeze' for the time being till a more long-term political solution is found in Gaza. Hamas continuing in its security role in Gaza may be unacceptable to Israel and all others including the Palestine Authority, but the disarming of Hamas needs to be seen in the context of the process of lasting peace in Gaza. If 'freezing' achieves the immediate aim of 'practically disarming' Hamas, it should be discussed as a viable option.

The next sticky issue is governance. As per the '20-Point Plan', Gaza is to be governed by a technocratic, apolitical committee, made up of qualified Palestinians and international experts, with oversight and supervision by a 'Board of Peace', headed by President Trump. Finding the right set of Palestinians to run the government and excluding Hamas leaders from any role is going to be a big challenge. Plus, the ability of the government to coordinate with the ISF and bring about stability followed by reconstruction and rehabilitation is also going to be a big challenge.

The Most Important Question

All the processes in the '20-Point Plan' fall short of a concrete road map to a viable and sovereign Palestinian state. Israel's PM has categorically stated that Israel is not going to accept any Palestine state. This was also earlier passed as a resolution in the Israeli Parliament. Plus, the increase in violence by settlers in the West Bank and continuing encroachment of territory by Israel there is steadily making any future viability of a 'Two-State Solution' difficult, if not improbable. If the whole process of the Peace Plan does not lead to resolving the core issue of the state of Palestine, can peace be permanent, is a question that needs to be answered.

Looking Ahead

Talks on Phase 2 of the Gaza ceasefire are critically important for long-term peace. The violent terror attack on Bondi Beach in Sydney, Australia, on 14 December, targeting Jews celebrating the annual festival of Hanukkah, is a reminder that Israel's fight against terror transcends the borders of Gaza and requires a deeper and long-term strategy. The start could be with a solution towards lasting peace in Gaza.

62

Can 'Board of Peace' Deliver Lasting Peace in Gaza?

It is February 2026 and the ceasefire in Gaza is holding on despite occasional reports of violations from both sides. Negotiated as part of Trump's '20 Point Peace Plan', the ceasefire which came into effect on 10 October 2025 has now completed four months and has been successful in implementation of most of the key requirements of Phase 1 of the plan. All the hostages (dead and alive) have successfully been returned to Israel with the mortal remains of the last hostage, police officer Ran Gvili, successfully retrieved on 26 January 2026, from a cemetery in northern Gaza. Israeli forces have pulled back to a designated 'Yellow Line' in Gaza and critical humanitarian aid is trickling into Gaza. Plus, the crucial Rafah Crossing into Egypt, vital for evacuation of patients requiring urgent medical aid, was opened on 2 February nearly two years after Israel closed it. Being operated by the European Union Border Assistance Mission, it allows a small number of Palestinians to enter and leave the Gaza Strip daily.

Taking the process of the peace plan forward, a number of important developments have taken place over the past one month. The Board of Peace has been nominated, an interim government of Gaza is now in place and the first summit meeting of the Board of Peace too has been held on 19 February with a number of countries pledging money and troops. There are, however, many crucial questions still to be answered, important among them is the prospect of long-term peace and security of Gaza and mechanisms to ensure that Israel does not face a repeat of 7 October, ever again.

Will the Board of Peace be able to deliver on its mandate? Can it ensure long-term peace and stability in Gaza and Israel? What happens to other key requirements like disarming of Hamas, demilitarisation of Gaza and deployment of an international force in Gaza?

The Governance

The most important piece of the puzzle in pursuit of peace in Gaza is the question of governance. As per the 20 Point Plan, the Board of Peace is the apex body to be chaired by President Trump. Soon after the announcement of the 20 Point Plan on 29 September 2025, the plan was presented at the Peace Summit held at Sharm el-Sheikh in Egypt on 13 October where, in the presence of more than 20 world leaders, the leaders of Egypt, Qatar, Turkiye and the USA issued a joint statement backing the Gaza ceasefire deal and committing to 'enduring peace' in the region. The 20 Point Peace plan was later endorsed by the UN Security Council on 17 November 2025, vide Resolution 2803 (2025).

The Board of Peace was finally unveiled on 16 January 2026 wherein an Executive Board was constituted—the international body that will oversee all the processes of governance, security, reconstruction and demilitarization in Gaza. The Executive Board will operate under the Board of Peace, which will be chaired by President Trump. Former UN envoy Nickolay Mladenov was nominated as the Board of Peace 'High Representative' for Gaza, to act as the on-the-ground link between the Board of Peace and the National Committee for the Administration of Gaza (NCAG). He will support the Board's oversight of all aspects of Gaza's governance, reconstruction, and development, while ensuring coordination across civilian and security pillars.

The other members nominated in the Executive Board were Steve Witkoff, the US envoy to the region, Jared Kushner; President Trump's senior adviser and son-in-law, Turkish Foreign Minister Hakan Fidan, Qatari minister Ali Al-Thawadi, Egyptian intelligence chief General Hassan Rashad, former British Prime Minister Tony Blair, billionaire businessman Marc Rowan, UAE Minister of State at the Ministry of Foreign Affairs, Reem al-Hashimy, Israeli-Cypriot real estate tycoon, Yakir Gabay, and former UN Gaza envoy, Sigrid Kaag. While regional players like Turkey, Qatar and the UAE found prominence, the key country found missing in the Board was Saudi Arabia.

In addition to the Executive Board, two close advisers to Jared Kushner—Aryeh Lightstone, who has served as Kushner's representative in Israel in recent months, and Josh Gruenbaum, who authored the Gaza reconstruction plan, were nominated as 'senior advisers to the Board of Peace'.

On the security front, Major General Jasper Jeffers from the USA was appointed as the commander of the International Stabilization Force (ISF) in Gaza. He was tasked to oversee all security matters related to the Palestinian technocratic government, assist in efforts to demilitarize the Gaza Strip, and supervise the safe transfer of humanitarian aid and reconstruction materials to the people in Gaza.

However, the most important part of this process was the nomination of the NCAG, a non-political body composed of Palestinian technocrats, responsible for managing daily civil-service affairs. Dr. Ali Sha'ath, an academic with a doctorate in engineering with Palestinian roots and years of experience in public administration, was nominated as its head. On 18 January, the other 11 members of the NCAG too were announced. They include Engineer Ayed Abu Ramadan, Abdel Karim Ashour, Ayed Yaghi, Ali Barhoum, Hanaa Terzi, Engineer Osama al-Saadawi, Jabr al-Daour, Engineer Omar al-Shamali and Adnan Abu Warda. Maj Gen Sami Nasman was assigned to monitor interior and security while Bashir al-Rayes was designated for finance. The NCAG will commence its work initially from Cairo before moving into Gaza. As expected, there were no members from Hamas or the Palestinian Authority in the NCAG.

With the Executive Board and the NCAG nominated, the first important step towards ensuring peace and reconstruction in Gaza has been completed. Is it, however, enough? The other key component in the process is the security arrangement, which is still in a flux.

Security Arrangements

While General Jasper Jeffers from the USA was appointed as the commander of the ISF in Gaza, there is no clarity on the composition of the ISF yet. The US Central Command (CENTCOM) hosted a conference in Doha on 16 December, which was attended by over 40 countries, to discuss various elements of the ISF. However, the talks were largely inconclusive as the countries failed to agree on the composition and the mandate. Most of the countries expressed concern over the crucial aspect of being involved in the de-militarisation of Hamas.

There were reports that Pakistan had offered to deploy upto 20,000 troops but that has been outrightly rejected by Israel. During the Board of Peace Meet on 19 February, ISF Commander Maj. Gen. Jasper Jeffers announced that the ISF will consist of 20,000 soldiers along with 12,000 police officers with the primary mandate to do two things: stabilize the security environment in Gaza and enable civilian governance. Initially, the ISF HQ will be located at the Civil-Military Coordination Centre in Kiryat Gat, in Southern Israel. During the meet, Indonesia, Morocco, Kazakhstan, Kosovo and Albania committed to contributing troops while Egypt and Jordan agreed to train Palestinian police. Indonesia emerged as the largest contributor, promising 8,000 troops. However, there is lack of clarity whether the troops will actively engage to de-militarise Hamas or just play the role of peace keeping, separating the Israeli forces and Hamas.

Financing the Peace

Finance is the next big issue in the reconstruction and rehabilitation of Gaza. According to the UN Development Programme (UNDP)'s Jaco Cilliers, Special Representative of the Administrator for the programme of assistance to the Palestinian people, the estimated cost of damage across the Gaza Strip is US$70 billion. To kickstart the massive operation of reconstruction, around US$20 billion will be required in the next three years alone. These funds are going to be hard to come by.

At the Board of Peace Meet on 19 February, presided by President Trump, a pledge of US$17 billion only could be mustered, including US$ 10 billion by the USA. However, much of these pledges are amounts spread over many years and some are conditional to issues like 'final resolution that fulfils Palestinian aspiration for statehood and recognition and the Israeli aspiration for security and integration.' The removal of the rubble or debris itself in Gaza, estimated at anything between 37 and 65 million tonnes could take upto 10 years and massive investment. When the possibility of unexploded mines and munitions is added to it, the risks, costs and time go up significantly.

Key Hurdles to Lasting Peace in Gaza

The peace process in Gaza is therefore likely to be hard and arduous. The assembly and deployment of the ISF could take up the whole of 2026, and that is if the USA is able to get the countries to commit enough troops and resources for it. The Rules of Engagement will pose the next challenge as most of the countries have made it clear that they would not like to engage in a military engagement against Hamas to demilitarise it. Hamas, on the other hand, has made it very clear that it has no plans to demilitarise, at least till the time Israeli forces continue to occupy Gaza. Israel meanwhile, has made it clear that there is no going back from the 'Yellow Line' till the military threat from Hamas is completely eliminated. With neither willing to compromise, how the peace process will move ahead is a big question.

The Executive Board and the NCAG too will find it difficult to execute their mandate in a situation of fragile peace and repeated incidents of ceasefire violations. As per the Gaza Ministry of Health, more than 600 people have been killed and over 1,600 injured in Israeli strikes since the ceasefire in October 2025. Israel too has lost the lives of four soldiers in Hamas ambushes during the same period.

The next issue of concern is the Board of Peace itself. Many countries including some key American allies like the UK, Germany and France see it as an attempt by President Trump to upstage international institutions like the UN. The initial framework and the charter of the Board of Peace projects it as an international organization designed to 'secure enduring peace in all areas threatened by conflict' but does not mention Gaza or Palestine. Instead, it projects the Board as a standing global body capable of operating across multiple conflict zones and coordinating peace and stabilization efforts worldwide. Plus, the fact that President Trump has given himself sweeping powers to run the Board, have caused grave concern among the nations.

Looking Ahead

Lasting peace in Gaza looks remote. Hamas is not ready to lay down arms. Without it happening, Gaza cannot be completely demilitarised. Without it, Israeli forces will not vacate Gaza or pull back from the Yellow Line. The ISF is yet to take shape and both the numbers as well as rules of engagement are likely to remain key friction points. Although initial financial commitments look good, in effect they would be grossly inadequate unless a concerted all-round pledge takes shape.

Without all the above, the Executive Board or the NCAG will be unable to execute their mandate on the ground. Israel is clearly frustrated at the slow pace of developments, especially the security situation. It is already drawing up plans for a renewed offensive in Gaza with its Southern Command put in charge of it. Hinting at the military's offensive plans recently, Defence Minister Israel Katz was quite emphatic that Israel was determined to disarm Hamas, threatening to 'dismantle' the terror group if it did not agree to lay down its arms.

The odds of Gaza therefore returning to another period of conflict are therefore live and real. Even if the IDF offensive does not go in, with the way things stand, Gaza could well turn into a zone of frozen conflict, with no winners – clearly an unwinnable war.

SECTION X

India and the Gaza War

63

India's Fine Balancing Act

The sudden and audacious attack by Hamas in the early hours of 7 October 2023 took Israel by complete surprise and shocked the world. With more than 1,300 killed by Hamas on the first day, including infants, women and the elderly, it marked the single bloodiest day in Israel's history. Indian PM Modi was among the first world leaders to condemn the terror attack and extend support to its strategic ally, Israel.

India, like Israel, has been a victim of terror in the past and therefore terror attacks are an absolute redline for India. Soon after the 7 October attack, PM Modi highlighted India's stand during the Ninth G20 Parliamentary Speakers' Summit (P20 Summit) in Delhi on 13 October, stating "*Wherever terrorism happens, for whatever reason, in whatever form, it is against humanity*".

Apart from its support to and solidarity with Israel in its fight against the 7 October terror attack, another very important foreign policy priority of India has been to evacuate its trapped citizens in any war-torn area. In recent years, wherever there has been a conflict or war, India has been among the first to launch operations to evacuate its citizens. Living up to it, India launched '*Operation Ajay*' on 12 October 2023. With an estimated 18,000 citizens including students and tourists trapped in the war zone in Israel and only air routes available to evacuate, it was a challenge. By 14 October, two Indian Air Force planes had landed back carrying more than 200 passengers each. The stories of these people evacuated from the war zone are heart rending as they describe the destruction caused by the war and their immeasurable gratitude that the Indian government has been able to pull them out safely.

India's Fine Balancing Act

While the immediate rescue of its people from the conflict zone was a top priority, maintaining a fine balance in the Gaza war was another foreign policy priority for India. Apart from PM Modi being among the first global leaders to denounce the

Hamas terror attack on 7 October itself, an official statement from the government reiterating India's steadfast support to the 'Two-State Solution' on 13 October laid to rest any doubts that may have crept in on India's stated foreign policy on Palestine. India was also prompt in providing humanitarian aid to Gaza. At the Munich Security Conference in February 2024, when asked, Dr. Jaishankar, the External Affairs Minister, was categorical that India backs the two-state solution, condemns terror, seeks the return of the hostages and the creation of a humanitarian corridor and that Israel should be mindful not to cause civilian casualties.

In the context of the Ukraine war, Dr. Jaishankar said that if approached, India could explore playing the role of a mediator. As regards the Gaza war and the region, both are critically important to India. In case the conflict spreads and escalates further, it would have serious consequences for India because of the close inter-dependency that it has with the region owing to its energy security needs, trade, diaspora and most importantly, threat of spillover of security threats into its neighbourhood. India has already deployed naval ships in the Arabian Sea to safeguard its cargos against any Houthi threat in the area. There are reports that much of its cargo is being diverted along longer routes and that the insurance costs too are rising, which will have a direct impact on Indian exports. The India-Middle East-Europe-Economic-Corridor (IMEC) corridor connecting India to Europe through the Arabian Peninsula has also got stuck due to the war and was one of the prominent points of discussion between India and the UAE as well as India and Greece recently during high level talks.

India however has a unique position in this war. It enjoys close ties with Israel as well as the Arab leadership and the Palestinian Authority. PM Modi and Netanyahu enjoy a close personal rapport and understand each other well too. As Dr. Jaishankar stated at Munich, India could pitch in, if asked, to mediate in the war. For India, this war is neither its creation nor its direct problem but a prolonged conflict will definitely hurt Indian interests in the region. The question is whether and when will India be asked to pitch in and what role will India thereafter assign for itself?

64

As War Continues in Gaza, a Lesson for Israel from India

It is November 2023 and the war in Gaza has already taken a heavy toll on innocent civilians on both sides. In over 45 days of the war, Israel has conducted over 7,500 strikes by air and artillery, moved ground troops and tanks into Gaza cutting off Northern Gaza and caused heavy destruction in the Gaza Strip. The Red Cross and Palestinian Health Ministry have reported that the death toll in Gaza has already crossed 14,500 persons which includes more than 6,000 children.

Israel's insistence on 'flattening Gaza to the ground' and 'eliminating Hamas from the face of the Earth' has meant that it has not exercised any restraint while choosing targets and striking them irrespective of the heavy collateral damage and casualties it may cause. Its strikes on hospitals in Gaza, UN-run facilities, and schools and refugee camps have caused global outraged calls for an immediate ceasefire; besides, calls for access to humanitarian aid are growing louder by the day. WHO, UN Relief and Works Agency, UN Population Fund and UNICEF, put out a joint statement on 4 November stating that almost 420 children are being killed or injured in Gaza every day. The UN General Assembly, in its special session on 27 October, adopted a resolution sponsored by Jordan, calling for an "immediate, durable and sustained humanitarian truce". It also demanded "continuous, sufficient and unhindered" provision of life-saving supplies and services for civilians trapped in the enclave.

On 4 November, US Secretary of State Blinken undertook his second visit to Israel in the past month and advised PM Netanyahu against punitive strikes that caused death and destruction of civilians and reiterated an appeal for a humanitarian pause so that essential aid could be delivered to the suffering population. On 15 November, the UN Security Council too passed a resolution, sponsored by Malta, calling for "urgent and extended humanitarian pauses and corridors throughout the Gaza Strip" to allow aid delivery and medical evacuations.

Special meetings of BRICS and OIC too have asked for an early ceasefire and delivery of humanitarian aid. All regional countries including Saudi Arabia, the UAE, Iran and others have unequivocally condemned Israeli strikes causing mass civilian casualties. The Arab Islamic Committee, a joint delegation of Arab and Muslim nations comprising ministers of Saudi Arabia, Egypt, Jordan, and the Palestinian Authority are on a global tour to rally support for a ceasefire and have already visited China on 20 November and Paris on 22 November.

As a result, pressure is mounting on Israel to exercise restraint and permit delivery of humanitarian aid. Despite that, on 17-18 November, Israel struck two schools in Northern Gaza including one run by the UNRWA leading to over 50 deaths, mostly children and severely injuring over 200 coupled with absolute destruction of the school facilities. Once again, it was promptly condemned by the UN and regional countries.

With the raid and blockade of Al Shifa Hospital in Gaza not being able to provide conclusive evidence that the hospital and the tunnels behind were actually being used by Hamas as command centres, how does Israel justify the deaths of hundreds of children and patients there due to lack of critical medical care, leading to their burial in a mass grave in the hospital's backyard? Has Israel achieved its military and political objectives or is it still a work in progress? More importantly, does an end state of this war leave any space for a two-state solution which ensures a viable and independent state of Palestine?

There are many more questions, with very few concrete answers. Like Israel, India too has grappled with the threat of terror for the last three decades and the manner in which India has slowly but steadily brought about peace and stability, especially in the Kashmir Valley, could offer some answers for Israel in the current conflict.

Indian Lessons for Israel

India got its independence in August 1947 while the state of Israel was formed in May 1948. Both nations had to face armed conflicts shortly thereafter in 1948. While the ceasefire in the case of Israel resulted in it occupying more territory than what was earmarked as its national boundaries, India had to accept division of territory in Jammu & Kashmir with one part of Kashmir going under Pakistan's occupation. Both nations fought major wars later – Israel in 1967 and 1973 while India fought wars against Pakistan in 1965, 1971 and 1999 (Kargil) and in 1962 against China. There have been other minor conflicts which both nations have fought against their adversaries, including their fight against terror unleashed on them from across the borders. Also, both nations have adversaries who use 'terror as an instrument of state policy'. Both nations have also faced hostage and hijack situations endangering the lives of its citizens more than once.

However, the methods and strategy used by India and Israel in countering these threats differ vastly. While India has always exercised restraint and has mostly avoided crossing the borders or ceasefire line or Line of Control, (LoC) with Pakistan, Israel has been more aggressive in its methods used in countering its threats. India has propagated peaceful co-existence and has made several attempts to make peace and Israel too, while offering peace solutions, has usually followed a strategy of seeking 'peace through security' and has often taken the battle right into enemy territory.

India, which has been fighting terror since 1990 in Jammu & Kashmir, mostly emanating from Pakistan, had to deploy a large number of security forces to counter it. Like Israel, in fact learning from Israel, India came up with a 'Line of Control Fence' which acts as physical barrier for terrorists infiltrating into India. Surveillance sensors coupled with active military deployment on the fence has ensured that infiltration levels have dropped significantly in the past decade.

In the early decades of fighting terror in the Kashmir Valley, India was confronted with a situation where the terrorists (local and foreign) enjoyed support from the locals making the task of the security forces difficult. However, India exercised restraint and followed the strategy of minimum force to achieve its objectives. India has also not been known for use of air strikes to target terror groups hiding amongst civilian populations, and definitely never any strikes on hospitals, schools, UN facilities, etc., on either side of the LoC. While conducting operations in the Indian side of Kashmir, Indian forces have exercised utmost restraint to ensure minimum collateral damage, even at great loss to its own soldiers sometimes. India has never enforced any blockades where it prevented delivery of critical humanitarian and medical aid for people in the region. On the contrary, 'Operation Sadbhavana', a campaign launched by the Indian Army in the early 2000s to win the hearts and minds of the people in Kashmir, has been hugely successful in winning back the support of locals in Kashmir and alienating the terrorists.

At the height of the Kargil war in 1999 too, when India was taking heavy casualties due to challenges posed by the enemy and terrain, India did not cross the LoC by ground or air to conduct operations. This may have dealt a tactical disadvantage militarily but the strategic advantage that accrued by keeping the war limited to Kargil and not blowing into an 'India-Pakistan war' was huge as it kept at bay other powers from getting directly involved. After the 26/11 Mumbai terror attack also, despite it being traced back to Pakistan, India exercised restraint and did not launch full-scale military operations. Incidentally as Israel is still recovering from its 7/10 terror attack, India marks 15 years of its 26/11 this year.

Israel could do well to learn from some of these Indian experiences. Yes, Israel had the full right to self-defence when Hamas unleashed terror on it on 7 October. Yes, Israel is located in a dangerous neighbourhood with terror threats from all sides. A small nation and a small population make Israel's task that much harder too. Israel may also argue that unlike India, it has always been a fight for its existence. But terror does not necessarily have to be fought with greater terror. There has to be a difference between the conduct of an internationally recognized and responsible nation and a terror group.

War has to be fought with a cool and calculated mind and not based solely on revenge. Military response should be calibrated and force applied commensurate to the effect desired. Strikes resulting in damage to a hospital, school or refugee camp and deaths of innocent children and women are best avoided even at the cost of prolonged operations and delayed achievement of objectives. Also, as President Biden said, Israel should not to repeat the mistakes that the USA made during its 'War on Terror' in Iraq and Afghanistan.

While India learnt from Israel how to react proactively to terror strikes and launch surgical strikes across the borders like Uri in 2016 and Balakot in 2019, Israel could do well to take a leaf out of the Indian book on how to conduct operations against terror without inflicting mass civilian casualties and facing condemnation from the international community.

65

Some Lessons for India from the Gaza War

Few nations in the world share the kind of security environment on their borders that Israel and India encounter. Both are surrounded by disputed borders, ideological hostility, and armed non-state actors operating with direct or indirect state backing. Both have faced frequent wars born due to unresolved territorial disputes and both have fought cross-border terrorism for decades. And yet, the threat of cross-border terror refuses to die down and threatens to erupt without warning and at scales that have shocked the nation. The 13 December 2001 Delhi Parliament attack, 26/11 Mumbai attack, and 22 April 2025 Pahalgam terror attack are some examples in India.

The 7 October Hamas terror attack across Gaza too was a typical high intensity cross-border terror strike, something that Israel has been dealing with for decades. For India, the attack holds valuable lessons and is a vivid reminder that terror attacks often come without warning and are, more often than not, a case of missed signals and a sense of complacency. Also, such attacks are increasingly taking new forms and the use of drones, tunnels, para gliders, etc., add to the need for scaled-up and multi-modal vigilance. Plus, a sense that border fencing duly controlled by sensors and physically kept under surveillance would be adequate has also been proved wrong by the Hamas attack.

It is a perfect case study in how a determined non-state actor can combine low-cost tools with surprise, mobility, and shock to impose a heavy price on a stronger state. Having encountered a similar terror attack on 22 April 2025 in Pahalgam, Kashmir, in which a group of terrorists slipped through the Line of Control between India and Pakistan and killed 26 innocent tourists in cold blood, a study of the Hamas terror strike and the Gaza war can offer key insights into how India should build various instruments of its national security strategy where there is 'zero tolerance for terror' and that any strike emanating from across the border will be considered an 'act of war'.

Lesson No. 1: Complacency Can Cost Dearly

The Hamas terror strike did not happen out of the blue. It was a result of months and years of preparations, some of which were in plain sight of the IDF deployment. However, Hamas was successful in lulling it and the intelligence agencies into not only thinking that Hamas was no longer targeting Israel but was also successful in diverting the attention of the IDF military and intelligence towards the West Bank. It may be recalled that the last conflict with Hamas across Gaza was fought in May 2021 and Hamas had deliberately kept its powder dry ever since.

Maps, documents, sketches, etc., seized later from Hamas hideouts explain the in-depth preparations for the attack. Also, as has been later revealed, there were adequate intelligence inputs which were deemed as 'routine' and 'disconnected'; if they had not been filed due to complacency, it could have averted the terror attack.

In India too, there have been many instances where, after a terror attack, an investigation revealed that there were several small, innocuous and seemingly disconnected inputs that were ignored as routine. Also, both in India and Israel, a large number of intelligence agencies operate, but often in isolation. Sharing of important inputs is not a norm and therefore important pieces of information, which could have stitched together a bigger story, are often missed.

A key and first lesson for India and any other nation facing constant threats of cross-border terror is to believe that no input is insignificant and be lulled into complacency.

Lesson No. 2: Constant Update of Geological and Seismic Data Essential

Hamas had built up an extensive tunnel network, called the 'Gaza Metro', which runs upto estimated 500 km. It was this tunnel network that was used to store weapons, move cadres, hide hostages and use concealed entry points to surprise the IDF and inflict damage on it. With advanced satellite imagery and geological tools available with countries, it is quite surprising how Israel either ignored the tunnel network or was oblivious to it. India too has discovered tunnels across the border in Punjab and Rajasthan a number of times which have basically been used to smuggle weapons and drugs. With the threat of cross-border terror constant and increasing, the possibility of terror groups in Pakistan emulating the Hamas model is not a far-fetched possibility.

As a lesson from the Gaza war, regular geological surveys by latest satellite imagery is very important to identify and dismantle any such network before it becomes a threat. India also needs to invest more in ground-penetrating radar, acoustic sensing, and AI-based detection to create a formidable anti-tunnel capability.

Lesson No. 3: Border Security Architecture Needs Constant Evolution

India has developed a dynamic multi-layered security grid in Kashmir with a decentralised operational authority but a centralised coordination and command mechanism. It has worked well but there have also been gaps and slippages along the way. The fact that it involves multiple security agencies starting from the Army, Rashtriya Rifles (a specialised force raised mainly for counter-terror operations in Kashmir), State and Central police forces as well as the Border Security Force, is a challenge both in coordination as well as operational efficiency. Plus, there are multiple layers of intelligence agencies working on the ground. Add to that is the ever increasing scope and involvement of technical intelligence.

The 22 April 2025 Pahalgam terror attack was a clear example of how the terrorists successfully infiltrated more than 100 km inland from the Line of Control, crossing and deceiving several layers of operational and intelligence agencies deployed in a grid. It was also a case wherein there was a possible thinning out of troops from one area to beef up the security grid in another. Similarly, Hamas was able to penetrate through several layers of operational and surveillance grid to inflict damage on 7 October.

The key lesson which emerges is that the border security architecture has to constantly evolve as per the threat. In India's case, the dynamic grid has to cater for cases where even if the terrorists are able to infiltrate one or two layers of defence, the subsequent layers should be able to box them in and neutralise the threat.

Lesson No. 4: Deterrence is not Absolute

Israel had fought a number of episodic conflicts in Gaza. In the last conflict which ended in May 2021, Israel had delivered a deadly blow to the military capabilities of Hamas. As Hamas did not initiate any conflict thereafter, there may have been a belief in Israel that the deterrence was working.

In India's case too, India launched surgical strikes across the border after terror attacks in Uri and Pathankot in 2016. After the Pulwama terror attack in February 2019, India undertook airstrikes on the JeM terrorist camp in Balakot, delivering a telling blow to the terror group. If India thought that this deterrence had worked, it was proved wrong when the Pahalgam terror attack took place in April 2025, which led to India undertaking a short and precise military operation, 'Operation Sindoor', into Pakistan. India also resolved to treat any future cross border-terror attack into India as an act of war.

However, will this threat or deterrence work forever? It is unlikely. That is why it is paramount to adopt a proactive counter-terror strategy, something that Israel had done successfully over the years. Any terror threat that is likely to manifest should be taken out before it can cause damage. India should adopt a strategy wherein any terror camp or terrorist launch pad where terrorists are clearly identified as armed and likely to infiltrate should be taken out before any such infiltration can manifest itself.

Lesson No. 5: Civilian Protection and the Possibility of Hostages

One of the major deterrents for Israel to reach an early conclusion on the ceasefire with Hamas was due to the 251 hostages held by Hamas. Despite having a policy of 'no negotiations with terrorists', Israel has had to often compromise whenever Hamas has taken Israeli hostages. This time, the number was large.

In the case of India, while a hostage situation of that kind has not yet manifested, its anti-infiltration and counter-terror strategy will have to incorporate the possibility of such an occurrence. As terror groups incorporate modern technology and weapons which include the use of drones, cyber, etc., the focus of threat may shift from targeting mainly security forces and government infrastructure to population centres which create more psychological effect and media attention; in such a situation, hostage taking becomes a possibility.

India should therefore focus on greater integration of civil defence and emergency response in overall security planning. This includes hardened shelters, evacuation protocols, civilian alert systems, and pre-positioned resources to protect non-combatants when conflicts erupt.

Lesson No. 6: Militaries Require Clearly Defined and Achievable Objectives

The Gaza war went on for almost 24 months before the final ceasefire in October 2025. It ended up being the longest conflict fought by Israel and resulted in unprecedented casualties to the IDF. At the end of it,, Israel had not achieved all its objectives. Reason? Of the four military objectives that Israel set in Gaza, two were clearly unrealistic. While Hamas has been severely degraded and its top leadership eliminated, it is far from being 'eliminated from the face of the Earth'. Its ability to launch repeated attacks across Gaza continues to irritate Israel and cause damage and casualties. Also, Gaza was bombarded and virtually 'flattened to the ground", but the possibility of it being rebuilt and re-used by Hamas or any other group in the future to launch attacks on Israel cannot be ruled out, unless Israel decides to continue its occupation there forever.

Contrary to it, in Operation Sindoor, Indian armed forces had clearly defined military objectives. The operation was launched to target the terrorist outfits behind the Pahalgam attack. In striking nine locations in Pakistan, the Indian armed forces were precise in converting the military objective into action. The subsequent strikes on air defence targets and air bases in Pakistan were also based on clearly-defined directions to strike back in response, and harder than the Pakistani effort. At no point did the military objectives stretch to include other possibilities like extending this operation to resolve territorial issues in PoK or Pakistan by undertaking ground operations or using naval forces for active kinetic action. The precise directive given to the armed forces, and the freedom to convert that political intent into military action, was a key factor in raining heavy punishment on terror groups and military infrastructure in Pakistan. This was a very important factor in enabling an early ceasefire.

Lesson No. 7: Strategic Communication as Important as the Fighting Itself

When Israel commenced its counter-attack in Gaza on 7 October, the entire world was with it. Its strikes in Gaza targeting Hamas combat cadres were welcomed even by the regional countries. However, Israel soon started to lose the battle of the narrative when reports of its air strikes hitting schools, hospitals, UN buildings and journalists started appearing in the media. Hamas, fighting with its back to the wall, took advantage of the situation and soon, videos and photos of Israeli atrocities in Gaza were dominating global headlines. It even forced the UN General Assembly as early as in the first week of November 2023 to pass a resolution to halt such punitive actions. This is not to say that Israel did not cause these damages but the stories in the media and on international platforms suggested that this was all that it was doing. Slowly and steadily, the entire global narrative turned against Israel and made fighting for its military objectives difficult.

Similarly, India initially captured the narrative right after the 22 April Pahalgam terror attack. The Prime Minister cut short his visit to Saudi Arabia and led a scathing communications campaign against Pakistan. The revoking of the Indus Water Treaty and the focused diplomatic campaign meant that when Operation Sindoor was finally launched, India held the upper hand. Also, the fact that India provided proof of the strikes in Pakistan through satellite images and videos of targets that were struck meant that Pakistan had little choice but to accept the losses.

However, where India lost the narrative was when it failed to seize the initiative to declare a ceasefire before President Trump did on his X handle on 10 May and also when it refused to divulge the losses to its aircraft leading to all kinds of speculation and letting Pakistan seize the narrative which, along with the USA, put India on the back foot at every successive media bite.

A clear lesson emerged from these conflicts highlighting the importance of maintaining information dominance not only at the start but also to maintain the dominance by proactive and credible communication strategy throughout, even after the ceasefire. Modern wars are fought on two fronts – the battlefield and the information sphere. Military commanders must treat communication as a weapon system, and governments must prepare for a credible strategic communication involving media, technology, and public diplomacy. Speed, authenticity, and coherence in messaging are now as important as accuracy in military targeting.

Conclusion

The Gaza war is over but India's war against terror continues. The Delhi car blast in November 2025 is a reminder that the threat of terror is not only external but has permeated into some sections of our society too. India requires a comprehensive, whole-of-nation approach strategy to defeat terror. Lessons from the Gaza war in fighting Hamas offer valuable inputs as India strengthens its resolve to formulate such a strategy while reinforcing that any act of cross-border terror will be treated as an 'act of war'.

66

Does India have a Role in the Gaza Peace Plan?

It is December 2025 and the ceasefire in Gaza is largely holding on although it is disrupted by occasional reports of Hamas allegedly violating it and Israel undertaking punitive retaliatory measures. The ceasefire, which came into effect on 10 October 2025 has so far been successful in achieving its initial objectives. Humanitarian aid in the form of food, water, medicines and fuel have started trickling in through UN agencies, although not in the numbers that are required to address the dire humanitarian crisis prevailing in Gaza. Also, hundreds and thousands of families are slowly returning to their destroyed homes in Gaza to pick up the threads of their lives once again in the hope that the nightmare of death and destruction of the past two years will never be repeated.

The Ceasefire

The ceasefire came about as a result of the US-sponsored '20-Point Trump Peace Plan' announced on 29 September 2025. There were fears and apprehensions that, like many ceasefire proposals in the past, this peace plan too may crumble soon. However, with Hamas agreeing to release all living hostages in one go, a key element of Israel was met, leading to the go-ahead.

In the first month of the ceasefire, many of the 'low hanging fruits' have been harvested which include pulling back of Israeli forces to a designated 'Yellow Line' in Gaza and cessation of Israeli air and artillery strikes and ground operations. The 20 living hostages have safely returned to Israel while the bodies of 28 dead hostages are being slowly returned to Israel by Hamas. Plus, critical aid has started trickling into Gaza.

However, the subsequent progress of the peace plan hinges on three vital components. The first is the establishment and positioning of the International Stabilisation Force (ISF); second is the disarming of Hamas and demilitarisation of Gaza; and thirdly, Gaza is to be governed by a technocratic, apolitical committee made up of qualified Palestinians and international experts with oversight and supervision by the new international transitional body, the 'Board of Peace,' headed and chaired by President Donald J. Trump. Each of these is a challenge in itself but, for the peace plan to have any chance of success, each of these have to be implemented.

Where Does India Stand?

PM Modi had skipped the high-profile Gaza Peace Summit convened in Sharm el-Sheikh on 13 October, where President Trump announced a 'new rebuilding' in Gaza while signing an agreement on the future of the peace process with Egypt, Turkey and Qatar. India was represented by Minister of State for External Affairs, Kirti Vardhan Singh. However, India did attend the 'Summit' meeting of the Board of Peace held in Washington on 19 February 2026 as an 'Observer', which was presided over by President Trump. More than 50 countries were represented and pledges of US$ 17 billion were made by countries, including US$ 10 billion by the USA.

There are a few issues that stand out with regard to India's role in Gaza. Firstly, as regards the Gaza peace plan, India was among the first countries to welcome Trump's 20-Point Plan as also the ceasefire in Gaza. Secondly, if there is any country that is trusted on both ends of the spectrum in Gaza, it is India. While some Arab and Muslim countries are mistrusted by Israel, any Western influence or participation is doubted by the Palestinians. Thirdly, the Indian army has years of experience of operating in two UN Missions across Israel's borders; UNIFIL in Lebanon and UNDOF in Golan Heights bordering Syria. Fourthly, with the 20 Point Plan having been endorsed at the UNSC which includes provision of deployment of the ISF in Gaza, any 'legal' hurdles which could have inhibited India's chances of contributing to the ISF in Gaza, too are gone.

India has huge stakes in the peace process in West Asia as it looks to expand trade and security ties not only with the region but across to Europe. One of the key projects that could transform India's growth outlook is the India-Middle East-Europe Economic Corridor (IMEC), a transformative project that was announced at the G20 Summit in Delhi in September 2023. However, the war in Gaza stalled the project. As the peace process takes shape, it would be in India's interest to be 'inside' rather than 'outside' this process in Gaza.

The visit of the Israeli Foreign Minister to Delhi on 4 November is important in this context. During the visit, India and Israel signed an agreement on advanced cooperation in defence equipment and technology but equally important was the discussion on the Gaza peace process. Speaking at a media event after the official talks, Israel's Foreign Minister, Gideon Sa'ar, hinted at India's role in the Gaza peace plan, stating that "It's a stage-by-stage plan, realistic and implementable. India, as a world leader, has a key role in ensuring it remains on track."

Looking Ahead

The first meeting of the Board of Peace held on 19 February had promised to shape the foundation for taking the peace process forward. However, the pre-emptive strikes launched by Israel and the USA against Iran on 28 February have not only plunged the entire region into a conflict, which is escalating by the day, but is also threatening to put all the efforts of the Gaza peace process on a back burner. With Hezbollah joining Iran in counter-attacking Israel in the current conflict, all previous assessments and claims that Hezbollah had been decimated by Israel in November 2024, have been proven wrong. This is likely to have an impact on how Israel takes the Gaza peace process forward once this war is over, if Hamas does not agree to disarm and demilitarise completely.

For India, it is back to 'wait and watch', hoping that the war in Iran will soon get over and that there will be recalibration towards long term peace in the region, including Gaza and Palestine. There is also likely to be a complete overhaul of the security architecture of the Gulf region as the American security guarantees have fallen woefully short, resulting in the Gulf nations being exposed to the damage and destruction, being caused by Iranian missiles and drones. Will the Gulf nations continue with American miliary presence and its security guarantees in the future too or will they opt for a more inclusive, regional and collaborative security architecture? Will or can India have a role, even in an advisory capacity, in a new evolving security architecture? Will or can India finally step up and be part of a collaborative security arrangement in the Gulf region where Indian armed forces have a direct and active role?

The war in Iran has exposed the fragilities of the security in the Gulf region and is forcing the region to think 'out of the box'. What role will India have in this new arrangement, will evolve over time. However, it may perhaps be the right time for India to step up and be counted.

Annexures

Annexure 1

Full text of Biden's speech laying out hostage and ceasefire deal for Israel-Hamas war, 31 May 2024

01 June 2025, Washington

I want to give an update on my efforts to end the crisis in Gaza.

For the past several months, my negotiators of foreign policy, intelligence community, and the like have been relentlessly focused not just on a ceasefire that would eve- – that would inevitably be fragile and temporary but on a durable end to the war. That's been the focus: a durable end to this war.

One that brings all the hostages home, ensures Israel's security, creates a better "day after" in Gaza without Hamas in power, and sets the stage for a political settlement that provides a better future for Israelis and Palestinians alike.

Now, after intensive diplomacy carried out by my team and my many conversations with leaders of Israel, Qatar, and Egypt and other Middle Eastern countries, Israel has now offered – Israel has offered a comprehensive new proposal.

It's a roadmap to an enduring ceasefire and the release of all hostages.

This proposal has been transmitted by Qatar to Hamas.

Today, I want to lay out its terms for the American citizens and for the world.

This new proposal has three phases – three.

The first phase would last for six weeks. Here's what it would include: a full and complete ceasefire; a withdrawal of Israeli forces from all populated areas of Gaza; a release of a number of hostages – including women, the elderly, the wounded – in exchange for the release of hundreds of Palestinian prisoners. There are American hostages who would be released at this stage, and we want them home.

Additional, some remains of hostages who have been killed would be returned to their families, bringing some degree of closure to their terrible grief.

Palestinians – civilians – would return to their homes and neighbourhoods in all areas of Gaza, including in the north.

Humanitarian assistance would surge with 600 trucks carrying aid into Gaza every single day.

With a ceasefire, that aid could be safely and effectively distributed to all who need it. Hundreds of thousands of temporary shelters, including housing units, would be delivered by the international community.

All of that and more would begin immediately – immediately.

During the six weeks of ph- – of phase one, Israel and Hamas would negotiate the necessary arrangements to get to phase two, which is a permanent end to hostol- – to hostilities.

Now, I'll be straight with you. There are a number of details to negotiate to move from phase one to phase two. Israel will want to make sure its interests are protected.

But the proposal says if the negotiations take longer than six weeks for phase one, the ceasefire will still continue as long as negotiations continue.

And the United States, Egypt, and Qatar would work to ensure negotiations keep going – all agreements – all agreements – until all the agreements are reached and phase two is able to begin.

Then phase two: There would be an exchange for the release of all remaining living hostages, including male soldiers; Israeli forces would withdraw from Gaza; and as long as Hamas lives up to its commitments, a temporary ceasefire would become, in the words of the propo- – the Israeli proposal, "the cessation of hostilities permanently," end of quote. "Cessation of hostilities permanently."

Finally, in phase three, a major reconstruction plan for Ga- – for Gaza wou- – would commence. And any final remains of hostages who have been killed would be returned to their families.

That's the offer that's now on the table and what we've been asking for. It's what we need.

The people of Israel should know they can make this offer without any further risk to their own security because they've devastated Hamas form- – forces over the past eight months. At this point, Hamas no longer is capable of carrying out another October 7th, which – one of the Israelis' main objective in this war and, quite frankly, a righteous one.

I know there are those in Israel who will not agree with this plan and will call for the war to continue indefinitely. Some – some are even in the government coalition. And they've made it clear: They want to occupy Gaza, they want to keep fighting for years, and the hostages are not a priority to them.

Well, I've urged the leadership in Israel to stand behind this deal, despite whatever pressure comes.

And to the people of Israel, let me say this. As someone whose had a lifelong commitment to Israel, as the only American president who has ever gone to Israel in a time of war, as someone who just sent the U.S. forces to directly defend Israel when it was attacked by Iran, I ask you to take a step back and think what will happen if this moment is lost.

We can't lose this moment. Indefinite war in pursuit of an unidentified notion of "total victory" will not bring Israel in – will not bring down – bog down – will only bog down Israel in Gaza, draining the economic, military, and human- – and human resources, and furthering Israel's isolation in the world.

That will not bring hostages home. That will not – not bring an enduring defeat of Hamas. That will not bring Israel lasting security.

But a comprehensive approach that starts with this deal will bring hostages home and will lead to a more secure Israel. And once a ceasefire and hostage deal is concluded, it unlocks the possibility of a great deal more progress, including – including calm along Israel's northern border with Lebanon.

The United States will help forge a diplomatic resolution, one that ensures Israel's security and allows people to safely return to their homes without fear of being attacked.

With a deal, a rebuilding of Gaza will begin [with] Arab nations and the international community, along with Palestinian and Israeli leaders, to get it done in a manner that does not allow Hamas to re-arm.

And the United States will work with our partners to rebuild homes, schools, and hospitals in Gaza to help repair communities that were destroyed in the chaos of war.

And with this deal, Israel could become more deeply integrated into the region, including – it's no surprise to you all – including no – a po- – potential historic normalization agreement with Saudi Arabia. Israel could be part of a regional security network to counter the threat posed by Iran.

All of this progress would make Israel more secure, with Israeli families no longer living in the shadow of a terrorist attack.

And all of this would create the conditions for a different future and a better future for the Palestinian people, one of self-determination, dignity, security, and freedom. This path is available once the deal is struck.

Israel will always have the right to defend itself against the threats to its security and to bring those responsible for October 7th to justice. And the United States will always ensure that Israel has what it needs to defend itself.

If Hamas fails to fulfill its commitments under the deal, Israel can resume military operations. But Egypt and Qatar have assured me and they are continuing to work to ensure that Hamas doesn't do that. And the United States will help ensure that Israel lives up to their obligations as well.

That's what this deal says. That's what it says. And we'll do our part.

This is truly a decisive moment. Israel has made their proposal. Hamas says it wants a ceasefire. This deal is an opportunity to prove whether they really mean it.

Hamas needs to take the deal.

For months, people all over the world have called for a ceasefire. Now it's time to raise your voices and to demand that Hasa- – Hamas come to the table, agrees to this deal, and ends this war that they began.

Of course, there will be differences on the specific details that need to be worked out. That's natural. If Hamas comes to negotiate ready to deal, then Israel negotiations must be given a mandate, the necessary flexibility to close that deal.

The past eight months have marked heartbreaking pain: pain of those whose loved ones were slaughtered by Hamas terrorists on October 7th; hostages and their families waiting in anguish; ordinary Israelis whose lives were forever marked by the shattering event of Hamas's sexual violence and ruthless brutality.

And the Palestinian people have endured sheer hell in this war. Too many innocent people have been killed, including thousands of children. Far too many have been badly wounded.

We all saw the terrible images from the deadly fire in Rafah earlier this week following an Israeli strike against – targeting Hamas. And even as we work to surge assistance to Gaza, with 1,800 trucks delivering supplies these last five days – 1,800 – the humanitarian crisis still remains.

I know this is a subject on which people in this country feel deep, passionate convictions. And so do I. This has been one of the hardest, most complicated problems in the world. There's nothing easy about this – nothing easy about it.

Through it all, though, the United States has worked relentlessly to support Israelis' security, to get humanitarian supplies into Gaza, and to get a ceasefire and a hostage deal to bring this war to an end.

Yesterday, with this new initiative, we've taken an important step in that direction.

And I want to level with you today as to where we are and what might be possible. But I need your help. Everyone who wants peace now must raise their voices and let the leaders know they should take this deal; work to make it real, make it lasting; and forge a better future out of the tragic terror attack and war.

It's time to begin this new stage, for the hostages to come home, for Israel to be secure, for the suffering to stop. It's time for this war to end and for the day after to begin.

Thank you very much.

Annexure 2

Ceasefire Deal Between Israel and Hamas- January 2025

Practical procedures and mechanisms to implement the Agreement for the exchange of Israeli hostages and Palestinian Prisoners and the return to a sustainable calm which would achieve a permanent ceasefire between the two sides

1. Stage two preparations

The parties and the mediators' objective is to achieve a final consensus to implement the May 27 2024 Agreement on the exchange of hostages and prisoners and return to a sustainable calm which would achieve a permanent ceasefire between the Parties.

All procedures in the first stage will continue in stage 2 so long as the negotiations of the conditions of implementing stage 2 are ongoing and the guarantors of this Agreement shall work to ensure that negotiations continue until an agreement is reached.

2. Israeli forces withdrawal

Withdrawal of Israeli forces eastwards from densely populated areas along the borders of the Gaza strip, including Wadi Gaza (Netzarim axis and Kuwait roundabout).

The Israeli forces will be deployed in a perimeter (700) metres with an exception at 5 localised points to be increased no more than (400) additional meters that the Israeli side will determine, south and west of the border, and based on the maps agreed upon by both sides which accompany the agreement.

3. Prisoner Exchange

a. The 9 ill and wounded from the list of 33 will be released in exchange for the release of 110 Palestinian prisoners with life sentences.

b. Israel will release 1000 Gazan detainees from 8 October 2023 that were not involved in 7 October 2023

c. The Elderly (men over 50) from the list of 33 will be released in exchange for an exchange key of 1:3 life sentences + 1:27 other sentences.

d. Ebra Mangesto and Hesham el-Sayed - will be released according to an exchange key of 1:30, as well as 47 Shalit prisoners.

e. A number of Palestinian prisoners will be released abroad or in Gaza based on lists agreed upon between both sides.

4. Philadelphi corridor

a. The Israeli side will gradually reduce the forces in the corridor area during stage 1 based on the accompanying maps and the agreement between both sides.

b. After the last hostage release of stage one, on day 42, the Israeli forces will begin their withdrawal and complete it no later than day 50.

5. Rafah Border Crossing

a. The Rafah crossing will be ready for the transfer of civilians and for the wounded after the release of all women (civilian and soldiers). Israel will work toward the readiness of the crossing as soon as the agreement is signed.

b. Israeli forces will redeploy around the Rafah Crossing according to the attached maps.

c. 50 wounded military individuals will be allowed to cross daily accompanied by (3) individuals. Each individual crossing will require Israeli and Egyptian approval.

d. The crossing will be operated based on the August 2024 discussions with Egypt.

6. Exit of ill and wounded civilians

a. All ill and wounded Palestinian civilians will be allowed to cross via Rafah border crossing, according to section 12 in the 27 May 2024 agreement.

7. Return of unarmed internally displaced (Netzarim Corridor):

a. The return is agreed based on the 27 May 2024 agreement section 3-a and 3-b.

b. On day 7, the internally displaced pedestrians will be allowed to return north, without carrying arms and without inspection via Rashid street. On day 22, they will be allowed to return north from the Salahudin street as well, without inspection.

c. On day 7, vehicles and any non-pedestrian traffic will be allowed to return north of Netzarim corridor after vehicle inspection which will be performed by a private company which will be determined by the mediators in sync with the Israeli side, based on an agreed upon mechanism.

8. Humanitarian aid protocol:

a. Humanitarian aid procedures under the agreement will be done subject to the humanitarian protocol agreed upon under the supervision of the mediators.

(Source: Middle East Eye, 15 January 2025)

Annexure 3

The 20-Point Peace Plan

United Nations Security Council Resolution 2803 (2025)

17 November 2025

Adopted by the Security Council at its 10046th meeting, on 17 November 2025

The Security Council,

Welcoming the *Comprehensive Plan to End the Gaza Conflict* of 29 September 2025 ("Comprehensive Plan")(annex 1 to this resolution), and applauding the states that have signed, accepted, or endorsed it, and further *welcoming* the historic *Trump Declaration for Enduring Peace and Prosperity* of 13 October 2025 and the constructive role played by the United States of America, the State of Qatar, the Arab Republic of Egypt, and the Republic of Türkiye, in having facilitated the ceasefire in the Gaza Strip,

Determining that the situation in the Gaza Strip threatens the regional peace and the security of neighboring states and *noting* prior relevant Security Council resolutions relating to the situation in the Middle East, including the Palestinian question,

1. *Endorses* the Comprehensive Plan, *acknowledges* the parties have accepted it, and *calls on* all parties to implement it in its entirety, including maintenance of the ceasefire, in good faith and without delay;
2. *Welcomes* the establishment of the Board of Peace (BoP) as a transitional administration with international legal personality that will set the framework, and coordinate funding for, the redevelopment of Gaza pursuant to the Comprehensive Plan, and in a manner consistent with relevant international legal principles, until such time as the Palestinian Authority (PA) has satisfactorily completed its reform program, as outlined in various proposals, including President Trump's peace plan in 2020 and the Saudi-French Proposal, and can securely and effectively take back control of Gaza. After the PA reform program is faithfully carried out and Gaza redevelopment has advanced, the conditions may finally be in place for a credible pathway to Palestinian self-determination and statehood. The United States will establish a dialogue between Israel and the Palestinians to agree on a political horizon for peaceful and prosperous coexistence;
3. *Underscores* the importance of the full resumption of humanitarian aid in cooperation with the BoP into the Gaza Strip in a manner consistent with relevant international legal principles and through cooperating organizations, including the United Nations, the International Committee of the Red Cross, and the Red

Crescent, and ensuring such aid is used solely for peaceful uses and not diverted by armed groups;

4. *Authorizes* Member States participating in the BoP and the BoP to: (A) enter into such arrangements as may be necessary to achieve the objectives of the Comprehensive Plan, including those addressing privileges and immunities of personnel of the force established in paragraph 7 below; and (B) establish operational entities with, as necessary, international legal personality and transactional authorities for the performance of its functions, including: (1) the implementation of a transitional governance administration, including the supervising and supporting of a Palestinian technocratic, apolitical committee of competent Palestinians from the Strip, as championed by the Arab League, which shall be responsible for day-to-day operations of Gaza's civil service and administration; (2) the reconstruction of Gaza and of economic recovery programs; (3) the coordination and supporting of and delivery of public services and humanitarian assistance in Gaza; (4) any measures to facilitate the movement of persons in and out of Gaza, in a manner consistent with the Comprehensive Plan; and (5) any such additional tasks as may be necessary to support and implement the Comprehensive Plan;
5. *Understands* that the operational entities referred to in paragraph 4 above will operate under the transitional authority and oversight of the BoP and are to be funded through voluntary contributions from donors and BoP funding vehicles and governments;
6. *Calls upon* the World Bank and other financial institutions to facilitate and provide financial resources to support the reconstruction and development of Gaza, including through the establishment of a dedicated trust fund for this purpose and governed by donors;
7. *Authorizes* Member States working with the BoP and the BoP to establish a temporary International Stabilization Force (ISF) in Gaza to deploy under unified command acceptable to the BoP, with forces contributed by participating States, in close consultation and cooperation with the Arab Republic of Egypt and the State of Israel, and to use all necessary measures to carry out its mandate consistent with international law, including international humanitarian law. The ISF shall work with Israel and Egypt, without prejudice to their existing agreements, along with the newly trained and vetted Palestinian police force, to help secure border areas; stabilize the security environment in Gaza by ensuring the process of demilitarizing the Gaza Strip, including the destruction and prevention of rebuilding of the military, terror, and offensive infrastructure, as well as the permanent decommissioning of weapons from non-state armed groups; protect civilians, including humanitarian operations; train and provide support to the

vetted Palestinian police forces; coordinate with relevant States to secure humanitarian corridors; and undertake such additional tasks as may be necessary in support of the Comprehensive Plan. As the ISF establishes control and stability, the Israel Defense Forces (IDF) will withdraw from the Gaza Strip based on standards, milestones, and timeframes linked to demilitarization that will be agreed between the IDF, ISF, the guarantors, and the United States, save for a security perimeter presence that will remain until Gaza is properly secure from any resurgent terror threat. The ISF shall, (A) assist the BoP in monitoring the implementation of the ceasefire in Gaza, and enter into such arrangements as may be necessary to achieve the objectives of the Comprehensive Plan; and (B) operate under the strategic guidance of the BoP and will be funded through voluntary contributions from donors and BoP funding vehicles and governments;

8. *Decides* the BoP and international civil and security presences authorized by this resolution shall remain authorized until Dec. 31, 2027, subject to further action by the Council, and any further reauthorization of the ISF be in full cooperation and coordination with Egypt and Israel and other Member States continuing to work with the ISF;
9. *Calls upon* Member States and international organizations to work with the BoP to identify opportunities to contribute personnel, equipment, and financial resources to its operating entities and the ISF, to provide technical assistance to its operating entities and the ISF, and to give full recognition to its acts and documents;
10. *Requests* the BoP provide a written report on progress related to the above to the UN Security Council every six months;
11. *Decides* to remain seized of the matter.

ANNEX 1: President Donald J. Trump's Comprehensive Plan to End the Gaza Conflict

1. Gaza will be a deradicalized terror-free zone that does not pose a threat to its neighbors.
2. Gaza will be redeveloped for the benefit of the people of Gaza, who have suffered more than enough.
3. If both sides agree to this proposal, the war will immediately end. Israeli forces will withdraw to the agreed upon line to prepare for a hostage release. During this time, all military operations, including aerial and artillery bombardment, will be suspended, and battle lines will remain frozen until conditions are met for the complete staged withdrawal.
4. Within 72 hours of Israel publicly accepting this agreement, all hostages, alive and deceased, will be returned.

5. Once all hostages are released, Israel will release 250 life sentence prisoners plus 1700 Gazans who were detained after October 7th 2023, including all women and children detained in that context. For every Israeli hostage whose remains are released, Israel will release the remains of 15 deceased Gazans.
6. Once all hostages are returned, Hamas members who commit to peaceful co-existence and to decommission their weapons will be given amnesty. Members of Hamas who wish to leave Gaza will be provided safe passage to receiving countries.
7. Upon acceptance of this agreement, full aid will be immediately sent into the Gaza Strip. At a minimum, aid quantities will be consistent with what was included in the January 19, 2025, agreement regarding humanitarian aid, including rehabilitation of infrastructure (water, electricity, sewage), rehabilitation of hospitals and bakeries, and entry of necessary equipment to remove rubble and open roads.
8. Entry of distribution and aid in the Gaza Strip will proceed without interference from the two parties through the United Nations and its agencies, and the Red Crescent, in addition to other international institutions not associated in any manner with either party. Opening the Rafah crossing in both directions will be subject to the same mechanism implemented under the January 19, 2025 agreement.
9. Gaza will be governed under the temporary transitional governance of a technocratic, apolitical Palestinian committee, responsible for delivering the day-today running of public services and municipalities for the people in Gaza. This committee will be made up of qualified Palestinians and international experts, with oversight and supervision by a new international transitional body, the "Board of Peace," which will be headed and chaired by President Donald J. Trump, with other members and heads of State to be announced, including Former Prime Minister Tony Blair. This body will set the framework and handle the funding for the redevelopment of Gaza until such time as the Palestinian Authority has completed its reform program, as outlined in various proposals, including President Trump's peace plan in 2020 and the Saudi-French proposal, and can securely and effectively take back control of Gaza. This body will call on best international standards to create modern and efficient governance that serves the people of Gaza and is conducive to attracting investment.
10. A Trump economic development plan to rebuild and energize Gaza will be created by convening a panel of experts who have helped birth some of the thriving modern miracle cities in the Middle East. Many thoughtful investment proposals and exciting development ideas have been crafted by well-meaning international groups, and will be considered to synthesize the security and governance frameworks to attract and facilitate these investments that will create jobs, opportunity, and hope for future Gaza.

11. A special economic zone will be established with preferred tariff and access rates to be negotiated with participating countries.
12. No one will be forced to leave Gaza, and those who wish to leave will be free to do so and free to return. We will encourage people to stay and offer them the opportunity to build a better Gaza.
13. Hamas and other factions agree to not have any role in the governance of Gaza, directly, indirectly, or in any form. All military, terror, and offensive infrastructure, including tunnels and weapon production facilities, will be destroyed and not rebuilt. There will be a process of demilitarization of Gaza under the supervision of independent monitors, which will include placing weapons permanently beyond use through an agreed process of decommissioning, and supported by an internationally funded buy back and reintegration program all verified by the independent monitors. New Gaza will be fully committed to building a prosperous economy and to peaceful coexistence with their neighbors.
14. A guarantee will be provided by regional partners to ensure that Hamas, and the factions, comply with their obligations and that New Gaza poses no threat to its neighbors or its people.
15. The United States will work with Arab and international partners to develop a temporary International Stabilization Force (ISF) to immediately deploy in Gaza. The ISF will train and provide support to vetted Palestinian police forces in Gaza, and will consult with Jordan and Egypt who have extensive experience in this field. This force will be the long-term internal security solution. The ISF will work with Israel and Egypt to help secure border areas, along with newly trained Palestinian police forces. It is critical to prevent munitions from entering Gaza and to facilitate the rapid and secure flow of goods to rebuild and revitalize Gaza. A deconfliction mechanism will be agreed upon by the parties.
16. Israel will not occupy or annex Gaza. As the ISF establishes control and stability, the Israel Defense Forces (IDF) will withdraw based on standards, milestones, and timeframes linked to demilitarization that will be agreed upon between the IDF, ISF, the guarantors, and the United States, with the objective of a secure Gaza that no longer poses a threat to Israel, Egypt, or its citizens. Practically, the IDF will progressively hand over the Gaza territory it occupies to the ISF according to an agreement they will make with the transitional authority until they are withdrawn completely from Gaza, save for a security perimeter presence that will remain until Gaza is properly secure from any resurgent terror threat.
17. In the event Hamas delays or rejects this proposal, the above, including the scaled-up aid operation, will proceed in the terror-free areas handed over from the IDF to the ISF.

18. An interfaith dialogue process will be established based on the values of tolerance and peaceful co-existence to try and change mindsets and narratives of Palestinians and Israelis by emphasizing the benefits that can be derived from peace.
19. While Gaza re-development advances and when the PA reform program is faithfully carried out, the conditions may finally be in place for a credible pathway to Palestinian self-determination and statehood, which we recognize as the aspiration of the Palestinian people.
20. The United States will establish a dialogue between Israel and the Palestinians to agree on a political horizon for peaceful and prosperous co-existence.

Annexure 4

Charter of the Board of Peace

(as on 16 January 2026)

Preamble

Declaring that durable peace requires pragmatic judgment, common-sense solutions, and the courage to depart from approaches and institutions that have too often failed;

Recognizing that lasting peace takes root when people are empowered to take ownership and responsibility over their future;

Affirming that only sustained, results-oriented partnership, grounded in shared burdens and commitments, can secure peace in places where it has for too long proven elusive;

Lamenting that too many approaches to peace-building foster perpetual dependency, and institutionalize crisis rather than leading people beyond it;

Emphasizing the need for a more nimble and effective international peace-building body; and

Resolving to assemble a coalition of willing States committed to practical cooperation and effective action,

Judgment guided and justice honored, the Parties hereby adopt the Charter for the Board of Peace.

Chapter I: Purposes and Functions

Article 1: Mission

The Board of Peace is an international organization that seeks to promote stability, restore dependable and lawful governance, and secure enduring peace in areas affected or threatened by conflict. The Board of Peace shall undertake such peace-building functions in accordance with international law and as may be approved in accordance with this Charter, including the development and dissemination of best practices capable of being applied by all nations and communities seeking peace.

Chapter II: Membership

Article 2.1: Member States

Membership in the Board of Peace is limited to States invited to participate by the Chairman, and commences upon notification that the State has consented to be bound by this Charter, in accordance with Chapter XI.

Article 2.2: Member State Responsibilities

(a) Each Member State shall be represented on the Board of Peace by its Head of State or Government.

(b) Each Member State shall support and assist with Board of Peace operations consistent with their respective domestic legal authorities. Nothing in this Charter shall be construed to give the Board of Peace jurisdiction within the territory of Member States, or require Member States to participate in a particular peace-building mission, without their consent.

(c) Each Member State shall serve a term of no more than three years from this Charter's entry into force, subject to renewal by the Chairman. The three-year membership term shall not apply to Member States that contribute more than USD $1,000,000,000 in cash funds to the Board of Peace within the first year of the Charter's entry into force.

Article 2.3: Termination of Membership

Membership shall terminate upon the earlier of: (i) expiration of a three-year term, subject to Article 2.2(c) and renewal by the Chairman; (ii) withdrawal, consistent with Article 2.4; (iii) a removal decision by the Chairman, subject to a veto by a two-thirds majority of Member States: or (iv) dissolution of the Board of Peace pursuant to Chapter X. A Member State whose membership terminates shall also cease to be a Party to the Charter, but such State may be invited again to become a Member State, in accordance with Article 2.1.

Article 2.4: Withdrawal

Any Member State may withdraw from the Board of Peace with immediate effect by providing written notice to the Chairman.

Chapter III: Governance

Article 3.1: The Board of Peace

(a) The Board of Peace consists of its Member States.

(b) The Board of Peace shall vote on all proposals on its agenda, including with respect to the annual budgets, the establishment of subsidiary entities, the appointment of senior executive officers, and major policy determinations, such as the approval of international agreements and the pursuit of new peace-building initiatives.

(c) The Board of Peace shall convene voting meetings at least annually and at such additional times and locations as the Chairman deems appropriate. The agenda at such meetings shall be set by the Executive Board, subject to notice and comment by Member States and approval by the Chairman.

(d) Each Member State shall have one vote on the Board of Peace.

(e) Decisions shall be made by a majority of the Member States present and voting, subject to the approval of the Chairman, who may also cast a vote in his capacity as Chairman in the event of a tie.

(f) The Board of Peace shall also hold regular non-voting meetings with its Executive

Board at which Member States may submit recommendations and guidance with respect to the Executive Board's activities, and at which the Executive Board shall report to the Board of Peace on the Executive Board's operations and decisions. Such meetings shall be convened on at least a quarterly basis, with the time and place of said meetings determined by the Chief Executive of the Executive Board.

(g) Member States may elect to be represented by an alternate high-ranking official at all meetings, subject to approval by the Chairman.

(h) The Chairman may issue invitations to relevant regional economic integration organizations to participate in the proceedings of the Board of Peace under such terms and conditions as he deems appropriate.

Article 3.2: Chairman

(a) Donald J. Trump shall serve as inaugural Chairman of the Board of Peace, and he shall separately serve as inaugural representative of the United States of America, subject only to the provisions of Chapter III.

(b) The Chairman shall have exclusive authority to create, modify, or dissolve subsidiary entities as necessary or appropriate to fulfill the Board of Peace's mission.

Article 3.3: Succession and Replacement

The Chairman shall at all times designate a successor for the role of Chairman. Replacement of the Chairman may occur only following voluntary resignation or as a result of incapacity, as determined by a unanimous vote of the Executive Board, at which time the Chairman's designated successor shall immediately assume the position of the Chairman and all associated duties and authorities of the Chairman.

Article 3.4: Subcommittees

The Chairman may establish subcommittees as necessary or appropriate and shall set the mandate, structure, and governance rules for each such subcommittee.

Chapter IV: Executive Board

Article 4.1: Executive Board Composition and Representation

(a) The Executive Board shall be selected by the Chairman and consist of leaders of global stature.

(b) Members of the Executive Board shall serve two-year terms, subject to removal by the Chairman and renewable at his discretion.

(c) The Executive Board shall be led by a Chief Executive nominated by the Chairman and confirmed by a majority vote of the Executive Board.

(d) The Chief Executive shall convene the Executive Board every two weeks for the first three months following its establishment and on a monthly basis thereafter, with additional meetings convened as the Chief Executive deems appropriate.

(e) Decisions of the Executive Board shall be made by a majority of its members present and voting, including the Chief Executive. Such decisions shall go into effect immediately, subject to veto by the Chairman at any time thereafter.

(f) The Executive Board shall determine its own rules of procedure.

Article 4.2: Executive Board Mandate

The Executive Board shall:

(a) Exercise powers necessary and appropriate to implement the Board of Peace's mission, consistent with this Charter;

(b) Report to the Board of Peace on its activities and decisions on a quarterly basis, consistent with Article 3.1(f), and at additional times as the Chairman may determine.

Chapter V: Financial Provisions

Article 5.1: Expenses

Funding for the expenses of the Board of Peace shall be through voluntary funding from Member States, other States, organizations, or other sources.

Article 5.2: Accounts

The Board of Peace may authorize the establishment of accounts as necessary to carry out its mission. The Executive Board shall authorize the institution of controls and oversight mechanisms with respect to budgets, financial accounts, and disbursements, as necessary or appropriate to ensure their integrity.

Chapter VI: Legal Status

Article 6

(a) The Board of Peace and its subsidiary entities possess international legal personality. They shall have such legal capacity as may be necessary to the pursuit of their mission (including, but not limited to, the capacity to enter into contracts, acquire and dispose of immovable and movable property, institute legal proceedings, open bank accounts, receive and disburse private and public funds, and employ staff).

(b) The Board of Peace shall ensure the provision of such privileges and immunities as are necessary for the exercise of the functions of the Board of Peace and its subsidiary entities and personnel, to be established in agreements with the States in which the Board of Peace and its subsidiary entities operate or through such other measures as may be taken by those States consistent with their domestic legal requirements. The Board may delegate authority to negotiate and conclude such agreements or arrangements to designated officials within the Board of Peace and/or its subsidiary entities.

Chapter VII: Interpretation and Dispute Resolution

Article 7

Internal disputes between and among Board of Peace Members, entities, and personnel with respect to matters related to the Board of Peace should be resolved through amicable collaboration, consistent with the organizational authorities established by the Charter, and for such purposes, the Chairman is the final authority regarding the meaning, interpretation, and application of this Charter.

Chapter VIII: Charter Amendments

Article 8

Amendments to the Charter may be proposed by the Executive Board or at least one-third of the Member States of the Board of Peace acting together. Proposed amendments shall be circulated to all Member States at least thirty (30) days before being voted on. Such amendments shall be adopted upon approval by a two-thirds majority of the Board of Peace and confirmation by the Chairman. Amendments to Chapters II, III, IV, V, VIII, and X require unanimous approval of the Board of Peace and confirmation by the Chairman. Upon satisfaction of the relevant requirements, amendments shall enter into force on such date as specified in the amendment resolution or immediately if no date is specified.

Chapter IX: Resolutions or Other Directives

Article 9

The Chairman, acting on behalf of the Board of Peace, is authorized to adopt resolutions or other directives, consistent with this Charter, to implement the Board of Peace's mission.

Chapter X: Duration, Dissolution and Transition

Article 10.1: Duration

The Board of Peace continues until dissolved in accordance with this Chapter, at which time this Charter will also terminate.

Article 10.2: Conditions for Dissolution

The Board of Peace shall dissolve at such time as the Chairman considers necessary or appropriate, or at the end of every odd-numbered calendar year, unless renewed by the Chairman no later than November 21 of such odd-numbered calendar year. The Executive Board shall provide for the rules and procedures with respect to the settling of all assets, liabilities, and obligations upon dissolution.

Chapter XI: Entry into Force

Article 11.1: Entry into Force and Provisional Application

(a) This Charter shall enter into force upon expression of consent to be bound by three States. (b) States required to ratify, accept, or approve this Charter through domestic procedures agree to provisionally apply the terms of this Charter, unless such States have informed the Chairman at the time of their signature that they are unable to do so. Such States that do not provisionally apply this Charter may participate as Non-Voting Members in Board of Peace proceedings pending ratification, acceptance, or approval of the Charter consistent with their domestic legal requirements, subject to approval by the Chairman.

Article 11.2: Depositary

The original text of this Charter, and any amendment thereto shall be deposited with the United States of America, which is hereby designated as the Depositary of this Charter. The Depositary shall promptly provide a certified copy of the original text of this Charter, and any amendment or additional protocols thereto, to all signatories to this Charter.

Chapter XII: Reservations

Article 12

No reservations may be made to this Charter.

Chapter XIII: General Provisions

Article 13.1: Official Language

The official language of the Board of Peace shall be English

Article 13.2: Headquarters

The Board of Peace and its subsidiary entities may, in accordance with the Charter, establish a headquarters and field offices. The Board of Peace will negotiate a headquarters agreement and agreements governing field offices with the host State or States, as necessary.

Article 13.3: Seal

The Board of Peace will have an official seal, which shall be approved by the Chairman.

IN WITNESS WHEREOF, the undersigned, being duly authorized, have signed this Charter.

(Source: Full text: Charter of Trump's Board of Peace, Times of Israel, 18 January 2026)

Index